PLATO OF ATHENS

PLATO
OF ATHENS

A LIFE IN PHILOSOPHY

ROBIN WATERFIELD

OXFORD
UNIVERSITY PRESS

OXFORD
UNIVERSITY PRESS

Oxford University Press is a department of the University of Oxford. It furthers
the University's objective of excellence in research, scholarship, and education
by publishing worldwide. Oxford is a registered trade mark of Oxford University
Press in the UK and certain other countries.

Published in the United States of America by Oxford University Press
198 Madison Avenue, New York, NY 10016, United States of America.

© Robin Waterfield 2023

Library of Congress Cataloging-in-Publication Data
Names: Waterfield, Robin, 1952- author.
Title: Plato of Athens : a life in philosophy / by Robin Waterfield.
Description: New York, NY : Oxford University Press, 2023. |
Includes bibliographical references and index.
Identifiers: LCCN 2023004737 (print) | LCCN 2023004738 (ebook) |
ISBN 9780197564752 (hardback) | ISBN 9780197564776 (epub)
Subjects: LCSH: Plato. | Philosophers—Greece—Athens—Biography. |
LCGFT: Biographies. Classification: LCC B393 .W37 2023 (print) |
LCC B393 (ebook) | DDC 184—dc23/eng/20230211
LC record available at https://lccn.loc.gov/2023004737
LC ebook record available at https://lccn.loc.gov/2023004738

DOI: 10.1093/oso/9780197564752.001.0001

Printed by Sheridan Books, Inc., United States of America

For Kathryn
my best friend and co-author of my books

"Plato himself, shortly before his death, had a dream of himself as a swan, darting from tree to tree and causing great trouble to the fowlers, who were unable to catch him. When Simmias the Socratic heard this dream, he explained that all men would endeavor to grasp Plato's meaning. None, however, would succeed, but each would interpret him according to their own views."

—*Anonymous Prolegomena to Platonic Philosophy* 1.29–37

Contents

Preface

The prospect of writing a biography of Plato is daunting, and many have judged it a lost cause. The sources are mostly thin and unreliable, the information sporadic and often uncertain, the chronology of his written works impossible to determine with precision. No official Athenian documents survive that mention him. Moreover, Plato hardly refers to himself in the dialogues (as his written works are called) and never speaks in his own name. Nevertheless, as I hope this book demonstrates, a book-length treatment is both possible and desirable. As well as unearthing biographical details, one has to delve into many areas that have the potential fundamentally to impact what one thinks of Plato, such as: What kind of writer was he? How should we read the dialogues he wrote? Is what we call "Platonism" true to its origins? Plato is a household name—a rare status for a philosopher— and he effectively invented the discipline we call philosophy. It would be good to gain some idea of the man himself.

Naturally, many books on Plato start with a chapter or a few paragraphs on his life, but, as far as I am aware, the last dedicated biography in English of any length was published in 1839, when B. B. Edwards translated the *Life of Plato* by Wilhelm Tennemann and included it in his and E. A. Park's *Selections from German Literature*.[1] The book you hold in your hands shares with this predecessor little except a critical approach. That is, I do not just write down "facts" and conclusions

---

1. Despite its title, Ludwig Marcuse's entertaining *Plato and Dionysius: A Double Biography* (1947) falls well short of a full biography of the philosopher and is hardly a *critical* biography anyway.

but also to a certain extent, suitable for a book designed for a general audience, explain what the evidence is and how I understand it, because nothing is uncontroversial in Plato studies. But otherwise my book is different in that it ranges wider and is longer than Edwards's fifty-six pages. And since the main fact about Plato's life is that he was a writer, my book will also serve as an introduction to his work. I do mean "introduction": finer points of interpretation and philosophical complexities play no part, and I have toed a fairly conservative line on most issues that exercise interpreters of Plato. This is not a book about Plato's philosophy but about Plato, though, as a biography of a philosopher, references to aspects of his thought are inevitable. But I focus more on general characteristics than the particulars and the ever-contended details. I am more likely to tantalize readers with suggestive and intriguing ideas of Plato's than elaborate them or spell out their pros and cons.

After about 2,400 years, Plato's books have scarcely aged; they are as brilliant, witty, profound, and perplexing as they have always been. Most of them are not only inspired but inspiring; they are very enjoyable to read, and even the few drier ones contain ingenious and delightful passages. No philosopher is as accessible to non-specialists as Plato. I hope that this book will stimulate readers to turn next to reading the dialogues themselves and to find out more about Plato's work. To this end, I have appended a fairly long bibliography. In terms of my personal biography, the book is a kind of summation, the fruit of many years of thinking and writing about Plato (not that he has always been my exclusive focus). Almost the first article I had published, more than forty years ago, was on the chronology of Plato's dialogues—a topic that, naturally, has exercised me in this biography. So, although I now disagree with the thesis of that article, the book completes a circle for me.

Acknowledgments

My gratitude to Stefan Vranka of Oxford University Press extends this time beyond his usual editorial wisdom, since it was he who invited me to write the book and later he gave me sound advice. Lori Meek Schuldt was once again my excellent copy-editor. Debra Nails offered early encouragement and sent me notes that effectively constituted a second edition of her indispensable *The People of Plato*. I am grateful to William Altman for a typescript copy of his book *Plato and Demosthenes: Recovering the Old Academy*; to Matthew Farmer for a helpful email about fourth-century comic references to Plato; to David Fideler for permission to use the photograph on p. 126; to Kilian Fleischer for letting me see the pages relevant to Plato's life from his forthcoming edition of Philodemus's *Index Academicorum*, and for consequent email exchanges; to Dorothea Frede for a copy of an unpublished talk; to Ian Maclean for the calculation on p. 71; and to James Romm for telling me about the papyrus fragment of *Letter 8*.

The book was written under COVID-19 restrictions. It is in any case my usual practice to ask friends and colleagues to send me offprints of articles of theirs that are unavailable in the online archives, but, denied access to libraries, it was especially important this time. I am particularly grateful to Andrew Erskine, Alexander Meeus, and James Lockwood Zainaldin for making material available to me from their university libraries; to all those—too many to name—who responded to the request for material that I posted on the Liverpool listserv for classicists; and to John Dillon and Sir Richard Sorabji for checking references in the Neoplatonic commentators when the texts were unavailable to me.

Maps

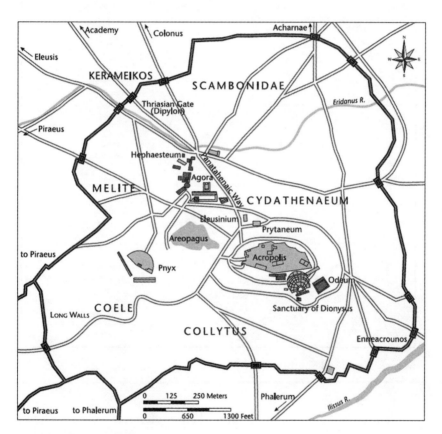

Map 1. The city of Athens

Map 2. Sicily and Southern Italy

List of Plato's Dialogues

All Plato's works are conventionally called "dialogues," even though some scarcely involve any give and take between interlocutors, and one, *Apology of Socrates*, is an alleged transcript of the defense speeches Socrates, Plato's teacher, gave at his trial in 399 BCE. Throughout the book I use the standard means of precise reference to Platonic texts. I might refer, for instance, to *Lysis* 222a–c. These numbers and letters refer to the pages and sections of pages of the edition of Plato's works by Henri Estienne (aka Stephanus) that was published in Geneva in 1578. This edition was in three volumes, each with separate pagination. Each page was divided into two columns, with the Greek text on the right and a Latin translation on the left. The column with the Greek text was divided into (usually) five sections labeled "a" to "e" by Stephanus. So *Lysis* 222a–c is a chunk of text that occupied some or all of sections a–c of page 222 in one of Stephanus's volumes (the second, as it happens). This convention is followed in all editions of Plato's works and by those who write about him.

We have the complete works of Plato. There is, these days, a high degree of unanimity among scholars as to which dialogues are genuine and which are not. I count twenty-eight as genuine. This is a good number of titles, but Plato was not an especially prolific writer: these twenty-eight dialogues amount to somewhat over 540,000 words,[1] which is about the same as David Foster Wallace's *Infinite Jest*. By contrast, we have about a million words from Aristotle's pen, and if we

---

1. J. Ziolkowski, "Plato's Similes: A Compendium of 500 Similes in 35 Dialogues; Chart D," accessed October 26, 2022, https://plato.chs.harvard.edu/chartD.

had his lost works, the figure would probably be nearer three million. But prolificness is not the only criterion by which to judge a writer; Plato was creative and original in everything he wrote.

Here is an alphabetical list of the genuine dialogues, many of them named after one of the lead characters who appears in the work. Most of them feature Socrates as the main driver of the discussion.

First Alcibiades
Apology of Socrates (often shortened to *Apology*)
Charmides
Cratylus
Critias
Crito
Euthydemus
Euthyphro
Gorgias
Hippias Major
Hippias Minor
Ion
Laches
Laws
Lysis
Menexenus
Meno
Parmenides
Phaedo
Phaedrus
Philebus
Protagoras
Republic (the first chapter of *Republic* probably started life as a
    separate short dialogue called *Thrasymachus*)
Sophist
Statesman (or *Politicus*)
Symposium

Theaetetus

Timaeus

The Platonic corpus contains other works as well. Ignoring those that were recognized as spurious even in antiquity, we have *Second Alcibiades*, *Cleitophon*, *Epinomis*, *Hipparchus*, *Lovers* (or *Rival Lovers*), *Minos*, and *Theages*. Of these, *Second Alcibiades*, *Hipparchus*, *Lovers*, and *Minos* are, I would say, certainly not by Plato. *Cleitophon* and *Theages* probably are not Platonic, but they are of considerable interest as fourth- or early third-century dialogues, possibly even composed by members of Plato's Academy, and the same may be true for *Hipparchus, Lovers*, and *Minos*. *Epinomis*, a kind of appendix to *Laws*, was written by Plato's student and secretary, the mathematician Philip of Opus, as a commentary on and development of certain parts of *Laws* and *Timaeus*. At some point in the past two hundred years, almost every single dialogue that I count as genuine has been regarded as spurious by some scholars, but the two that still most commonly fall under suspicion are *First Alcibiades* and *Hippias Major*. On the authenticity of some of Plato's letters, see pp. xxx–xxxv.

Timeline

For the chronology of Plato's written works, see pp. 74–94.

469 BCE Birth of Socrates

431–404 Peloponnesian War

430 Birth of Adeimantus, brother

429 Birth of Glaucon, brother

426 Birth of Potone, sister

424 or 423 Birth of Plato

423 Death of Ariston, father

422 Perictione (mother) marries Pyrilampes

421 Birth of Antiphon, half-brother

413 Death of Pyrilampes

411–410 Oligarchic regime in Athens

407 Birth of Speusippus, nephew

404 Peloponnesian War ends with defeat of Athens

404–403 Regime of the Thirty Tyrants in Athens; Plato comes of age

399 Trial and death of Socrates

c. 396 Plato with Euclides in Megara

395–386 Corinthian War

390s First dialogues written, and proto-*Republic*

384 Plato with Pythagoreans in southern Italy; meets Dion and
Dionysius I in Syracuse

383 Foundation of Academy in Athens

c. 370 Eudoxus joins Academy

367 Aristotle arrives in Athens

366–365 Plato's second visit to Syracuse, to Dion and Dionysius II

361–360 Plato's third visit to Syracuse

359 Philip II ascends to the Macedonian throne

357 Dion seizes power in Syracuse

354 Assassination of Dion

349 Plato visits southern Italy?

347 Death of Plato; Speusippus head of Academy

338 Xenocrates head of Academy

86 Destruction (?) of physical Academy by Roman troops
    under Sulla

529 CE Emperor Justinian orders closure of Academy and other
    schools of pagan philosophy

Introduction

Plato's importance as a philosopher is universally acknowledged. He was the first Western thinker systematically to address issues that still exercise philosophers today in fields such as metaphysics, epistemology, political theory, jurisprudence and penology, ethics, science, religion, language, art and aesthetics, friendship, and love. He was the heir to a long tradition of thinking about the world and its inhabitants, but the use he made of this inheritance was original. In effect, he invented philosophy, and he did so at a time when there was little vocabulary or framework for doing so—no words for "universal," "attribute," "abstract," and so on. Moreover, he founded a school, the Academy, which was dedicated not just to philosophy, but to scientific research and practical politics, and fostered thinkers of the stature of Aristotle and Eudoxus, whose multiple influences on subsequent thinkers were profound. The Academy taught philosophy and encouraged research for almost a thousand years, a span still unsurpassed by any other educational establishment in the West.

The range of topics Plato addressed, the depth with which he addressed them, and the boldness of his theories are astonishing. It is not just that he raised questions that still provoke us, but he also asked, as a philosopher must, whether it is possible to come up with secure answers to the questions, and even whether knowledge is possible at all. He was concerned not just with conclusions but with how we reach them. He had certain definite doctrines, or theories perhaps, but even they might find themselves tested in the dialogues. This sense of philosophy as an ongoing quest is one of the most attractive features of his work. What is more, these ideas are generally presented in a way that is accessible to every intelligent reader because Plato's brilliance as a philosopher was matched by his talent as a writer. In later centuries, many thinkers have written philosophical dialogues, but none of those dialogues has captured the fluency and conversational realism of Plato's work at its best.

I said just now that Plato raised questions that still provoke us, but the "us" in that sentence consists chiefly of practicing philosophers. It is more to the point to say that he raised questions that *should* still provoke us—all of us, not just philosophers. In a world in which even liberal democracies can be distorted by fanatical, incompetent, and emotionally immature leaders, should we perhaps not pay more attention to Plato's prescriptions for turning out political leaders who are both competent and principled? In a world in which information and misinformation are more widespread than ever before, especially thanks to social media and the Internet, should we not reconsider Plato's insistence that our actions should be based on knowledge, not belief or opinion? When many perpetuators of popular culture drag us down to the level of the lowest common denominator, let's reflect on Plato's reasons for loathing both trivialization and the unthinking acceptance of ideas and practices even when they are widely sanctioned by society. Plato was an idealist in that he believed that perfection, or at least a far better state of affairs, is achievable in every area of human life, starting with personal reformation. Should we not similarly devote our energies to improving ourselves and the world around us, so that each generation bequeaths to the next conditions that are healthier and more sustainable than what went before?

Plato's work generated discussion and responses throughout antiquity and in every generation since. There is still such an enormous output of scholarly books and articles every year that it would take more than a single lifetime to master all the publications and all the languages required to read them. He is read and studied in, I dare say, every country in the world. The indexes of a good proportion of the nonfiction books on any reader's shelf will have an entry for Plato.

Plato was not just important but super-important. And so he has been judged by some of the greatest intellects of recent times.

Perhaps the most famous such assessment is that of the English philosopher Alfred North Whitehead (1861–1947), who wrote in *Process and Reality*, published in 1929: "The safest general characterization of the European philosophical tradition is that it consists of a series of footnotes to Plato." I believe this to be correct, in the sense that Plato invented what we call the discipline of philosophy, though like all great thinkers and innovators, he also built on the work of his predecessors. He could have echoed Isaac Newton: "If I have seen further, it is by standing on the shoulders of giants."

But let's be clear on what Whitehead was saying: every great Western thinker, from Aristotle onward, has been indebted to Plato. Aristotle's debts are more close and obvious than those of, say, Judith Butler, but the foundations of even Butler's work were laid down by Plato. If the mark of genius, rather than merely great intelligence, is that the field in which the person works is forever changed, or a new field created, then Plato was a genius. In saying that he invented philosophy, Whitehead and I are not saying that he got everything right. Of course not: that would make all subsequent philosophy even more of a waste of time than many people already think it is! And in any case, it is the job of philosophy to inquire, more than it is to come up with solutions. Plato launched philosophical investigation.

Whitehead's estimation of Plato is so famous that it has long had the status of a cliché. But it is not commonly noted that Whitehead was preceded on the other side of the Atlantic by Ralph Waldo Emerson, leader of the Transcendentalists. Whitehead was ensconced within the establishment, while Emerson was more of an outsider; perhaps this is why the latter's saying has been forgotten. "Out of Plato," Emerson said, in his chapter on Plato in *Representative Men* (1876), "come all things that are still written and debated among men of thought." We note his "all things," a measure of Plato's great importance.

I could add testimonials from many others, such as Georg Wilhelm Friedrich Hegel (1770–1831), who said in his *Lectures on the History of Philosophy* that Plato and Aristotle "above all others deserve to be called the teachers of the human race." I could add testimonials from thinkers and commentators of our own time, but it is the way of things that current philosophers and scholars have not yet passed the test of time and attained the stature of Whitehead, Emerson, and others. So I rest my case on these quotations from earlier thinkers, and on the fact that *Republic* at least, and often more of Plato's works, are invariably included in the canon of Great Books of the World. Nor is this reverence for his books a new phenomenon. Most ancient Greek literature has been lost, sometimes by accident, but more often because it was felt to be not worth preserving, in the sense that, in the centuries before the invention of the printing press, no one was asking scribes to make copies. Yet we have the complete set of Plato's dialogues; not a single word that he published has been lost. Every generation of readers in antiquity and the Middle Ages felt that Plato's work was worth preserving.

In short, without Plato, European culture would be poorer, or at least it would have had to struggle to attain the same richness. Plato cannot be dismissed as just a dead white male. It is safe to say that, apart from the Bible, no body of written work has had such an impact on the Western world as Plato's dialogues. Over the centuries, Platonism has reappeared in some form or other in philosophical contexts—in much early Jewish, Christian, and Islamic thought; in the ideas of the Cambridge Platonists such as Henry More and Ralph Cudworth; in the slightly later seventeenth-century dispute between John Locke and Gottfried Leibniz; even in the late nineteenth-century "platonism" of Gottlob Frege's mathematical philosophy. But that is not my point, which is that Plato bears some responsibility for forming and tuning the way *all* of us think, whatever our gender, skin color, cultural background, or philosophical or political affiliation. In saying this, I am not promoting the chauvinistic notion that the only discipline worthy of the name "philosophy" is the Western version, founded by Plato; but I am saying that, whether or not we know it, our minds have been affected by him. Moreover, I have suggested that he still has important lessons for us—that he should *continue* to affect the way we think about many of the issues that currently trouble or perplex us. This book, then, attempts to contextualize the work of this important thinker and to uncover as much as possible what else he did other than write books.

The Sources

How do we know about Plato's life? What are the sources, and how reliable are they? In Plato's case, they are peculiarly intriguing. There are three kinds of source: biographies written in antiquity, letters written in antiquity under Plato's name, and Plato's own published works. All three of these sources are problematic in their own distinct ways. There are also countless references to Plato by other ancient writers, but they are concerned with philosophy rather than biography.

Ancient Biographies of Plato

Six ancient Lives of Plato exist in whole or part. Philodemus of Gadara, in the first century BCE, included a critical account of Plato's life in the part of his massive *History of the Philosophers* that was dedicated to the history of the Academy. What remains of this text, however, is fragmentary: it exists only on carbonized papyrus rolls from Herculaneum in Italy, burned and preserved by the eruption of Mount Vesuvius in 79 CE, and the delicate and highly technical work of reading the papyri is still ongoing. Moreover, what remains deals largely with the Academy; most of the details of Plato's life are missing, and little is added in this respect to what we can gather from the other Lives, which have survived complete. These surviving Lives are, in chronological order: *On Plato and His Teaching* (second century CE), by the novelist and Platonist Apuleius of Madaurus; the third chapter of the *Lives of the Eminent Philosophers* (third century CE) by the biographer Diogenes Laertius; the opening sections of *Commentary on Plato's First*

Alcibiades (sixth century CE) by the Platonist scholar Olympiodorus the Younger; an anonymous *Prolegomena to Platonic Philosophy* (sixth century CE); and the entry "Plato" in the *Dictionary of Wise Men Distinguished in the Field of Intellectual Studies* (sixth century CE), by Hesychius of Miletus.[1]

Three features of these biographies catch our attention straight away. First, they were all written centuries after Plato's life. Second, with the exception of the one written by Diogenes Laertius, they are all very short: Apuleius devotes about eight hundred words to Plato's life before turning to his teachings, while Hesychius gives our philosopher about six hundred words, including a summary of his ideas; Olympiodorus and the *Anonymous Prolegomena* come in at somewhat over two thousand words, and Diogenes at about four thousand, before turning to his philosophical theories. Third, they all rely heavily on anecdotes, and they retell many of the same anecdotes, which shows that they were writing at the end of what was already a long tradition, during which these "facts" about Plato's life became dogma, often of an entertaining kind. So I am little concerned to identify the particular sources on which these extant Lives drew; they all drew ultimately on "the tradition."

The tradition's roots go back to the fourth century BCE because biographies, memoirs, and commemorative poems were written by some of Plato's followers and others in the decades immediately after his death in 347: Aristotle and Speusippus wrote poems; Speusippus, Xenocrates, and Philip of Opus wrote biographies, probably of an encomiastic nature; Erastus of Scepsis and a certain Asclepiades wrote memoirs. In the next generation, Dicaearchus of Messana, Satyrus of Collatis, and Neanthes of Cyzicus wrote biographies, and Clearchus of Soli wrote an encomium, perhaps trying to counteract the effect of hostile accounts of Plato, because they too started early: Theopompus of Chios wrote a work *Against the School of Plato*, in which he seems

---

1. There is also a biographical entry (Π 1707) in the encyclopedia known as the *Suda*, dating from the tenth century CE, but it is very short and tells us nothing we did not know from elsewhere.

to have charged Plato with writing many falsehoods and focusing on stuff that was useless; Idomeneus of Lampsacus wrote a book *On the Followers of Socrates* that recounted gossipy scandals; Aristoxenus of Taras's *Life of Plato*, as far as we can tell from the few surviving fragments, drew on gossipy anecdotes and accused Plato of plagiarism and much else besides; Phaenias of Eresus must have included something about Plato in his *On the Socratics*; the Sicilian historian Philistus wrote a hostile account of Plato's visits to Sicily; and comic playwrights were ridiculing Plato even during his lifetime, though not all their remarks were hostile: he is mocked above all for his obscurity, his dependence on wealthy patrons, and the uselessness of philosophy, but these were standard slurs about intellectuals.[2]

None of these works from the fourth or early third centuries survive except for a few snippets, but there can be no doubt that they are the ultimate sources for what we find in the extant biographies. After all, many of them were written by people whom later writers could take to be authoritative, especially Speusippus and Xenocrates. Speusippus was Plato's nephew and succeeded him as head of the school, and Xenocrates succeeded Speusippus.

Other Lives were written over the centuries; the tradition was being perpetuated. But, like their fourth- and third-century predecessors, these works are lost, and it is the later, extant Lives that form the foundation of what we know or think we know about Plato's life.[3] Leaving aside their accounts of Plato's philosophy, they all cover much the same topics: Plato's birth, name, ancestry, and early education (my chapter 1); his association with Socrates and other thinkers (chapter 2); his travels, especially to Sicily (chapters 3, 4, and 7); the foundation of the Academy (chapter 5); and his death (chapter 8).

---

2. Many of these comic fragments were collected by Diogenes Laertius (*Lives of the Eminent Philosophers* 3.26–28) and Athenaeus of Naucratis, the author of *Savants at Dinner* (first/second centuries CE), at 11.504e–509e and elsewhere.

3. I do not have firsthand acquaintance with the Arabic Lives or the occasional biographical details included in the *Syriac Chronicle* of the Christian bishop Gregory Bar Hebraeus in the thirteenth century, but to judge by what I have read about them, they do not add anything of substance.

I shall be drawing on the extant Lives in their proper contexts, but unfortunately little of this ancient biographical tradition is reliable; the general picture of the trajectory of Plato's life is more or less sound, but when it comes to details, the tradition often turns gossipy or downright fanciful. These writers were the ancient equivalent of celebrity gossip journalists. Common sense is the best tool with which to assess anecdotes, and it is not difficult to dismiss out of hand the notion that members of the Academy, Plato's school, used to blind themselves so that they would not be distracted from philosophy, or that Plato died of shame when he was unable to answer a riddle. Students of ancient biography well know that sometimes the slanders and jibes of comic poets seep as factoids into biographical tradition. It is as though Monty Python's "Philosophers Song" were taken to be biographical fact: "Plato, they say, could stick it away: half a crate of whisky every day." One constantly has to be on the lookout for this kind of nonsense. What is more interesting is what the anecdotes tell us in general about Plato: he was huge in his day, a major celebrity, idolized enough for legends to have arisen about him and for his detractors to go to extreme lengths to try to topple him from his pedestal; and his fame, equal to that of Homer, continued after his lifetime for many centuries.

The Platonic Letters

Of the extant letters supposedly written by Plato, the thirteen that were included alongside the dialogues in the Platonic corpus, possibly as early as the late third century BCE, have the best claim to authenticity, but they are in bad company: most ancient letters attributed to famous men and women are spurious. And indeed, the authenticity of any of Plato's letters is one of the most hotly contested issues in Platonic scholarship. It is one of those issues that is subject to scholarly fashion. At the moment the scholarly consensus, while falling well short of unanimity, is that even the most plausible of them are forgeries, but

in the middle of the twentieth century the consensus was the other
way around, and there are signs today that the pendulum is swinging
back again. They are not "forgeries" in the sense that there is anything
malicious about them, as though the writer were trying to blacken
Plato's name in some way. More accurately described, they are "pseudepigrapha," or works written under an assumed name. We are talking
here of imposture, not fraud; the writer is more likely to be honoring
Plato than disrespecting him. The majority of the letters are written to
or about the Syracusan and southern Italian rulers and statesmen with
whom Plato interacted on his visits to the central Mediterranean.

There remains a significant minority of scholars who believe that
some of the letters are genuine. Most of them are easily dismissed as inauthentic, for stylistic or anachronistic reasons. In the case of the corpus
of Platonic dialogues, a core of authentic dialogues gained an accretion
of spurious ones. This is likely what happened in the case of the letters
too: over the decades, inauthentic letters written under Plato's name
were added to a core collection of a few genuine ones. This is a common
phenomenon. To take two other fourth-century writers, the same happened with Demosthenes's speeches and Speusippus's letters: the corpus
consists of both authentic and inauthentic works. The arguments for and
against the authenticity of Plato's letters are often highly technical, and
for the purposes of this book I will not go into them to any great extent.
Since, as I have said, the scholarly consensus is that none of the Letters
are genuine, I will not undertake the dispiriting task of eliminating those
that I too reject. I will just explain why I accept the three that I accept.

Insofar as we can guess, the reasons why people impersonated Plato
and others varied. They might have wanted to fill a gap in the historical record by composing a letter containing the missing facts or
alleged facts. They might have done it just for fun, or to be able to present themselves as the discoverers of an important document, which
they hoped to sell to a library.[4] Writing such a letter might have been

---

4. The growth of libraries such as the one in the Museum of Alexandria in Egypt in the
   third century BCE stimulated the production of forgeries. They were one of the reasons

a school exercise. Especially in the case of letters written under a philosopher's name, it might have been a way of giving authority to a point of doctrine the writer wanted to communicate.

The first point to note is that none of these reasons are such as to induce any forger to write at length. This immediately puts in the spotlight the most important of the Platonic epistles, *Letter 7*, because it is long. In the standard pagination of Plato's works, it occupies twenty-eight Stephanus pages,[5] which makes it longer than eleven of the dialogues. Second, forged letters tend to be bland; the writer does not want to commit himself to saying anything that would betray the fact that he is making it up. *Letter 7* is not bland. It is written with care and a high degree of literary skill; it expresses far more of Plato's personality and feelings than is usual in forgeries; it contains insights into Sicilian history that are not available elsewhere; and its perspective on Plato's philosophical teachings is complex and unusual. The details of Plato's youthful turn toward philosophy are completely plausible, as even those who doubt the letter's authenticity agree. The letter is just too elaborate to be a forgery.

Given Plato's stature, it would be a bold forger who would pretend to know so much about his character and thinking. No forger would have dared to speak about Socrates, Plato's teacher, as casually as the letter does. No forger would have dared to suggest that knowledge of Plato's metaphysical teaching is not imparted by the written word—that is, by the published dialogues—but results "from long acquaintance with the matter and from being embedded in it," when "suddenly, like a light that is kindled by a leaping spark, it is born in the soul and at once becomes self-sustaining." And Plato adds that "there is certainly no written work of mine that covers the issues I consider important, nor will there ever be."[6]

---

the residents of the museum developed the tools of scholarship and literary criticism: they had to determine which texts were genuine and deserved to be housed in the library.

5. See the List of Plato's Dialogues, pp. xv–xvii, for an explanation of this term.
6. *Letter 7* 341c–d.

These remarks have generated a great deal of scholarly discussion, but there does not seem to me to be anything surprising in them. Despite the vivid language, they say no more than that knowledge or understanding, as distinct from information, cannot be gained from books. The turning of belief into knowledge, and of knowledge into secure knowledge, takes time and reflection on what has been learned from books or lectures, which needs to be absorbed and made one's own. Plato preferred live conversation and internal dialogue to the passive reception of the written or spoken word, and one of the primary reasons he wrote dialogues rather than treatises is that he wanted to encourage us, his readers, to think for ourselves and to come to understanding by ourselves.

Three other factors weigh in favor of the authenticity of *Letter 7*. One is chronological: he talks of the necessity of resettling Sicily, where the Greek cities had become drastically underpopulated as a result of warfare and forced migration. This was a true crisis in Sicilian affairs, but it was sorted out by the early 330s. So the letter assumes a situation that was salient in Plato's day but was resolved fifteen or so years later. The second factor is the style in which the letter is written. Sophisticated and plausible computer-based analyses of Plato's style, undertaken in the 1980s, suggest that Plato was the author. It would be impossible for a forger to imitate Plato's style so faithfully in a work of this length. In a looser sense, too, its style is typical of Plato, in that it introduces important philosophical issues as a kind of digression. This is typical of Plato: topics interweave, disappear, return. All the central aspects of *Republic*—the images of Sun, Line, and Cave; the fundamental importance of goodness in the world; the educational program designed for philosophers—are contained within a digression. And the third factor is that the certainly spurious *Letter 2* imitates *Letter 7*,[7] which would be odd if both were forgeries.

While certainty may be impossible, the cumulative effect of these points suggests that *Letter 7* was genuinely written by Plato. For the

---

7. *Letter 2* 312d–314c, imitating elements of the philosophical digression of *Letter 7* 341a–344d.

purposes of this book, it gives us a wealth of detail about Plato's life, especially his involvement in Syracusan politics. It is a justification of his life as a whole, written as an autobiography; in particular, given Plato's long association with Syracusan tyrants, he needed to defend himself against the charge of favoring tyranny. Read as authentic, *Letter 7* is an impressive and thrilling document that brings us as close to Plato as we could possibly hope to get, and it shows us a man who was not just a theoretician but who wanted to see whether his theories were viable in the real world.[8]

I also accept the genuineness of *Letter 3* and *Letter 8*, which are consistent with *Letter 7* both stylistically and factually. The authenticity of *Letter 8* is also made more likely by the publication of a papyrus fragment containing a couple of lines from the Letter, that dates from the middle of the third century BCE.[9] They are nowhere near as long as *Letter 7*—each of them occupies about six Stephanus pages— but the decisive factor is that they seem to come from the same hand. These three letters are generally accepted as genuine by the majority of the minority of scholars who think that any of the letters are genuine. What distinguishes them from the other ten letters in the collection is that they are pamphlets or manifestos disguised as letters; they are designed to be read not just by their nominal addressees but also by the general public in Sicily and Athens. Plato was doing much the same as his contemporary Isocrates, who also wrote an autobiographical defense of his life and who also wrote open letters on political matters—including one to Dionysius I, the first of the Syracusan tyrants whom Plato met. Both *Letter 7* and *Letter 8* are addressed to the friends of Plato's friend and disciple Dion, but *Letter 3* is addressed to the Syracusan tyrant Dionysius II and consists largely of a series of stinging rebukes, probably in response to a lost denigration of Plato published by Dionysius. Together, then, these three

8. Apart from occasional short quotations from the letter, I translate a few paragraphs in the course of Chapter 7.
9. C. Gallazzi, "Plato: *Epistulae VIII* 356a, 6–8," in F. Hoogendijk and B. Muhs (eds.), *Sixty-five Papyrological Texts* (Brill, 2020), 1–4.

letters, joined especially by Plutarch's *Life of Dion* (and Cornelius Nepos's brief *Life of Dion*, too, though it adds very little), will form the basis of my account of Plato's visits to Syracuse, and *Letter 7* also supplies us with details about Plato's earlier life. That Plato did go to Sicily is not doubted even by those who reject the letters because, although Plutarch draws heavily on the letters, he also adds details not found in them.

The wealth of detail we have for these Sicilian visits might seem to create a regrettable imbalance: we are far better informed about them than about most of the rest of his life. But I do not think the imbalance is misleading. The visits to Sicily were exceptional in what seems to have been an otherwise quiet and scholarly life. One may compare the life of J. R. R. Tolkien: apart from the products of his brilliant imagination, he lived the ordinary, uneventful life of an Oxford don. We have Plato's writings, we know of his Sicilian interventions, and these were the two most significant elements in an otherwise peaceful and reclusive life.

The Dialogues as a Source for Plato's Life

We can glean little about Plato's life or character from the dialogues. It is not just that, like a playwright, Plato never once speaks in his own name, but also that the attempt is hazardous. The eighteenth-century Scottish philosopher David Hume developed a skeptical philosophy that left his brain in a whirl, having proved to his own satisfaction that no theories can be fully proved and that sense data are unreliable. Nevertheless, he confessed in *A Treatise of Human Nature* that in real life he shed the skeptical persona he adopted in his philosophical writing: "Most fortunately it happens, that since reason is incapable of dispelling these clouds, nature herself suffices to that purpose, and cures me of this philosophical melancholy and delirium . . . I dine, I play a game of backgammon, I converse, and am merry with my friends."

In short, it is often difficult to infer much about a writer from his work. Vladimir Nabokov, the author of *Lolita*, was not obsessed with underage girls. Plato is most famous for holding the view that the only true ontological reality lay with Forms,[10] the immaterial entities that allow us to identify the things of this world and to think with concepts. But I am sure that when he stubbed his toe on a rock, his first thought was not "This rock is unreal." And apart from the difficulty of reading a writer's character from his writerly persona, there is in addition the frequent difficulty of deciding exactly where Plato stood on various issues, even fundamental ones. Nevertheless, the risk of reading Plato's characteristics from his written work is one I shall have to take from time to time; I shall do so as little as possible, but it is a risk that all biographers of writers have to take.

Politics, with a particular focus on political leadership, was central to Plato's interests, not least because it had been central to his teacher Socrates's interests. Plato devoted not only *Republic* and *Laws* to the topic, which together make up almost 40 percent of his total output, but also his third longest work (*Gorgias*) and the mid-length *Statesman*. Then there are political aspects to several other dialogues as well, especially *Menexenus*, *Crito*, and *Critias*. Seeing that politics is a real-world subject (unlike metaphysics, for instance), and seeing that Plato spent quite a lot of time personally trying to establish responsible leadership in the great Sicilian city of Syracuse, I shall track his views on certain political issues, especially leadership and the relation between leadership and law, insofar as they can plausibly be seen as influencing and being influenced by the circumstances of his life. Politics will therefore loom somewhat larger in this book than other branches of philosophy, and since politics and ethics (how people should live)

10. Also sometimes called "Ideas," in older books. Neither translation is happy. "Form" implies shape and materiality, whereas the *eidē* are immaterial, and "Idea" implies that *ideai* (the other word Plato uses) are no more than mental constructs, whereas they exist independently of the human mind. It is closer to being a theory of "types," with the particulars that fall under each type being its "tokens," and indeed in later dialogues Plato uses a different term, *genos*, which means "kind" or "type." But the vocabulary of "Forms" is firmly entrenched in modern scholarship.

were intertwined in ancient philosophy, I shall be dipping into Plato's ethics as well. These are branches of philosophy with practical application, suitable for mention in a biography.

What about references to contemporary events in the dialogues? What do they tell us about the sequence of Plato's life? The pickings here are slim. A number of dialogues—in dramatic order: *Theaetetus*, *Euthyphro*, *Sophist*, *Statesman*, *Apology of Socrates*, *Crito*, and *Phaedo*—all refer to the preliminaries to Socrates's trial, the trial itself, and his time in prison in 399, awaiting death. So they were written later than 399. Where the rest of the dialogues have a recognizable setting, their dramatic dates fall in the fifth century, during Socrates's lifetime, and can therefore tell us nothing about the dates of their writing. But there are a very few anachronistic references to fourth-century events.[11] So we know that *Laws*, or a stretch of it, was a work of his old age because it refers to an event in the 350s. *Menexenus* refers to the Peace of Antalcidas of 386 that brought the Corinthian War to an end, and *Symposium* to an event of 385/4. *Theaetetus* refers to Theaetetus's death from dysentery and battle wounds in 391.[12] *Philebus* refers to some views of Eudoxus of Cnidus, who arrived in Athens to study, research, and teach in Plato's Academy c. 370; *Meno* appears to reference an anti-Socratic pamphlet published c. 390.

On a couple of occasions, Plato gives his age away. In *Republic*, he says that the philosopher rulers of his imaginary city-state must be at least fifty years old, and it seems unlikely that he would have written that unless he himself were at least fifty. Similarly, *Laws* pretends to be a conversation between three elderly men, and at one point Plato suggests, paradoxically, "In youth everyone's vision is least keen, but in old age it is at its sharpest."[13] And that is about all the direct help the dialogues themselves give us toward determining the stages of Plato's

---

11. I do not count *Meno* 90a as one of these. The wording is opaque, but it probably refers to an event of c. 404, a couple of years before the dramatic date of the dialogue.

12. The reference is not to an action of 369, as is commonly stated. Born c. 415, it is unlikely that Theaetetus would have been on active service in 369.

13. *Laws* 715d–e.

writing career. The dialogues occupy a fictional universe of Plato's making, set loosely in fifth-century Athens and centering on Socrates but with little attention to the outside world.

Plato refers to himself only three times in the dialogues, but none of these passages is very informative. We learn from two mentions in *Apology of Socrates* that he was present at Socrates's trial in 399 and was among those who offered to help him pay his fine, if the court decided to penalize him with a fine;[14] and in *Phaedo* he mentions that he was prevented by illness from being with Socrates on the last day of his life in prison.

Otherwise, Plato is more or less invisible in the dialogues. He often even effaces himself completely: the text of *Theaetetus*, for instance, is said to have been written down by Euclides of Megara, leaving Plato to act merely as an unacknowledged copyist. The fundamental reason for his aloofness is a good one: it makes us, the readers, avoid the immediate assumption that one point of view—the author's—is authoritative. As the *Anonymous Prolegomena to Platonic Philosophy* puts it: "In our minds, that sit in judgment, we side now with the questioner, now with the questioned."[15] We are forced to think for ourselves whom we agree with, and even to examine our own beliefs—to engage with the texts and turn ourselves into philosophers, creating a second dialogue in addition to the one we are reading. So Plato has Socrates say:[16]

> If you take my advice, you'll care little for Socrates but much more for the truth. If you think I'm speaking the truth, agree with me; but if not, resist me with every argument you can muster, taking care that in my zeal I don't deceive you and myself alike, and go off like a bee leaving behind its sting.

This sense that as readers we are actually taking part in the dialogues is what is chiefly responsible for the great intellectual pleasure of reading Plato. The degree of his anonymity must not be exaggerated, however;

---

14. The story in Diogenes Laertius, *Lives of the Eminent Philosophers* 2.41, that Plato was moved to get to his feet during the trial and address the court is certainly false.
15. *Anonymous Prolegomena to Platonic Philosophy* 15.
16. *Phaedo* 91c.

after all, readers have always known that they are reading something "by Plato." Plato is always present in the dialogues; it is just that he is never visible. But his self-effacement does mean that the dialogues are not a good source for his life and character, and we have to rely largely on the authentic letters and on external sources, supplemented by what we know of contemporary Athenian society and history. It will never be possible to write the kind of biography of Plato that is enabled by more recent philosophers, such as Immanuel Kant or Bertrand Russell, where we have voluminous personal correspondence detailing their daily lives and thinking; but despite the difficulties and limitations, a portrait of the man emerges.

I

Growing Up in Wartime Athens

Plato was born in the Athenian year 428/7 BCE.[1] So states almost every book and article on Plato, but the claim is very likely to be wrong. Because of Plato's great fame and the degree of reverence he inspired, his name attracted legends and hyperbolic praise. The aspect of this praise that is relevant to the date of his birth is that he was considered to be under the special protection of the god Apollo, who was the god, among other things, of revelation and intellectual clarity. It was said that bees, agents of Apollo's servants the Muses, sat on baby Plato's lips and filled his mouth with honey, as a token of his future eloquence and erudition.

The notion that Plato had an Apollonian nature was current even in his lifetime, or very soon after, because Speusippus, his nephew and his successor as head of the Academy, already knew the story that Plato's real father was Apollo; he may have invented it for the eulogy he delivered at Plato's funeral. It was said that Plato's human father tried to force himself on his new young wife (women in Athens were frequently married at about the age of fifteen) but "failed"—or in other words, was afflicted with impotence. When he stopped trying, he was warned in a dream not to have intercourse with his wife for

[1]. We write Athenian years like this because their New Year's Day fell in our midsummer (on the day of the first new moon after the summer solstice). But when we can, we also date events by our Gregorian calendar, projected back onto ancient Athens; we say, for instance, that the Athenian expedition to Sicily was launched in 415.

ten lunar months, so as not to spoil the purity of Plato's divine birth. Early Christian writers, who found much of Plato's work compatible with their own beliefs, interpreted this as parthenogenesis. "The prince of wisdom was born by virgin birth," gushed Saint Jerome.[2] He was clearly following the biographical tradition that made Plato the firstborn of the family, but in fact his mother was no virgin: Plato was her fourth child.

This legend had two consequences. The relatively trivial one is that Plato's birthday was dated to 7 Thargelion in the Athenian calendar (sometime in late May in ours) because that was supposed to be when Apollo was born. It was probably Speusippus who, after Plato's death, chose this day as Plato's birthday, to make it the day on which annual rites of remembrance would be performed by members of the Academy, the school founded by Plato. Later Platonists such as Plutarch of Chaeronea (first/second centuries CE) and Plotinus (third century CE) celebrated Plato's birthday on this day, and Socrates's on the day before.[3] The more important consequence concerns the year of his birth. The only fixed date that we have for Plato's life, confirmed by historians, is that he died in the year 348/7. By the time he died, he was famous enough for historians to note the date, but they were left to guess about the year of his birth. There were nine Muses, so his birth was projected back to 428/7, 81 (9 × 9) years from his death.[4] He was even said to have died on his birthday, thus completing exactly eighty-one years and no more.

Later, another factor came into play and perpetuated this date for Plato's birth. In the second century BCE, the scholar Apollodorus of Athens, who worked in the Museum of Alexandria in Egypt, devised

2. Jerome, *Against Jovinianus* 1.42–43.
3. Plutarch, *Moralia* 717a–b (*Table Talk*); Porphyry, *Life of Plotinus* 2.40. We are also told, by the *Anonymous Prolegomena* (6.16–18), that the Athenians collectively used to celebrate Plato's birthday and sing, "On this day the gods gave Plato to humankind."
4. 348/7 + 81 = 429/8, but the Greeks counted inclusively, so that, for instance, today being Saturday, next Saturday is eight days away, because this Saturday is included in the counting as day one.

an influential chronographic system that divided people's lives into twenty-year chunks, with their acme coming at age forty. In Plato's case, then, he was born in 428/7, met Socrates in 408/7, founded the Academy in 388/7, traveled to Sicily in 368/7, and died in 348/7. Apollodorus himself was aware of the rigidity of his scheme, but he offered it to help historians correlate events around the world at least roughly. For precise biographical purposes, however, we can place little trust in Apollonian schemes or dating systems based on Apollodoran numerology.

There are several factors that point to a birth date later than 428/7. The most important is that there is no evidence that he fought in any of the last battles of the Peloponnesian War in 406 and 405, so he was probably still under the age of twenty. Athens was critically short of manpower at the time, so he would certainly have been called up. Young Athenian men did a form of military service when they were eighteen and nineteen, but within the borders of Attica (the countryside of which Athens was the urban center); they did not serve abroad until they were twenty. So Plato seems to have still been under twenty in 405. This clue is backed up by *Letter 7*.[5] He says that he was planning to begin to play a part in Athenian public life (as many well-born young men would) when he came of age—that is, after the age of twenty. It so happened that when the Peloponnesian War ended in 404, the victorious Spartans imposed on Athens an oligarchy of thirty men, commonly known as the Thirty Tyrants (more on them later). Plato admits that he was attracted to their program of the moral reform of Athens and says that since some of the Thirty and their adjutants were friends and relatives of his, they invited him to join them. The clear implication is that in 404 he either was old enough to play a political role or soon would be, whereas, as we have seen, he was not old enough in 405. So he was born at the earliest in 424/3.

<hr>

5. *Letter 7* 324b–d.

The Peloponnesian War

Plato's childhood coincided with the terrible war that was fought between the city of his birth and Sparta.[6] The purpose of the war was to decide whether Athens (at the head of a mighty alliance of states around the Aegean basin) or Sparta (at the head of a scarcely less powerful alliance, chiefly made up of other Peloponnesian states) would be the leading city-state in Greece, with the right to enrich itself at the expense of its subject states. The war began in 431. From 421 until 413, during Plato's young childhood, there was an uneasy peace between the two sides. The Athenians, however, were still involved throughout these years in campaigns abroad, and in 415, at the instigation of the ambitious aristocrat Alcibiades and his political allies, who played the populist card, they chose to invade the island of Sicily, where the most powerful city was Syracuse, a potential ally of Sparta.

This was a disastrous decision. It was utterly unrealistic to expect to be able to rule as troubled and as large an island as Sicily from distant Athens. Two years later, the Athenian expeditionary force was wiped out with the loss, over the course of the expedition, of forty thousand men—Athenians, allies, and mercenary auxiliaries. Athenian manpower, already reduced by the plague that swept through the city and the army in the early 420s and by battlefield losses, was further reduced, to perhaps a third of what it had been at the start of the war, and the city was almost insolvent. In the same year, 413, the Spartans again renewed hostilities because in the previous year the Athenians had broken the peace accord by taking part in an invasion of Spartan territory.

The Sicilian expedition brought to the surface the anger of many members of the Athenian wealth elite. They had sound reasons for disgruntlement, not least the fact that they were being called on to

---

6. The only good thing about the war was that it was written up by Thucydides, whom many people rate as the greatest historian there has ever been.

finance military operations just at the time when the war had cut them off from much of their wealth. In 411 an oligarchy seized control of the government and delegated executive power to a council of four hundred sympathizers drawn from the ranks of the disgruntled rich. The transition was relatively peaceful, but after only a few months the people rose up against the council, which had signally failed to keep any of its promises, and democracy was restored. Plato was old enough to pay critical attention to the turmoil; his family belonged to the same stratum of society as the oligarchs, and at least some of them may have had some sympathy for the cause.

In military terms, the handwriting was on the wall for Athens; with the Sicilian expedition, Athens had effectively engineered its own defeat. There was a brief flurry of renewed hope between 411 and 408, when Alcibiades achieved significant successes at sea, but after that, hope died. The Persians, who wanted to reclaim their mastery of the Greek city-states of Asia Minor, most of which were in the Athenian alliance, started to underwrite the Spartan war effort. This assistance made it possible for the Spartans to develop a powerful fleet, when naval superiority had been the essential underpinning of Athenian hopes and successes throughout the war. Everyone knew that Athens was going to lose, and the end came in 404. The Athenian navy had been annihilated the previous year, leaving Athens vulnerable. The Spartans besieged the city into starvation and then imposed the rule of the Thirty.

In his teenage years, then, Plato was living in a city that was sunk in gloom and the certainty of defeat. When he was born, Athenians could still claim to live in the wealthiest and arguably the most powerful state in the Greek world; by the time he came of age, its financial resources had been drained and it had been humbled by defeat. It must have been both depressing and terrifying.

He witnessed the famous Athenian democracy at its most extreme and irresponsible, with the people thinking only of their own power, not what was good for the city as a whole. They enthusiastically voted for the invasion of wealthy Sicily; they relished Alcibiades's victories

but banished him after a single defeat. In a vote that was probably
unconstitutional, and was certainly ill advised, they condemned eight
of their ten elected generals to death after a sea battle in 406; the
Athenians had won the battle, but a rising storm had made it impossible for the generals to rescue more than two thousand Athenians and
allies who were floundering in the water and subsequently drowned.
Most of the oarsmen in the Athenian navy were from the poorer
strata of Athenian society, as were the people at home who voted to
condemn the upper-class generals. In later years Plato was never sympathetic to democracy, though toward the end of his life he came to
recognize that the people must be allowed to have a say in the political life of their community; in his youth he saw the disastrous effects
of rule by people who were not political experts, and he always clung
to the ideal of the truly knowledgeable political leader. He would
probably have agreed with Alcibiades, who described the Athenian
democracy as "acknowledged folly."[7]

The Athens of Plato's youth was a city in disarray. Moral standards
were in flux, as they often are in times of war, and in later life Plato
always promoted high moral standards. The city was divided against
itself, along both class and generational lines, and Plato always insisted that unity and concord were crucial for political stability, and
that stability was crucial for people to be able to flourish and fulfill
themselves. "Could we describe anything as worse for a community,"
asks Socrates in Plato's *Republic*, "than what tears it apart and destroys
its unity? And could we describe anything as better for a community
than what binds it together and unifies it?" He says that a divided
community does not even deserve to be called a community, specifically citing dissension between rich and poor as the primary division,
from which all others flow.[8]

7. Thucydides, *The Peloponnesian War* 6.89.6.
8. Quotation from *Republic* 462a–b. Reference to *Republic* 422e–423a.

Plato's Immediate Family

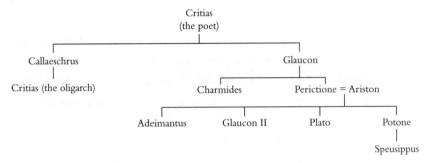

Figure 1.1 The Family of Plato

Plato's family was very distinguished (see figure 1.1). Both his father and his mother could name illustrious statesmen of earlier centuries among their ancestors and, in the manner of aristocratic Athenian families, his father's family even traced their lineage back to the god Poseidon. Plato, however, was, or came to be, dubious about such claims.[9] The family's wealth was based, as was typical of the long-established families of the Athenian elite, on their ownership of land. Plato's father was Ariston, son of Aristocles, of the deme Collytus and the tribe Aegeis, and his mother was Perictione, daughter of Glaucon. Plato had two older brothers, Adeimantus and Glaucon, and an older sister, Potone. Adeimantus was probably born in 430 and Glaucon the following year, since both were old enough to take part in a battle outside the borders of Attica in 409. A poem addressed to them began: "Sons of Ariston, godlike offspring of an eminent sire."[10] Potone was born around 426, and then Plato in 424 or 423. Potone married a man called Eurymedon, and in or around 407 gave birth to a son, Speusippus, who would become a famous philosopher in his own right and succeed Plato as head of the Academy. By the 360s, if we can

9. *Timaeus* 40d–e.
10. *Republic* 368a.

trust information from the pseudo-Platonic *Letter 13*, Plato had four grandnieces, the children of the children of his siblings.

At some point the story arose that Plato's given name was Aristocles, after his grandfather, and that Plato was a nickname that stuck. The ancient biographers and others tell us that he was named "Plato" because he was fat or stocky (Greek *platus*) or perhaps "broad" in the sense of having a capacious intellect. Once they had concluded that "Plato" was a nickname, they had to invent a change of name for him, and so they decided, not unreasonably, that Plato had originally been named Aristocles after his grandfather. But this is nonsense: we know of many Platos in Athens and elsewhere in the fifth and fourth centuries (including another famous one, a writer of comedies). It was a perfectly normal name.[11] Besides, the common practice of naming a son after his grandfather was reserved for the eldest son. So the future philosopher's full name was Plato, the son of Ariston, of the deme Collytus and the tribe Aegeis (see figure 1.2).[12]

All full Athenian citizens belonged to a hereditary deme and tribe. A deme was a parish—there were 139 in Attica—but a person might belong to a deme without living there. He was registered in the deme in which his ancestor had been enrolled at the time of the reform of Athenian society along democratic lines at the very end of the sixth century, whether or not he or his family was still based there. Plato's deme, Collytus, was located within the city walls, southwest of the Acropolis; he may well have been raised there as a child and young man, in the heart of the city. And for administrative purposes all Athenian citizens belonged to one of ten tribes; fellow tribesmen took part in various civic and religious rituals together, and fought side by side on the battlefield. All ten tribes were named after legendary local

11. See also the story on pp. 201–2.
12. We may have a garbled trace of the truth in the story (Olympiodorus, *Commentary on Plato's First Alcibiades* 2.36) that it was one of his teachers, Ariston of Argos, who invented the alleged nickname, Plato. In fact, it was another Ariston, his father, who so named him.

Figure 1.2 Plato. This bust is a Roman copy of the head of a statue that was set up in the garden of the Academy, the school that Plato started, soon after his death. Altes Museum, Berlin.

heroes and kings. Aegeis was dedicated to Aegeus, an early king who was remembered as the father of Theseus (and after whom the Aegean Sea is named).

Plato was probably born on the island of Aegina in the Saronic Gulf, southwest of Athens. The island was taken over by the Athenians in 431, the first year of the Peloponnesian War. They expelled the islanders, who, out of long hostility toward Athens, were on good terms with the Spartans, Athens's enemies, and they resettled the island with their own citizens, including Ariston. Aegina, lying close to the Peloponnese, would make a useful naval base for the Athenians. But before long the family relocated back to Athens, perhaps feeling that it was too dangerous to remain. Ariston probably retained the land he had been allotted on the island, but as a distant landlord, leaving the estate to be run largely by slaves. This was common practice, especially for people who wanted to stay close to the political center, Athens. However, after their victory in the Peloponnesian War in 404, the Spartans returned the island to the former inhabitants, or those that had survived: during the war, the Athenians had raided the place where the wretched Aeginetans had been settled by the Spartans, and slaughtered as many of them as they could lay their hands on. Aeginetan hostility toward Athenians may on one occasion have had a direct impact on Plato's life, as we shall see later.

Not long after returning to Athens, Ariston died, either before or shortly after Plato's birth. Under Athenian law women could not own property, and all of Perictione's sons were still underage, so she was married off to her uncle Pyrilampes. This was not considered incestuous; it was a perfectly normal way of ensuring that the estate stayed in the family. So Plato never knew his natural father, and Pyrilampes was to all intents and purposes his father.

Pyrilampes was another man of distinction, famous for raising peacocks on his estate. He was the Athenians' first choice as ambassador to the Persian king or his satraps in Asia Minor, and thus he was often away. Persians and Greeks were neighbors, in the sense that the Great King's empire extended from Afghanistan and the Punjab to the west coast of what is now Turkey. The empire covered more than 10 percent of the planet, and early in the fifth century the Persians had tried to add the Greeks to their empire. They failed, thanks to astonishingly brave resistance from a Greek coalition, led by Sparta and Athens, but Persia was still a threat, and the Greeks often felt the need to send ambassadors. It was while Pyrilampes was on one such mission for Athens that he acquired his famous peacocks; they were not the first that had ever been seen in Athens—earlier ambassadors to the east had also received them as gifts—but they were still delightfully exotic.

Plato paid a compliment to his stepfather in one of his dialogues, while explaining why the good looks of one of Pyrilampes's nephews were typical of the family: "Whenever he went to the court of the Persian king or was on some other diplomatic mission in Asia, he was held to surpass all other men in the continent for his beauty and stature."[13] The assumption that a fine exterior indicated a fine interior was more or less universal in ancient Greece.

Pyrilampes died in his sixties in 413, but by then Adeimantus was old enough to act as head of the family, so Perictione was not required to marry again. Pyrilampes and Perictione had a son called Antiphon, born around 421. We know virtually nothing of the activities of this half-brother. Plato makes him the narrator of his dialogue *Parmenides*, which presumably indicates an interest in philosophy, but nothing seems to have come of it, and in later life he was more interested in horse breeding than abstract thinking—and some of *Parmenides* is highly abstract.

We know very little of the lives of Plato's brothers. Glaucon certainly, and Adeimantus probably, had political ambitions, but neither of them became prominent. But they put in occasional appearances in Plato's dialogues, most famously as Socrates's main interlocutors in *Republic*. Glaucon also features in conversation with Socrates in one of the Socratic works written by Plato's contemporary, Xenophon, and was credited with writing dialogues featuring Socrates. Whether genuine or not, none of these dialogues has survived. Adeimantus was close enough to Socrates to be among the onlookers at his trial in 399, along with Plato. At any rate, we can safely guess that both Glaucon and Adeimantus knew Socrates, and therefore their main contribution to Plato's adult life, and to posterity, is likely to have been that at some point they introduced their younger brother to his teacher. Plato must have known that *Republic* would be one of the greatest books he would write; his making his brothers Socrates's interlocutors—and

13. *Charmides* 158a.

they are far from being the least intelligent of Socrates's interlocutors in the dialogues—was surely a way of thanking them.

Plato's Extended Family

Following Ariston's death, Plato was in effect under the protection of his mother's family, which included, besides Pyrilampes, two other prominent political men. Critias was Perictione's first cousin. He was a well-known author of poems and plays and an admirer of the Spartan constitution and way of life, which he praised in a couple of works.[14] In terms of the main polarity of ancient Greek politics in the Classical period, oligarchy versus democracy, he was an oligarch, and his place in history was assured when he became one of the leaders, and probably the ideologue, of the Thirty Tyrants. Pyrilampes, however, was a democrat. In wartime years, it is easy for politics to divide a family.

So when Plato said in *Letter 7* that he had relatives among the Thirty, he was thinking in the first instance of Critias. But he was also thinking of Perictione's brother, Charmides. The Thirty set up a board of ten men to administer Piraeus, the port of Athens, and Charmides was one of the ten. Along with Critias, he had been suspected of involvement in an abortive oligarchic coup in 415, and after that episode he fled the city and was condemned to death in absentia. I have suggested that the main trigger for the oligarchic revolution of 411 was that the rich were being reduced to relative poverty, and we know that Charmides had suffered in this way.[15] He was still in exile in 411, otherwise it seems likely that he would have been involved in the oligarchic coup that took place then.

Critias's ties to Plato's immediate family became even closer when he gained Glaucon as his boyfriend. In upper-class Athenian society,

14. Plato himself, in later life, expressed admiration for the Spartan constitution; at *Letter 8* 354b–c, and in *Laws* he was impressed enough by many aspects of Spartan society to incorporate them into his imaginary city-state. But there remained other aspects that he despised.
15. Xenophon, *Symposium* 4.30–32.

"Greek love" (a term for homosexuality coined in the eighteenth century) was not regarded as perverted, against a standard of hetero-sexuality as normal. Although, naturally, men did sometimes become long-term lovers (as were the Athenian playwright Agathon and a cer-tain Pausanias, who appear in Plato's *Symposium*), the most common form of homoeroticism was *paiderastia*—"sexual desire for boys" from about the age of fourteen. It was accepted that a noble youth had a kind of beauty and that older men would be attracted to him and would try to win honor by winning his favors. But a man's attraction to a boy said nothing, in our terms, about his sexuality; it did not ne-cessarily make him gay or bisexual as opposed to heterosexual. When Greeks thought about sex, they focused less on the genders of the people involved than on their roles—who was the penetrator and who was penetrated. In any case, the relationship was not necessarily sexual.

If an affair took place, whether sexual or not, the partners would likely be faithful to each other and would typically stay together for a few years, while the boy was still beardless. What the boy got out of the affair—and this too is why it was an upper-class phenomenon—was a form of patronage. In return for "gratifying" his lover, as the Greeks ra-ther delicately put it, he would expect the older man to act as an extra guardian in public life, to introduce him to the best social circles, and later, perhaps years after the sexual side of the affair was over, to help him gain entry into the political life of the city-state. As a high-born youth, it is very likely that Plato had a male lover as a patron.

Plato wrote two superb dialogues celebrating male homosexual love and its philosophical potential and ramifications, *Symposium* and *Phaedrus*, and homoeroticism features in other dialogues as well.

> And just at this moment, I saw inside Charmides's clothes. I was on fire! I was in ecstasy! I realized what a true expert on love Cydias was, when in speaking of a beautiful boy he warned that "one should beware of going as a fawn into the presence of a lion, and being seized as a por-tion of meat." I certainly felt as though I'd been caught by some such creature.[16]

16. *Charmides* 155d–e.

Plato never wrote in this vein about heterosexual love. As a result, he has often been co-opted by the gay community as a member himself. But what I have just said puts this in context. Plato may have been gay, in our terms,[17] but he may simply have been giving an unusual philosophical twist to the kinds of relationships he saw around him in Athens. Athenian upper-class men did not usually marry for love but rather for the political and commercial connections their wives could bring to the family. So their best chance of feeling passion was in a relationship with a boyfriend or a mistress, and it is precisely the energy of real passion that interested Plato in *Symposium* and *Phaedrus*, especially the possibility of its being channeled toward philosophical and life-changing ends. He never married, but, in an ancient Athenian context, despite being unusual, that is a meaningless criterion for assessing a person's sexuality. Ironically, however, in the city-state he imagined in *Laws*, he would make it compulsory for a man to marry between the ages of thirty and thirty-five.

Early Education

We have no direct evidence for Plato's early education, but it would have conformed to Greek norms. Education was designed above all to socialize children—to indoctrinate them into the values of their society. It is not surprising, then, that Plato was in many ways a man of his times. In real life he kept slaves—five house slaves are mentioned in his will, and each of his farms would have been worked and run by a half dozen or so slaves, as all farms of any size were—and not only did the imaginary societies of Callipolis and Magnesia (those, respectively, of *Republic* and *Laws*) both have institutional chattel slavery,

17. But, if so, he was not "glad to be gay," to judge by the number of times in the dialogues that he condemns sex between men: *Phaedrus* 250e–251a, 253c–256e; *Republic* 402e–403b; *Laws* 636c–d, 836c–841e. Both Diogenes Laertius (*Lives of the Eminent Philosophers* 3.31) and Athenaeus (*Savants at Dinner* 13.589c) say that he was in love with a courtesan called Archeanassa, but this is probably a false inference from the fact that an epigram to Archeanassa at some point became attributed to him.

but the punishments that Plato imagined for wrongdoing by slaves in Magnesia were harsher than those that existed under Athenian law.

Then again, even though in devising Callipolis the logic of his argument forced him to admit that a few female Guardians of the city could be the intellectual and moral equals of their male counterparts, and in Magnesia women are full citizens alongside men, in reality he seems to have thought women inferior to men. He held that if men undertook the activities that were traditionally reserved for women, they would prove to be better at them; that men are more intelligent than women; that plundering the corpses on a battlefield is the mark of a womanish mind; that a cowardly man would be reborn in his next incarnation as a woman; that women are more secretive and devious than men. Even in *Laws* women seem to be debarred from higher political offices. To put it at its harshest: Plato was less interested in women as women than he was in their potential to be men.

School education in ancient Greece was far from universal: there were not many students, and they were not required to do much. Schooling began in Athens around the beginning of the fifth century, but schoolteachers remained few and underrated in the Classical period, and unsupported by the state. Schools were not institutions separate from the teachers who ran them that could outlast a teacher's death, nor were they necessarily housed in dedicated buildings or rooms. Girls, and boys from poorer families, might gain a little elementary education at home; boys who were lucky enough to go outside the home were taught in a sporadic fashion, for a few weeks or a few years, by three kinds of teacher. A *grammatistēs* taught them reading, writing, and arithmetic, and made them study and even learn and recite substantial chunks of epic poetry, since Homer, especially, was regarded as a fount of wisdom in many areas (see figure 1.3). Plato would later criticize the expectation that by studying poetry people would be provided with role models to emulate; in his view, expressed especially in *Republic*, the gods and other characters described by Homer and others were often too corrupt to act as exemplars. The skill set provided by a *grammatistēs* was so fundamental that probably

Figure 1.3 School scene. In the center, a seated teacher checks the recitation of the pupil standing before him. Behind the boy is seated a slave who accompanied him in public, to make sure he did not cause or get into any trouble. To the left, another boy practices on his lyre.
Douris Painter (5th BCE)
bpk Bildagentur/Antikensammlung/Staatliche Museen, Berlin, Germany/Johannes Laurentius/Art Resource, NY

the sons of some poorer families also attended this kind of school; it did not cost much.

The other two schools were more specialized and more for elite children. A *kitharistēs* taught music, singing, dancing, and the lyric poets, so that the boys would be able to hold their own in a cultured symposium and take part in choral festivals. A *paidotribēs* supervised their physical education at a gymnasium (likely to be publicly owned) or "palaestra" ("wrestling-ground," likely to be privately owned), to prepare them for all forms of athletic contest and for warfare. "The sons of gentlemen are taught things like reading and writing, playing the lyre, wrestling, and other sports."[18] Plato was said to be good

18. *Theages* 122e.

at wrestling, though the anecdotal tradition goes too far when it claims that he competed in the panhellenic games and was even an Olympic victor. The ancient biographies appear to know the names of Plato's teachers: a certain Dionysius was his *grammatistēs*,[19] Dracon of Athens and Metellus of Acragas were his *kitharistai*, and Ariston of Argos was his *paidotribēs*. On the authority of Speusippus, who was said to have found this out from "family documents," we are told that Plato was studious and precocious.[20] Both qualities seem probable.

School education was seen as supplementary to the company of adults, from whom one could learn, by imitation, the behavior and patterns of thought that were expected of a citizen. Plato sketched this aspect of a child's education in *Protagoras*:[21]

> People start teaching and correcting their children when they are young and make it a lifelong practice. As soon as a child is capable of understanding what people say to him, his nurse, his mother, his minder, and his father himself strive to make him as good as may be. In everything they do and say, they're teaching him and showing him what's right and wrong, what's good and bad, what's pious and impious, what is and isn't acceptable behavior. . . . And then, when they send him to school, they tell the teachers to pay far more attention to seeing that the child learns good behavior than to seeing that he learns how to read and write or play the lyre.

To Plato's mind, however, this was a hit-or-miss system: the eminent Athenian statesmen Themistocles and Pericles were good men (let's suppose) and brought their sons up right, but the sons still turned out to be unexceptional.[22] Why? Is excellence (virtue, *aretē*) not teachable? This question may even have been the spur that made Plato a philosopher. It is prominent in *Meno* and *Protagoras* and puts in an occasional appearance elsewhere.

19. The dialogue *Lovers* is set in Dionysius's school.
20. Apuleius, *On Plato and His Teaching* 1.2.
21. *Protagoras* 325c–e.
22. *Meno* 93b–94c.

In Athens, attendance at the dramatic festivals was another part
of a boy's education—and perhaps one of the few that gave him
some notion of critical thinking, since the dramas, though set in
the legendary past, invariably raised social and political issues that
were relevant to contemporary Athens. Tragic poets were considered "the teachers of Greece."[23] Plato was growing up at a time
when the tragedian Euripides, the most philosophical of the playwrights, was at the height of his popularity. However, Plato would
later criticize drama as a form of rhetoric that could make people
believe certain things but could not impart knowledge.[24] Then, at
another kind of festival, professional reciters and interpreters of
epic poetry, known as "weavers of song" ("rhapsodes," such as Ion
in Plato's dialogue), would perpetuate and deepen their audience's
understanding of Homer and other poets. An equally important
aspect of a young Athenian's education was attending to the decisions of the people in the Assembly and the law courts, and listening to gossip and conversation in the Agora, the central square
of Athens, to learn what earned communal praise or dispraise. A
few boys, only from the aristocracy, were further socialized by
being taken under the wing of an older lover (see figure 1.4), as
previously mentioned.

For an upper-class child such as Plato, attendance at symposia was
also part of his education, when he was allowed at last to join his elder
brothers in his father's and others' *andrōn*—the "men's apartment" of
a house, where symposia were held. The word "symposium" literally
means "drinks party," but this has misleading connotations for the
modern reader: the Greeks did not sip sherry and nibble salted nuts,
and no women—or no respectable women, at any rate—were present
at a symposium. The consumption of alcohol was indeed the main
purpose of the party, but the evening meal was eaten first. There was

23. Olympiodorus, *Commentary on Plato's First Alcibiades* 2.53.
24. *Gorgias* 502b–d.

Figure 1.4 Homoerotic symposium scene. An older man (on the right, with a beard) and a teenager share a couch at a symposium.
Photo by Carole Raddato.

a distinct break after the meal while the room was cleared and rituals performed, and then the drinking started.

A lot of wine might be drunk, but it was well diluted. Few symposia were inebriated orgies; the point—at any rate, in cultured circles—was to remain on the creative edge of intoxication. Though there might be hired entertainment, put on by dancing girls, acrobats, or mimes, guests were also expected to entertain one another. Following a hymn to the gods, they settled down to make witty and elegant conversation, sing songs while accompanying themselves on the lyre, recite poetry and even their own compositions, break into dance, ask riddles, tell jokes, and play games such as *kottabos*, the flicking of drops from the bottom of one's cup at a target. This is how Plato would have been introduced to the refined salon world of highbrow literature and cultured men. In *Laws* he goes on at some length about the educational importance of properly conducted symposia.

The Youthful Poet

Plato is said to have studied painting, but that does not seem likely: it was not generally an upper-class pursuit. At least two of the writers who perpetuate this information point to a passage of *Timaeus* as evidence that Plato knew about painting. So here we have an explicit case of the risky tactic of inferring details of a person's life from what he says in his written works. More consistently, the biographical tradition says that, even when young, Plato intended to be a writer. There was little yet by way of a tradition of prose writing, and it was largely confined to not many works of medicine and historiography, technical treatises and handbooks, and published political or forensic speeches. Philosophy—the word in Plato's youth covered everything from logic to geography—was certainly being perpetuated in prose as well as poetry, but these works tended to be short and dogmatic. This was largely because, up until only a couple of decades before Plato's birth, literature was written for performance first and publication second. But by the time he was writing dialogues in the fourth century, books were being written directly for publication, so they could be longer and less dogmatic, in the sense that readers could linger over an argument and assess its validity and its impact on them.

Plato and some other followers of Socrates were going to revolutionize forever what could be done with philosophical prose. But he seems at first to have been attracted to writing poetry; perhaps he wanted to follow in Critias's footsteps and combine a political career with authorship. But the story that he destroyed his early tragedies after his "conversion" to philosophy[25] is such a cliché that we might be inclined to dismiss the whole set of tales as false, were it not for their plausibility. As a well-educated young man with literary aspirations, and also as a participant in symposia, it is very likely that he

---

25. In the ranking of occupations that occurs at *Phaedrus* 248d–e, poetry is placed sixth out of eight, while philosophy comes first.

tried his hand at poetry. "I've had a kind of fascinated admiration for Homer ever since I was young," he has Socrates say in *Republic*, surely speaking for himself.[26] And Plato certainly had a sense of the tragic; no one who reads the sequence of dialogues surrounding Socrates's trial and death (*Apology of Socrates, Crito, Phaedo*) can have any doubt about that.

Thirty-one epigrams have come down to us under Plato's name; three of them, however, are ascribed not to "Plato" but to "Plato the Younger," perhaps an otherwise unknown homonymous writer. The majority of the epigrams can be found in the *Greek Anthology*, a collection of thousands of poems that was finalized in the thirteenth or fourteenth century CE; there are also eleven, all love poems, in the biography written by Diogenes Laertius (nine of which also occur in the *Greek Anthology*). An epigram is a short, memorable poem, originally used for memorial purposes—perhaps on the base of a statue, commemorating the life of the sculpted person. By the third century, it had become an art form in its own right and was used especially for poignant reflection on love affairs. That is why none of the love poems attributed to Plato by Diogenes Laertius is genuine: they conform exactly to the standards established long after Plato's death and even longer after the time he was supposed to have composed them, in his youth or young manhood. At least one of the epigrams was actually composed by another poet early in the third century and somehow became attributed, in a slightly altered form, to Plato.

Overall, this is probably what happened. People knew of Plato's youthful literary aspirations, and they also knew that, according to the biographical tradition, he was supposed to have had love affairs with various men and women. So they made up epigrams under his name and addressed them to some of his alleged lovers and others he would have known: Agathon the playwright (at whose house the symposium of *Symposium* takes place); Dion, Plato's friend and student from Syracuse; Xanthippe, Socrates's wife; Phaedrus (called "Aster" in

26. *Republic* 595c.

the epigrams), after whom Plato named one of his dialogues. Most of the historical details are wrong: there is no way that Plato could have addressed a love poem to Socrates's wife, nor would he have treated Agathon and Phaedrus as his boy-loves when they were older than him. But whoever wrote those particular epigrams might have been pretending to be Plato impersonating Socrates, as he does in the dialogues.

> As I kissed Agathon, my soul was on my lips.
> The poor thing went there to cross the gap between us.

> You gaze at the stars, Aster, my star! If only I were heaven!
> I would gaze at you then with myriad eyes!

The one addressed to Dion is really a commemorative poem, but with a love twist at the end:[27]

> Tears were allotted by the Fates at their birth
> To Hecuba and the women of Ilium.
> But on you, Dion, who have fashioned
> A victory trophy out of noble deeds,
> The gods showered great hopes.
> Now you lie in your spacious country
> Honored by your fellow citizens.
> Dion, you drove my spirit mad with love!

The other epigrams—the ones not preserved by Diogenes—are mostly commemorative. It is possible that one or more of them may genuinely have been written by Plato, but there is no way to know. Here is a rather flat one commemorating the great poet Pindar, who was working early in the fifth century:

> The man lying here was pleasing to strangers
> And dear to his fellow citizens—
> Pindar, servant of the melodious Muses.

---

27. Curiously, when Apuleius quotes three of Plato's epigrams (not in his *On Plato and His Teaching* but in his *Defense against the Charge of Practicing Wizardry* 10.6–9), he quotes only the last line of this poem. Might it originally have been a one-line epigram on its own?

Another poem honors another famous poet:

> People say that there are nine Muses. How careless!
> Look at Sappho of Lesbos: she's the tenth.

A particularly poignant one salutes the inhabitants of the town of Eretria, on the island of Euboea. In a famous incident, the Eretrians had joined the Athenians in an attack on the Persians in Asia Minor early in the fifth century, in support of a rebellion against Persian rule by the Greek cities of Asia Minor. In 490 the Persians responded by sending an army that was famously defeated by the Athenians at the battle of Marathon. But before reaching Marathon, the Persians sacked Eretria and arranged for the transportation of its inhabitants to distant, landlocked Media, in what is now northwestern Iran.[28]

> Here we lie in the midst of the plains of Ecbatana,
> Who formerly sailed the deeps of the Aegean Sea.
> Farewell, far-famed Eretria, once our homeland!
> Farewell, Athens, neighbor of Euboea!
> Farewell, beloved sea!

These are good poems, but they are not outstanding. If any of them were written by Plato, he might have been looking back on his youthful poetic endeavors when he wrote:[29]

A third kind of possession and madness comes from the Muses. It takes hold of a delicate, virgin soul and stirs it into a frenzy for composing lyric and other kinds of verse, and so educates future generations by glorifying the countless deeds of the past. But anyone who approaches the doors of poetic composition without the Muses' madness, in the conviction that skill alone will make him a competent poet, is cheated of his goal. In his sanity both he and his poetry are eclipsed by the compositions of men who are mad.

---

28. I have translated the version found in Philostratus, *Life of Apollonius* 1.24, rather than the one found in the *Palatine Anthology*. The ascription of this poem to Plato is probably owing to the fact that he mentions the historical episode at *Menexenus* 240a–c and *Laws* 698c–d.

29. *Phaedrus* 245a.

Perhaps Plato felt that he was just too sane and rational to make a great poet.

Coming of Age

Athenian males were formally enrolled by their demes as citizens at the age of eighteen. Plato would therefore have been registered in 406 or 405. Aristotle has left us a description of the procedure, which was not substantially different in Plato's day than it was in his:[30]

> Men belong to the citizen body if they are of citizen parentage on both sides, and they are registered as members of their demes at the age of eighteen. When they are being registered, the deme members take a vote about them on oath, first to decide whether they have reached the age prescribed by the law (if they decide that they have not, the candidates return to the ranks of the boys), and secondly to decide whether they are free men and born as prescribed by the laws. . . . After this the Council scrutinizes those who have been registered, and if anyone is found to be below the age of eighteen it punishes the deme members who have registered him.

There was no register of births in Athens; the only way of assessing whether a young man was eighteen was by looking him over. The law that both parents had themselves to be Athenian citizens was relatively new, instituted in 451/0. As a matter of fact, by the time of Plato's enrollment, the regulation had been relaxed; loss of citizen life in the Peloponnesian War meant that the city could not be so exclusive, and the law was resuscitated only after the war was over. Plato fulfilled the requirements anyway: both his parents were citizens, he was not and never had been a slave, and he must have satisfied the committee as to his age.

---

30. Aristotle, *The Athenian Constitution* 42.1–2, translated by P.J. Rhodes. This work might not have been written by Aristotle but by one of his students; or it might have been written up by one of his students from his notes.

Having been enrolled as a citizen, Plato immediately became an "ephebe" or cadet. Resuming Aristotle's description, he goes straight on to describe the *ephēbeia*. It was more formal in his day than at the end of the fifth century, but the purpose was the same: to get the young men to learn by experience what it was to be an Athenian citizen. They first swore an oath:[31]

> I shall not bring shame upon my sacred weapons, nor shall I desert the man beside me, wherever I stand in the line. I shall fight in defense of things sacred and secular, and I shall not hand on the fatherland lessened, but greater and better as far as I am able and together with all. And I shall be obedient to those who exercise power reasonably at any time, and to the laws currently in force and any reasonably put into force in the future. If anyone destroys these, I shall not give him allegiance as far as is in my power and together with all. And I shall honor the ancestral religion.

After the solemn oath-swearing ceremony, Plato and his fellow cadets were taken on a tour of all the temples of Attica, to familiarize themselves with the sacredness of the landscape they were to defend. Then, for the next two years, they underwent military training within the borders of Attica. It is not entirely clear what their duties were in Plato's day, but they probably included garrison duty in Piraeus, the port of Athens, drilling, and weapons training. In the second year, they were given a shield and a spear by the state and were assigned the more dangerous task of patrolling the borders against enemies coming in and runaway slaves going out, while garrisoning the various forts that dotted the borderlands. They were expanding their horizons beyond the family environment that had nurtured them and learning that their duties extended to the entire citizen body. The importance of seeing a community as a whole was something that Plato never forgot.

---

31. P.J. Rhodes and R. Osborne, *Greek Historical Inscriptions, 404–323 BC* (Oxford University Press, 2003), no. 88.

Plato's Wealth

Perhaps the most important aspect of Plato's outer life is that he was wealthy. He came from a wealthy family and he remained wealthy all his life. There is a thread in the ancient biographies that portrays him as poor or impoverished, but this is wrong. It probably stems from the hostile tradition that had him always with cap in hand at the door of Sicilian tyrants. He may well have accepted such gifts, but as a token of respect, not because he was unable to live without them. Throughout his life, he never had to work to make money but lived off the labor of those who worked his estates. He was even said to have been the first not to charge for his teaching, though that distinction properly belongs to Socrates.[32] Plato was rich enough for the state to require him, on one occasion in the 360s, to perform what was called a "liturgy" (*leitourgia*, "public service"). It was customary in Athens for well-off private citizens to be required to help out with public expenses. There was no regular income tax, but there were a few wealth taxes. Some were occasional (for instance, raising money for warfare), but liturgies—between 97 and 118, depending on the year—were required every year.

In fourth-century Athens, out of a total population of about 220,000 (down from a peak of 340,000 just before the Peloponnesian War), there were perhaps two thousand men who were rich enough to be liable for liturgies, and of the two thousand a super-rich element of perhaps three or four hundred who were liable for the most costly liturgies. A "trierarch," for instance, was required to man, equip, and maintain a trireme (a warship) for a year, the hull of which was provided by the state. This extremely costly liturgy was undertaken on one occasion by Pyrilampes's son Demos, which gives some idea of the wealth that Pyrilampes brought to Plato's family when he married Perictione. The most expensive festival liturgy was the *chorēgia*,

32. *Anonymous Prolegomena to Platonic Philosophy* 5.24–25.

which involved recruiting a chorus for a dramatic or choral festival and paying for the trainers, the training, the rehearsals, the costumes, the scenery, and the equipment. This was the liturgy that Plato was called on to perform; he paid for the training of a chorus of boys for a festival. The boys' chorus may have been somewhat less burdensome to fund than a chorus of men for a tragedy, but it was not much less so.

The state assumed that Plato had at least several hundred drachmas to spare, and by complying with the order, Plato agreed. He was among the two thousand or so most wealthy men in Athens, truly a member of the top 1 percent. Even if we believe the story that Plato's liturgical expenses were covered by someone else,[33] that does not alter the fact that he was first called on by the state to fund the chorus, and that would not have happened if his property-holdings did not put him in the top bracket. Plato may have been required to do no more than put up the money, but it seems likely that he got more involved because when he came to formulate his imaginary city-state in *Laws*, he devoted quite a few pages to the educational importance of dance and the correct way to go about it.[34]

Diogenes Laertius records Plato's personal will, which appears genuine.[35] I say "personal will" because it includes no mention of the Academy, the school that Plato established, so he must have made separate arrangements for it, perhaps in the form of a permanent endowment. Or perhaps he left it to fend for itself, as it had during his lifetime; at any rate, his successors soon introduced fees for membership of the school. The bulk of his wealth seems to have come from two large farms in the countryside north and east of Athens, one inherited from his family and one that he bought himself.

33. By Dion, that is: Plutarch, *Life of Dion* 17.5, *Life of Aristeides* 1.4.
34. *Laws* 653d–658a.
35. Diogenes Laertius, *Lives of the Eminent Philosophers* 3.41–43. Diogenes included six wills in his biographies of philosophers, and where we can tell (especially with the Peripatetic wills), they are genuine.

This property has been left and these dispositions made by Plato.
The estate in Iphistiadae, abutted to the north by the road from the
temple at Cephisia, to the south by the sanctuary of Heracles in
Iphistiadae, to the east by the property of Archestratus of Phrearrhi, and
to the west by that of Philip of Chollidae: let no one be permitted to
sell or transfer it, but let it be the property of young Adeimantus [prob-
ably Plato's brother's grandson] for all usages and purposes. Then there
is the estate in Eiresidae that I bought from Callimachus, abutted to
the north by the property of Eurymedon of Myrrhinus, to the south
by that of Demostratus of Xypete, to the east by that of Eurymedon
of Myrrhinus, and to the west by the Cephisus river.[36] Three minas of
silver; a silver bowl weighing 165 drachmas; a small cup weighing 45
drachmas; a gold signet ring and gold earring, both together weighing
4 drachmas and 3 obols. Euclides the mason owes me three minas. I
grant Artemis her freedom. I leave four house-slaves: Tychon, Bictas,
Apollonides, and Dionysius. Household furniture as set down in the in-
ventory, of which Demetrius has a copy. I owe no one any money. My
executors are Leosthenes, Speusippus, Demetrius, Hegias, Eurymedon,
Callimachus, and Thrasippus.

The will shows that Plato was not cash rich, but that was common
in ancient Greece. There was never enough coined money to satisfy
demand, and there was a flourishing system of credit, from banks or
friends. Hence Plato takes care to say that he owes no money and that
Euclides the mason owes him the not inconsiderable sum of three
minas (300 drachmas, perhaps $20,000 today). Bullion was also used
alongside coined money, and so Plato listed the value of his most pre-
cious items. Plato's wealth was all to the good: it gave him leisure time.
Philosophy would be poorer if Plato had been poor.

Athenians such as Plato from the wealth elite were well educated
and were proud of their culture. It seems that Plato, along with many
of his peers, translated such pride into snobbery. In a brilliant stretch
of *Republic*,[37] he first bemoans the fact that the kind of people who

36. The will fails to say what is to happen to this estate. It is roughly in the district where
    the Academy was, and some scholars think it is the estate in which the Academy was
    situated. This seems unlikely. If Plato had been including the Academy in the will, he
    would have mentioned the library and other valuables. So this is a private estate, and
    it was presumably left along with everything else to Adeimantus.
37. *Republic* 494a–496a.

should take up philosophy are seduced away from it by the lure of worldly power and then vilifies the unsuitable people who, attracted by the prestige of philosophy, claim the field for themselves. He concludes with this savage little portrait:

> Do you think the impression these interlopers give is any different from that of a small, bald metalworker who's come into some money? He's just got himself out of debtors' prison, he's had a bath and is wearing brand-new clothes and a bridegroom's outfit, and he's about to marry his master's daughter because she's hard up and has no one to look after her.

By the same token, people from the working class in the fictional city-state of *Republic* are rigidly excluded from a share in government, on the grounds that their occupation makes it impossible for them to have the kind of lofty and long-term thoughts that are appropriate to political leaders. Plato mellowed somewhat in his later years, but, under the influence in the first instance of his childhood upbringing, he shared not just his class's pride in their wealth and education but also their snobbery about those who had to work for a living. In this sense, too, he was a man of his times.

Religion and Religiosity

The gods permeated all aspects of life in ancient Greece, so much so that there was no word for "religion," as though it were a separate activity. And the gods and a sense of divinity permeate so many of Plato's dialogues that it must reflect sincerely held beliefs. God and gods are mentioned more than a hundred times in *Republic* and twice that in *Laws*. Plato consistently has characters in his dialogues speak of the divine in ways that show how seriously they take it, and how much they see the gods as forces for good. Piety (treating superiors, whether divine or human, with due respect and reverence) is a regular member of the set of virtues that Plato regarded as fundamental. But he did not approve of all aspects of traditional religion. To start with, he did not believe all the tales about the gods, as found in what we call the Greek myths, which would have been a major aspect of his education in early childhood. Since he believed that the gods were only ever good, he came to reject stories of their lying, cheating, vindictiveness, and so on. "We'd better not admit into our city the story of Hera being tied up by her son, or the episode when Hephaestus is hurled away by his father for trying to save his mother from a beating, or any of the battles between gods that Homer has in his poetry."[38]

Greek religion was based on practice rather than belief. There was no sacred text to whose provisions one had to adhere, no commandments or creed in which one had to believe in order to be "orthodox," no Church to coordinate practice and develop doctrine. Religion was largely a matter of the appropriate performance of ritual. But ritual also rested on a bedrock of beliefs: that the gods exist, that they provide for us, that they know more and are more powerful than us, and that they can be moved by sacrifice and prayer. All these propositions were challenged or denied by thinkers and playwrights in the late fifth century, as Plato would have known from his youthful reading and attendance at the theater, but the only one that he denied was the last. He believed that since the gods are good and take thought for us, they will do what is right anyway, without our petitioning them. And if we do petition them, it should not be for worldly prosperity, but only be for help in what is, essentially, one's own doing. We have an example:[39]

> Dear Pan and all gods here, grant that I may become beautiful within and that my external possessions may be congruent with my internal state. May I take wisdom for wealth, and may I have just as much gold as a moderate person, and no one else, could bear and carry by himself.

On the other points, he held that the gods exist and, although we can never know them fully, we can be sure of their goodness and their care for humankind; that there is no way that the world is the product of chance, and the divine is ultimately responsible not just for the

---

38. *Republic* 378d.
39. *Phaedrus* 279b–c.

creation of the world, but also for its ongoing governance and orderliness; and that atheism is not just an intellectual error but a sure way
to damn our souls.[40]

But Plato was an innovative thinker; although he recognized the
importance of conventional religion for the masses, and left it more
or less untouched in his fictional cities, he supplemented it with more
philosophical views. Most radically, he talks in his dialogues not just of
the traditional gods of the Greek pantheon—Zeus and his extended
Olympian family—but also of God in the singular. A few other thinkers before and during his lifetime did the same; the lineage began
with Xenophanes of Colophon in the sixth/fifth century and included another follower of Socrates called Antisthenes. Plato was par-
taking in and giving impetus to a movement that would culminate
only a few decades after his death in the monotheism of the Stoics,
who saw the traditional gods more as the Semitic religions today see
angels—as agents of God's providence for the world. Plato sets off in
that direction, especially in the astral theology he outlines in late dialogues such as *Timaeus* and *Laws*, where the heavenly bodies are gods
that—in an almost astrological fashion—intermediate between God
and humankind.

The Olympian gods were present in the world, their influence immediately visible. Zeus made it rain; Poseidon caused earthquakes;
Demeter made cereal crops grow; and so on. The monotheistic
tradition of Greek thought was always an attempt to transcend this
worldly perspective. Given what we know of Plato's character from
his philosophy, with its otherworldly emphasis on the soul and the
transcendent Forms, his entry into the club of Greek monotheists
should hardly occasion surprise.

Building on this quasi-monotheistic foundation, Plato came to
hold the startling view that philosophy itself had a religious purpose,
assimilation to God.[41] Most ethical thinkers would maintain that the

---

40. Plato's main discussion of these points occurs in the tenth book of *Laws*.
41. *Republic* 500c, *Theaetetus* 176b–c, *Phaedrus* 253b, *Timaeus* 90d, *Laws* 716c.

perfectibility of a person lies in their fulfilling their human nature, not in transcending it. But Plato believed that human nature has a divine as well as a bestial aspect—that we are attracted to what is true as well as to what is pleasant—and that it is our purpose to develop the divine in us, to become godlike ourselves. He acknowledges, however, that there are few who will be interested in undertaking the hard, private work involved in such a path; for most people, religion will remain the public worship of the Olympian deities through festivals and sacrifices. But God is the paradigm of goodness and moral perfection, and this will inspire at least a few people to aim to be as like him as is possible for incarnate beings. Our souls are immortal, and the point of philosophy is to purify the soul until it is capable of achieving communion with God and breaking free of the constant cycle of reincarnations. Anyone who manages to be a philosopher in three successive incarnations will never have to be incarnated again.[42] As for the rest of us, incapable as we are of such immersion, Plato was convinced that even ordinary religion, the worship of the Olympian gods, was a force for good that kept people on the narrow path of morality. This polytheistic religion was what he was exposed to and practiced in his youth, and it is likely that he learned its benefits from his own experience.

Plato's mature thoughts about God and religion represent some of his most sincerely held views. Plato's God is a rational being, who guides the universe for the good of his creatures, especially human beings, and has left clues that this is what he does—clues that are visible to those with eyes to see. But despite being, as it were, Reason personified, Plato's God is capable of arousing the kind of emotional response that constitutes religious feeling, just because he does us nothing but good. Anything bad in our lives is our own fault, not God's. God is "the best kind of soul, that takes care of the universe as a whole and guides it along its path."[43]

42. *Phaedrus* 249a.
43. *Laws* 897c.

Another unconventional feature of Plato's take on religion is that he emphasizes aspects that, though traditional, were not mainstream. His talk of assimilation to God as the goal of life echoes an ecstatic and salvationist thread in Greek religion, in which one transcends the material world by purging oneself of impurities and becomes, in effect, a god oneself. But for Plato this state is achieved not by practices such as drug taking or trance-dance (famously practiced in Plato's day by the Corybantes of Asia Minor), but by rational inquiry. He agrees that it takes a kind of "god-given madness" to transcend the material world and glimpse the "Plain of Truth,"[44] but the work of trying to turn that glimpse into a permanent awareness is largely rational work.

We should picture Plato, then, conforming throughout his life to civic religion by performing private acts of worship and taking part in the calendrical Athenian rituals, just as, at the start of *Republic*, he has Socrates attending a festival in Piraeus. But at the same time, he was also urging himself and others not to carelessly accept conventional beliefs (this is a recurrent theme in his work) but to go farther and deeper, and even to attempt to bridge the gulf between humanity and immortality. It is "proximity [to transcendent Forms] that gives a god his divine qualities,"[45] and Plato constantly holds out the promise that a true philosopher can also get to know and contemplate the Plain of Truth, where the Forms subsist. This is not a literal place but Plato's way of expressing the idea that there is more to the world than our five senses can detect.

Personal Characteristics

So as a child Plato was studious and had literary pretensions, and as an adult he was wealthy, snobbish, and religious. Can we say anything more about his character and attributes? Here we have to rely largely

44. *Phaedrus* 245b, 248b.
45. *Phaedrus* 249c.

on the ancient biographies, but it is precisely in the area of Plato's personality and temperament that they are at their most unreliable; they infer characteristics from what he wrote in the dialogues, and they exaggerate and contradict themselves. Most of the details of his personality stem from the hostile tradition started in particular by Aristoxenus of Taras: Plato was physically repulsive, morally corrupt, and intellectually dishonest. He was a pederast, a whoremonger, and a slave to tyrants, despite being hungry for political power. None of his work is original; all is taken from other thinkers. There is no way of proving Aristoxenus wrong, but surely his vehemence betrays him.

Plato certainly had a sense of humor. There is plenty of banter, irony, and sarcasm in the dialogues, but there is little to make one laugh out loud. His humor is understated, that of Cervantes rather than P.G. Wodehouse. The dialogues with the strongest veins of humor overall are *Apology of Socrates*, *Euthydemus*, and *Symposium*. There are also occasional comic scenes, such as the grumbling doorkeeper in *Protagoras*, or this homoerotic one, close to the start of *Charmides*. Socrates calls young Charmides over because he is interested in the beautiful boys of Athens—beautiful in mind as well as body. Charmides's arrival "caused a lot of laughter, because each of us who was sitting down immediately began to push his neighbor, to make room for Charmides to sit next to himself, until we forced the man sitting at one end to stand up and dumped the one at the other end on the ground to the side."

Having dismissed the idea that his name refers to his stocky build, we are left in the dark as to what Plato looked like. There are busts in existence that are or might be of the philosopher, but they are all Roman copies of lost Greek originals, and in any case they show only head and shoulders (see figure 1.2). They conform to the canons of portraiture of philosophers: Plato has a fringe (rather too Roman in appearance to inspire confidence in its authenticity) and a thick beard. His features are stern, with a slightly downturned mouth and a forehead furrowed from deep thought. One source tells us that he was stoop-shouldered and that this was imitated by his admirers. Those who derive his name from his stocky build describe him as strong.

Some say that he had a weak voice. Some claim that he kept him-self celibate, others that he had multiple affairs. He was sober, even somber, serious, humble; he enjoyed olives, a peasant food, despite his wealth; he tried not to sleep too much. He was apparently slow to find fault with others, asking himself, "Might I not be like that?" Some recent scholars have inferred from his anonymity in the dia-logues and the tradition of his haughtiness that he was shy. And so on. I pass over sillier anecdotes in silence. The trouble with these stories is that they bear the stamp of stemming either from the hostile or the comic tradition, or from the responses to such hostility. In the hostile tradition, Plato is malicious, arrogantly disrespectful, jealous, dishonest, greedy; in the favorable tradition he is altruistic, a true friend, cour-ageous, and so on.[46] There is nothing much to be learned here. Even if we had the early accounts of Plato written by people who knew him, they would probably need to be taken with a liberal dose of salt. We know what fourth-century Greek encomiastic biographies were like: we have Isocrates's *Evagoras* and Xenophon's *Agesilaus*, for instance, which, with their rather tiresome catalog of their subjects' virtues, are closer to hagiography than biography.

So much for Plato, child and man. He could, perhaps, have been a dozen other high-born young men of his generation in Athens, if they matched him for intelligence. But two events that affected him very deeply and very personally would push him onto the path that has made him a household name even today. The first was the cruelty of the Thirty Tyrants, and the second was the condemnation of Socrates by the restored democracy.

46. For these and all other anecdotes, see Riginos, *Platonica* (listed in the bibliographic "Further Reading" at the end of the book, in the section on "Plato: Letters and Biographical Details").

2

The Intellectual Environment

The first stages of Plato's education in Athens, as we have seen, were haphazard and pretty basic, and in both *Republic* and *Laws* Plato recommends a great many changes.[1] When he began to be interested in philosophy, Plato must have been self-taught to a large extent. He would have engaged his brothers and others in conversation, read the books of those who had died or were absent, and attended the lectures and seminars of living men. In this, he was peculiarly blessed because Athens had already established its place as the cultural leader of the Greek world—so much so that the historian Thucydides described the city at the time Plato was growing up as "the school of Greece."[2] Artists and intellectuals of all stripes passed through the city or took up residence there. A flourishing book trade circulated available books, though full literacy was confined to the wealthier strata of Athenian society and to educated slaves. In a momentous shift, people were beginning to read to themselves, rather than having a slave read a work out loud to them.

The anecdotal tradition certainly assumes that Plato was widely read, to judge by the number of writers he is supposed to have plagiarized. Almost all *Republic* was taken from Protagoras of Abdera and

---

1. He even suggests at one point (*Laws* 811c–812a) that some of his own moralizing work would make suitable material for children's education. Perhaps the most important suggestion he makes is that children's educational environment should be "light-hearted rather than authoritarian" (*Republic* 536e–537a). Some examples are given at *Laws* 819b–c of this kind of playful teaching of mathematics.
2. Thucydides, *The Peloponnesian War* 2.41.1; see also Plato, *Protagoras* 337d.

Timaeus from Philolaus of Croton; Plato borrowed heavily from the Pythagorizing playwright Epicharmus of Cos; Plato was not allowed to attend meetings of Pythagorean groups in case he stole the ideas; he got the notion of writing his works as dialogues from Sophron the writer of mimes, whose skill at characterization he also imitated; he copied the work of his fellow Socratics Antisthenes and Aristippus and, more inexplicably, that of the mathematician Bryson of Heraclea. Plato was so original that the hostile tradition was desperate to impugn his originality. These accounts are not wrong, in the sense that, like any writer, Plato drew on many sources; they just put a hostile spin on it and exaggerated "learning from X" to "plagiarizing X." Plato rarely simply borrowed an idea from any of his teachers, even Socrates, without transforming it and putting it to work in his own way and in the context of his own philosophical principles.

Plato and the Presocratics

The "Presocratics" is the name given to a miscellaneous group of thinkers—proto-scientists, philosophers, even the occasional mystical prophet—who lived and worked, as the name implies, before Socrates. What unites them is the attempt to give a systematic account of the whole known universe and all its major features, from the setting of the stars to the rising of the Nile. In fact, despite the name, the kind of scientific work they were doing continued during and well past Socrates's lifetime. Among the Presocratics, Plato mentions by name Thales of Miletus, Heraclitus of Ephesus, Parmenides and Zeno of Elea, Empedocles of Acragas, Pythagoras of Samos (and the Pythagoreans), and Anaxagoras of Clazomenae. This is a fairly complete roll call of the leading lights, and at other points he refers to or borrows Presocratic doctrines without naming names. However, his failure to mention by name Democritus of Abdera, a very important thinker and prolific writer who was still working and writing in his lifetime, is a perennial puzzle, first mentioned by Diogenes Laertius. It is clear that Plato had read widely in the Presocratic treatises, and he was presumably also acquainted with the summary of the Presocratics' and others' theories prepared by the polymath Hippias of Elis toward the end of the fifth century.

What Plato chiefly took from the Presocratics was the basic principle that the world is not the playground of capricious gods but an ordered system that is comprehensible by the human mind and which therefore can be laid bare by reason and argument, rather than by the senses and faith. Otherwise, he is generally critical of their scientific work. Several of them were materialists who suggested that all the furniture of the world was derived from a single underlying substance or from a few such substrates. Anaximenes of Miletus, for instance, made air his primary cosmic substance and claimed that everything else was the result of the thickening or thinning of air. Plato calls this kind of notion childish and even atheistic;[3] in his view it is not the case that the only things that exist are bodies and their properties. In *Phaedo*, Plato gives Socrates a kind of intellectual autobiography, which might as well be his as Socrates's. He says that Socrates was excited by the work of Anaxagoras, who claimed that Mind was the creative and driving force of the cosmos, but found that he failed to follow up this insight and, like Anaximenes and others, relied on purely material and mechanical causes.[4] In *Timaeus*, the most Presocratic of the dialogues, Plato gave that kind of proto-scientific idea a more sympathetic hearing,[5] but on the whole he found little of value in it and thought they were delving into areas where the truth was unknowable.

The two Presocratic thinkers who exerted the greatest influence on Plato, and for whom he shows the greatest respect, are Parmenides ("venerable and awesome," Plato calls him)[6] and Heraclitus. Plato presents them as polar opposites—Parmenides and the Eleatics (as they are known) who followed him as the champions of stability and being,

3. *Sophist* 242c–243a; *Laws* 891c–892c.
4. *Phaedo* 96a–99c.
5. Especially *Timaeus* 49b–d.
6. *Theaetetus* 183e.

and Heraclitus as the prophet of universal change and becoming. The Eleatics also taught Plato how convincing powerful argumentation could be and how important it is to be aware of the hidden assumptions on which an argument might be relying. Important stretches of argument in the dialogue *Sophist* are dedicated to clearing up just such misconceptions—ironically, those generated and perpetuated by Eleatics.

Plato seems to have come across these two lines of Presocratic thinking early in his life, because the ancient biographies and anecdotes inform us that he had two other philosophy teachers besides Socrates: a Heraclitean called Cratylus and a Parmenidean called Hermippus.[7] Aristotle names no Parmenidean teacher but says that Cratylus was actually Plato's earliest teacher.[8] Whatever the source, both Eleatic and Heraclitean influences are clearly detectable in Plato's work. In his metaphysics, he combined an Eleatic faith in the existence of eternal and stable entities with the Heraclitean view that the world of the senses was in constant flux. Everything here is always changing over time, and nothing has even its dominant qualities securely, so we have to look elsewhere for entities that truly are what they are without qualification and so are knowable and definable. Anything I might call "beautiful" may not be beautiful to someone else, or in a different context, or at a different time, so how do we know how to use the term? It must, Plato thought, be because there exists an entity that acts for us as a permanent paradigm of Beauty. From the Eleatics, Plato learned the distinction between appearance and reality, on which he hung his crucial epistemological distinction between belief and knowledge.

7. Diogenes Laertius calls this person "Hermogenes," but this is wrong. It is easy to see how the mistake arose: Hermogenes joins Cratylus as Socrates's interlocutors in Plato's dialogue *Cratylus*. *Anonymous Prolegomena to Platonic Philosophy* gets the name right.
8. Aristotle, *Metaphysics* 987a32–33. Diogenes Laertius, *Lives of the Eminent Philosophers* 3.6, says that Plato attached himself to Cratylus and Hermogenes (*sic*) after Socrates's death, but everyone else seems to think the association was earlier. There is no reason why Plato could not have been attending the lectures of other thinkers even while being a member of Socrates's group.

As for Pythagoreanism, one of the ancient biographies goes so far as to claim that Plato's thought was a synthesis of Heraclitean, Pythagorean, and Socratic ideas: "He followed Heraclitus with regard to perception, Pythagoras with regard to knowledge, and Socrates with regard to politics."[9] Others simply portray Plato as a member of the Pythagorean school. These are exaggerations, but only exaggerations. Pythagoreanism influenced Plato's metaphysics—especially their insight that numbers have the kind of immateriality, permanence, and perfection that Plato ascribes to the metaphysical entities that he calls Forms, and his accounts of the fundamental principles of the universe—but Plato learned much more than this from Pythagoreans, as we shall see in chapter 6. Plato's most noteworthy act of homage to Pythagoreanism was his making a fictional Pythagorean, Timaeus of Locri, the spokesman of his account of the physical universe, as a way of acknowledging that it was inspired by similar Pythagorean work.

No doubt Plato's reading of and thinking about the Presocratics continued throughout his working life; his detailed acquaintance with Pythagorean ideas, for instance, seems to date from after his visit in the 380s to southern Italy, which was the center of Pythagoreanism. Indeed, Diogenes Laertius dates Plato's acquaintance with the two Pythagoreans who most influenced him to this visit. But it seems safe to say that Plato was steeping himself in Presocratic work from an early age, and that his agreements and disagreements with them fundamentally affected his thinking.

Plato and the Sophists

By the third quarter of the fifth century, a new breed of professional teachers began to arrive in Athens to provide a kind of higher education. Many of the sophists (as they came to be called, though, like "Presocratics," the generic label obscures specific differences) were

9. Diogenes Laertius, *Lives of the Eminent Philosophers* 3.8.

itinerant teachers, but several of them stayed in Athens for stretches of time. The word "sophist" was used for anyone judged to be wise, but by the last quarter of the fifth century it had come to mean more specifically an expert who was prepared to impart his expertise through teaching. The sophists taught a wide range of subjects—from mathematics to martial arts, and from history to music—with particular topics more popular in particular places. Much of their teaching was less theoretical than practical. This is the most important way in which their contemporary, Socrates, differed from the sophists: if Plato is to be trusted, Socrates had an interest in ethical and metaphysical theory as well as developing an effective method of argument and enquiry. Socrates also was not a professional; he took no money for his teaching because he felt that the most important things he had to pass on were encouragement and inspiration, not information or the key to worldly success.

The kind of success the sophists were claiming to teach was importantly different from the kind that had been valued before, which was based on charisma—on the aristocratic values of military prowess, eloquence, athleticism, benefaction, and good looks. Possession of this cluster of qualities gave a man *aretē*, excellence; under the influence of the sophists, the meaning of the word shifted to mean political and moral excellence—kinds of excellence that did not depend on blood or breeding but had to be earned and worked for. The sophists did not initiate this revolution, but they were foremost in perpetuating it.

Essentially, what a person needed now to be successful in Athens and other democratic states in Greece was the ability to argue well. Democracy generated a verbal culture, and a politician's very life, let alone his career, could depend on his ability to deliver a persuasive speech in the popular assembly or a law court. In Athens, then, some of the sophists were teachers of rhetoric and disputation (and hence of grammar, terminology, argumentation, and other subjects that support rhetoric and disputation). Some of them taught their students to argue both sides of a case with equal plausibility, contrary to the unreflective view that truth must lie only with one side or the other.

Skillful speaking was a good route to political power in democratic Athens.

The sophists latched onto and made extensive analytical use of the opposition between nature (*physis*) and convention (*nomos*—the same word means both official "law" and unofficial "custom"). Did the gods exist in reality or were they human inventions? How much trust can one put in man-made laws, seeing that they are readily changed and repealed, and differ from culture to culture? Was there such a thing as natural law instead, whose demands were or should be more binding on us? Is it a natural law, which it is only realistic to recognize, that the stronger state or individual will rule the weaker, or should the strong restrain themselves and deny their self-interest in accordance with conventional justice? But does this not make human law a kind of tyrant? And so on. Plato discusses and problematizes many of these issues in his dialogues, and the nature/convention distinction under-lies many of his arguments.

It was the sophists, then, who taught Athenian young men from the wealth elite—their fees were steep[10]—to think critically and ra-tionally. They were the first to probe areas that we would now define as sociology, psychology, and political science. Their teaching proved exciting to many young men in Athens. We do not know whether Plato attended any of their lectures or seminars, but it is highly likely; their heyday coincided with his youth. Perhaps young Hippocrates, who in *Protagoras* wakes Socrates early in the morning to be sure to get on time to a house where a number of sophists were meeting and displaying their wares, was a stand-in for young Plato. In that dialogue, he paints a vivid (and somewhat tongue-in-cheek) picture of soph-ists at work that seems to draw on personal experience. Protagoras of Abdera is pacing in the colonnade of a rich man's house, followed

10. One of the reasons the sophists flocked to Athens was its wealth, generated in the first instance by its empire. Wealth creates leisure, and leisure makes time for non-practical pursuits such as education. The Greek word for "leisure" is *skholē*, from which we get the word "school." Plato comments on the sophists' fees at *Meno* 91d, *Hippias Major* 282d–e, and *Apology of Socrates* 19d–20c.

by a group of young men (including Plato's uncle Charmides) who hang on his words; Hippias of Elis is seated in the opposite colonnade, surrounded by another group, while Prodicus of Ceos is in a nearby room with his admirers. Apart from these three, other sophists appear or are mentioned in the dialogues: Gorgias of Leontini, Polus of Acragas, Thrasymachus of Chalcedon, Evenus of Paros, Damon of Oa, and the brothers Euthydemus and Dionysodorus of Chios.

But the excitement that the sophists aroused was offset by a degree of suspicion, especially among those with conservative values. "Any decent Athenian gentleman," claims Anytus in Plato's *Meno*, "will do a better job of improving a young man than the sophists."[11] They were feared as slick—as *deinos*, a word that simultaneously meant "clever" and "frightening." The most famous orator of them all, Gorgias of Leontini, did nothing to allay such fears when he likened speech to a powerful drug that operates by a kind of deceit or bewilderment to stir or pacify emotions and change men's minds.[12] In an episode of edgy comedy in his play *Clouds*, produced in 423, Aristophanes portrayed a debate between Unjust Argument and Just Argument, in which Unjust Argument trounces his fuddy-duddy opponent with sophistic arguments.

There was potential here for real conflict, but it is not certain how far it went. It seems that around 430 a decree, proposed by a man called Diopeithes, was passed in Athens to the effect that "anyone who did not pay due respect to divine phenomena or who offered to teach others about celestial phenomena should be impeached."[13] It was the start of the Peloponnesian War, the Athenians were in the grip of a pandemic, and they turned against science and toward religion.[14] In itself, Diopeithes's decree was aimed at Presocratic scientists rather than sophists, and was perhaps a way to get at Pericles, the leading

11. *Meno* 92e. See also the remarks of another follower of Socrates: Xenophon, *On Hunting* 13.
12. Gorgias, *In Praise of Helen* 8–14.
13. Plutarch, *Life of Pericles* 32.1.
14. Despite Thucydides's fine description (*The Peloponnesian War* 2.47–54) identification of the famous plague has proved impossible, though the guesses are many.

Athenian statesman of the time, who counted Anaxagoras among his close friends. But the case seems not to have come to court, and Anaxagoras simply left Athens to avoid trouble. Protagoras, the earliest and most philosophical of the sophists, also seems to have come under attack, but again the evidence does not allow us to conclude that any case came to court. On the other hand, it is certain that another of Pericles's associates (a kinsman by marriage), the Athenian musicologist and political theorist Damon, was banished "for seeming to be too much of an intellectual."[15] And Diagoras of Melos, a poet of otherwise little consequence, fled into exile to avoid a trial for atheism.

There was clearly a degree of intolerance in Athens toward the end of the fifth century, exacerbated by the facts that most of the sophists were not Athenian and that they were making themselves outrageously rich, but a few near-prosecutions do not add up to persecution, and wealthy, leisured Athens was still a congenial place for artists and intellectuals. It would have been harder for Socrates and Plato to have thrived elsewhere. Intellectuals got into trouble only on those extremely rare occasions when they were felt to be politically undesirable or (what came to the same thing) to be in danger of offending the gods. The legal instruments that were available to be used against them were either Diopeithes's decree or the more flexible charge of impiety—the charge that would be brought against Plato's teacher, Socrates.

Plato agreed that the sophists were dangerous, but for different reasons. It is true that he felt that their work could lead some people to amoral and politically dubious conclusions, and he reacts strongly to this in *Gorgias* and the first book of *Republic*, where his main interlocutor is the sophist Thrasymachus. As far as Plato was concerned, there was no point to intellectual studies unless they led to an understanding of what the good is for human beings. But other sophists, such as Protagoras, held perfectly conventional moral and political positions, and Plato, preceded by Socrates, was delighted to learn from

15. Plutarch, *Life of Aristeides* 1.7.

the sophists that political science was a science, something that should
be left to experts rather than amateurs.

Plato's disagreement with the sophists was, first, with their teaching
methods—they treated their students as passive recipients of information rather than as active co-searchers after knowledge—and, second,
with their assumptions and arguments. They did not deepen understanding of political and moral issues because they were concerned
solely or chiefly with teaching people how to be successful in the
context of current politics and morality. To do that in democratic
Athens, they had to adopt the mob's standards and values, which Plato
considered to be largely corrupt. Their arguments could also tend to
favor relativism over absolute moral standards. As Protagoras put it,
"Man is the measure of all things," and part of what he meant is that
there is no absolute right or wrong, but only what seems to an individual or state to be right or wrong. We determine our own truths.
Hence, unlike many earlier wise men of Greece, the sophists did not
claim divine authority for what they were saying but spoke in their
own names.

Moreover, some sophists were concerned to win arguments at all
costs, and even just to score points against opponents to gain the
applause of the audience. At best, they were genuinely interested in
training the mind, but Plato thought that education should also train
character because a person with a bad character will use the intellectual attainments gained from the sophists for bad purposes. The sophists held debating contests and took up any position they could render
plausible, while Plato was looking for moral and political principles
that could survive the most searching examination. Why should the
ability to speak well qualify a person to be a political leader? A rhetor-
ician does no more than win others over to his point of view; he persuades people rather than giving them the truth. Should the criterion
not be whether or not he possesses political expertise, which in Plato's
terms is the ability to benefit all members of a community? The difference of approach is neatly summarized in a statement of Isocrates of
Athens, one of the fourth-century heirs of the sophists, that "plausible

belief about useful things is far superior to exact knowledge of useless things."[16] At several points in the dialogues, Plato confronts and even celebrates the accusation that philosophy as he understood it was impractical and useless. Nevertheless, as we shall see, Plato also felt that his principles were capable of practical application, and in Syracuse he made a famous attempt to demonstrate this.

Plato and Socrates

In Plato's opinion, Socrates was "the best, the wisest, and the most just" person of his time,[17] and he is said to have thanked his lucky stars that he was born in his time.[18] I have suggested that Plato was introduced to him by his brothers; in fact, among the ancient biographers, Apuleius of Madaurus says that it was his father, Ariston, who effected the introduction, since he was planning to hire Socrates as Plato's tutor. But Ariston was long dead. Perhaps Apuleius meant to name Pyrilampes, Plato's stepfather; but, still, it was in Rome and the provincial cities of the Roman empire in Apuleius's day that rich men hired famous philosophers as private tutors for their sons, not in fifth-century Athens. At any rate, from about the age of sixteen, perhaps, Plato knew Socrates. Socrates already had around him a group consisting mainly of young men. Born in 470/69, he is first mentioned as an influence on young people in a fragment of a comic play produced in the late 430s, and was famous enough by the time of Plato's birth to have been one of the butts of Aristophanes's satirical play *Clouds*, produced in 423. Although Socrates was not from the same social stratum as Plato's family, he had married well and was a familiar figure in some quarters of Athenian high society.

---

16. Isocrates, *Helen* 5. See also the criticisms of Isocrates's student, Theopompus of Chios, on pp. xxviii–xxix.
17. These are the closing words of *Phaedo*, an obituary after portraying Socrates's death in prison from drinking the poison hemlock. They are substantially repeated at *Letter 7* 324e.
18. Plutarch, *Life of Marius* 46.1.

It was said that, on the night before he met Plato, Socrates dreamed that he was cradling a fledgling swan in his lap, which grew wings and took off, singing sweetly enough to please both gods and men, and the next day, on meeting Plato, he recognized him as the swan of his dream. The swan was Apollo's bird, for the beauty of its song and for the legend that, since it sings most beautifully before dying, it is able to predict its death—Apollo being the god of prophecy as well as music. The ancient biographers are singularly unhelpful on the relationship between Socrates and Plato. They reflect the fact that it was important to both of them—to Socrates because now he had someone to carry on his work and to Plato because he had found his teacher. But most of the stories they tell either focus on Plato's conversion to philosophy by Socrates, who persuaded him in one anecdote not to go and become a professional mercenary soldier,[19] or stem from the tradition hostile to Plato and imply that Plato misrepresented Socrates's teachings. For instance: "They say that Socrates, after hearing Plato read *Lysis*, said, 'What a lot of falsehoods the young man tells about me.'"[20]

It is difficult to know what to say about Socrates because the historical person is elusive. He himself wrote nothing, but probably just because it was rare in those days for a person to commit his thoughts to writing, not because he was suspicious of the written word. Aristophanes's *Clouds*, though contemporary with Socrates, is more or less useless as evidence because his "Socrates" is a catch-all figure, an amalgam of comically exaggerated versions of sophist and Presocratic. We have the complete Socratic writings of two of his followers, Plato and Xenophon, but both of them were writing a kind of fiction: what Socrates might have said and done had he been in conversation with so-and-so about such-and-such a topic. When we read Plato's *Laches*, for instance, we should not think that Socrates ever

19. This is presumably to confuse Plato with his fellow Socratic, Xenophon, who did become a professional soldier, despite Socrates's advice, and wrote about his experiences in what many consider his best book, *The Anabasis* (*The Expedition of Cyrus*).
20. Diogenes Laertius, *Lives of the Eminent Philosophers* 3.35.

engaged the two Athenian generals, Laches and Nicias, on the topic of courage; he might have, but even so, Plato could not have been present at the conversation and no one recorded it. The conversation is Plato's idea of what might have taken place had such a meeting ever occurred. We do not know what Socrates himself thought about courage, only what Plato makes him say. All the philosophy of the dialogues should therefore be ascribed to Plato, not to Socrates.

The details must remain elusive, but the overall tenor of Socrates's work is clear. In a famous passage, the Roman statesman and philosopher Cicero said that he "was the first to call philosophy down from the heavens, transfer it to society and even introduce it into people's homes, and compel it to inquire about life and morality—about what things are good and bad."[21] Actually, since the earliest sophists predate Socrates, it was they who first "called philosophy down from the heavens" (that is, broke away from Presocratic proto-scientific cosmology) and focused on politics and human ethics. Socrates, from this perspective, was part of a movement that was being followed by the sophists and by the Presocratic thinker Democritus of Abdera; but it is probably safe to say that he was the most important element in that movement.

Aristotle's summary of Socrates's work is also useful:[22] "Although he confined his inquiry to ethics and did not study the nature of the universe as a whole, he still sought within the moral sphere for the universal and was the first to concentrate his attention on definitions." This is very much what we find Socrates doing in one set of Plato's dialogues, and to a lesser extent in Xenophon's accounts of Socrates as well. In *Laches*, for example, the issue is to define courage. One of Socrates's interlocutors suggests that courage is standing firm in battle. But Socrates comes up with a counter-example, thus proving that "standing firm in battle" is not a universal definition of courage. And so the search for a definition—which is really the quest for expert knowledge—goes on. It is thanks to Socrates that philosophy became

21. Cicero, *Tusculan Disputations* 5.4.10.
22. Aristotle, *Metaphysics* 987b1–4; see also *Metaphysics* 1078b7–32.

and remains inquisitive and self-reflective, whereas before his time it had been dogmatic. For Socrates, and then for Plato, philosophy was argument, not the production of untested and untestable grand ideas.

The Socratic search for definitions or the true meaning of terms was of fundamental importance to Plato. Immediately after his remark about Socrates, Aristotle goes on: "Hence his follower, Plato, judged that the entities thus defined could not be perceptible things, but must be of some different kind, since it is impossible for there to be a general definition of any sensible thing, seeing that they are constantly changing." The "different kind of entities" are the Platonic Forms, the metaphysical entities that are Plato's best-known contribution to philosophy. Plato believed that the only things that are stable and constant enough to be truly definable and knowable are these immaterial entities, that subsist in some heavenly realm, which in *Phaedrus* is called the Plain of Truth. Therefore, insofar as the goal of philosophy is knowledge, a philosopher has to get acquainted with Forms, the only true objects of knowledge. Reason assures a seeker that the Forms exist, and then he might be able to sense their existence as well. Diogenes the Cynic once cast doubt on the existence of Forms: "I can see a table and a cup, but not tablehood and cuphood." Plato replied: "That's right, because you have the eyes with which to see a cup and a table, but not the mind with which to comprehend tablehood and cuphood."[23]

When Aristotle said that Socrates confined his inquiry to ethics (*ēthika*), he meant that Socrates was concerned with character (*ēthos*)—with what forms it and what people can do to become better people. Ethics and politics were peculiarly linked in classical Greece. Everyone assumed, not unreasonably, that the fundamental influence on a person's character was the society in which they lived. So in *Republic* Plato accuses Athenian society of being the greatest cause of the corruption of promising young men, and he occupies himself with imagining an ideal state in which all the citizens would be

23. Diogenes Laertius, *Lives of the Eminent Philosophers* 6.53.

good to the best of their abilities—that is, would develop the virtues appropriate to their ways of life. And Aristotle's *Politics* is expressly a continuation of his *Nicomachean Ethics*: thorough ethical inquiry entails also describing the state that will best allow its citizens to flourish.

In this sense Socrates too was a political thinker, and all our sources for his work describe him as such. Socrates's political views were based on a simple premise, one that was shared by all his followers: "Socrates said that it was not those who held the scepter who were kings and rulers, nor those who were elected by unauthorized persons, nor those who were appointed by lot, nor those who had gained their position by force or fraud, but those who knew how to rule."[24] In this single sentence, he dismisses in turn the claims of monarchy, oligarchy, democracy, and tyranny to be legitimate constitutions, in favor of government by experts, however many there may be.[25] His intention was to reform the young men of Athens, who would be the next generation of political leaders. He saw politics as a profession and wanted leadership to be in the hands of such experts. These views on leadership were taken over wholesale by Plato.

If a political leader was an expert and was recognized as such, people would willingly obey him, Socrates believed, because they would see that he had their best interests at heart and that there was no one more effective than him at doing them good. This obedience is not coerced, then; Socrates did not envision a totalitarian state. Were there to be a Socratic leader, his first purpose would be the persuasion by rational argument of as many of the citizens in his care who had ears to hear that the focus of their lives should be on improving their souls, and his second purpose would be the establishment of legislative apparatus suitable for achieving this goal. This is, in broad terms, the agenda of Plato's two greatest political works, *Republic* and *Laws*.

---

24. Xenophon, *Memorabilia* 3.9.10; see also especially 3.6–7, and Plato, *Crito* 47a–d and *Apology* 25b.
25. I should say, since the term "tyrant" will frequently recur, that in Greek terms it simply means someone who gained power by unconstitutional means. Some were also tyrants in our sense of the word, oppressive rulers, but not all.

If we guess that Plato met Socrates when he was about sixteen and Socrates in his early sixties, then their association lasted eight or nine years before Socrates's death. This is a good length of time, and it is not surprising to find Plato describing Socrates not as his teacher but as his friend and companion.[26] When a teacher sees his role not just as imparting information but also encouraging a student to change his character and way of life, at a certain point that teacher becomes a friend (or an enemy). We can only guess what form their association took. It is likely that Plato and others met regularly as a group, presided over by Socrates. They would not only discuss and develop theories but, insofar as the work was intended to change their lives, they would undertake practical exercises based on their convictions and then report back on their experiences to Socrates and the rest of the group.

I admit that this conjecture is largely a retrojection back onto the Socratics of the practices of the Stoic school; but Xenophon seems to hint at such group work when he has Socrates say:[27] "In company with friends, I open and read from beginning to end the books in which the wise men of the past times have written down and bequeathed to us their treasures, and when we come across anything good we take it for ourselves; and we regard our mutual friendship as great gain."

Socrates's influence on Plato was enormous. It is no exaggeration to say that all Plato's philosophical work, in areas ranging from metaphysics to politics, echoes and elaborates ideas and approaches he learned from Socrates. That is why Socrates plays such a dominant role in the dialogues. Of the twenty-eight dialogues that I confidently count as authentic, Socrates is absent from only one, *Laws*, though he hardly plays a part in four others (*Sophist*, *Statesman*, *Timaeus*, *Critias*). And Plato also learned from Socrates how to go about writing and doing philosophy. Throughout the dialogues he consistently has Socrates engage people in conversation. His transformative new idea

26. *Letter 7* 324e, 325b.
27. Xenophon, *Memorabilia* 1.6.14.

was that the best way for people to search for the truth of any matter was not by writing treatises but by bouncing ideas off one another— or, internally, off oneself.[28] He believed that productive thinking of any kind had a conversational structure in that it proceeded by question and answer, by the to and fro of argument. In *Republic*, dialectic— the art of philosophical conversation—is said to be the "copestone" of the education that the Guardians of the imaginary city are to have.[29] When Antisthenes, another follower of Socrates, was asked what he gained from philosophy, he replied that it was the ability to converse with himself.[30]

The most famous kind of Socratic conversation involves short questions and answers, as Socrates seeks what follows from a given hypothesis and what conflicts with it. But some of his conversations involve longer speeches and even stretches of monologue. The overriding principle is summed up in his famous saying that "the unexamined life is not worth living."[31] It is better for me to come to the realization that a belief I hold is false than to carry on acting on that belief. Everyone always does what they think best for themselves, but without such examination, and ultimately without knowing what goodness is, people are liable to mistake where their advantage lies. And it turns out that what is always and everywhere good for a person is moral excellence—the virtues justice, courage, prudential wisdom, piety, and self-control. Socrates, followed by Plato, was constantly pushing the question: What is it to live well?

In short, if it is true to say that Plato invented philosophy, that is only because Socrates chose not to write his thoughts down. Not that Plato was ever merely a mouthpiece for Socrates. No writer of

28. For thinking—or at least the kind of thinking we call "thinking things through"—as internal conversation, see *Theaetetus* 189e, *Sophist* 263e, and *Philebus* 38c–e. At *Topics* 163b3–4 Aristotle recommends arguing with oneself if one cannot find someone to argue with. The English philosopher William Godwin (1756–1836) agreed: Truth "is struck out . . . by the collision of mind with mind" (*Political Justice*, vol. 1 [1793], 21). Nevertheless, like Plato, Godwin also committed his thoughts to paper.
29. *Republic* 534e.
30. Diogenes Laertius, *Lives of the Eminent Philosophers* 6.6.
31. *Apology of Socrates* 38a.

genius is a parrot—though, if the ancient biographers are right, he may be a swan! Be that as it may, as a result of his thinking about the Presocratics, Plato became and remained throughout his life opposed to materialism and mechanistic causation. As a result of his reflecting on the sophists, he became and remained throughout his life opposed to skepticism about the possibility of knowledge, to relativism, and to the commodification of wisdom. He insisted, with Socrates as his model, that a teacher should not take money for his teaching. And, thanks to Socrates, he became the philosopher that he was.

Plato's Colleagues: The First Socratics

Plato was not the only follower Socrates had. We know of thirty-three people who were Plato's contemporaries and who knew and worked with Socrates. We do not always know their relative ages, but it is safe to say that Plato must have known most or all of them, and known them in that peculiarly intimate and intense way that working together in a group creates. Not surprisingly, the majority of them were native Athenians, but there were also a number of foreigners, who would have taken up temporary residence in Athens.[32] Thirty-three is a good haul, but we know very little about most of them. Some are no more than names; in the case of those who became authors like Plato, we usually have little more than a name and a list of alleged book titles. Some of them appear as narrators or interlocutors in Plato's dialogues, but it would be rash to infer much about their

32. Athenians: Aeschines, a certain Antiphon, Antisthenes, Apollodorus, Aristodemus, the brothers Chaerecrates and Chaerephon, Charmides, Critias, Crito, Critobulus, Ctesippus, a certain Diodorus, Epigenes, Euthydemus, Hermogenes, Lysanias, Menexenus, Simon, Socrates the Younger, Theages, Theodotus, Xenophon, and Plato's brothers Adeimantus and Glaucon. Non-Athenians: Aristippus of Cyrene, Cebes of Thebes, Cleombrotus of Ambracia, Euclides of Megara, Phaedo of Elis, Phaedondas of Thebes, Simmias of Thebes, Terpsion of Megara. Probably some of the other people whom Plato has participate in his dialogues should also count as Socratics, but the tradition, as found in Diogenes Laertius, for example, has not accorded them that distinction.

characters or work from that. We know the most about Aeschines of
the deme Sphettus (also sometimes known as Aeschines Socraticus, to
distinguish him from a famous politician of the later fourth century),
Antisthenes, Aristippus of Cyrene, Critias, Euclides of Megara, and
Xenophon.

Critias we know about chiefly because of his involvement with the
Thirty Tyrants, and it is possible that, as an older man (born around 460),
he was only loosely attached to the Socratic circle. Crito, Chaerephon,
and Chaerecrates, however, who were certainly Socrates's followers,
were much the same age as Critias. Nevertheless, Critias probably belongs among the people who knew and admired Socrates and were
attracted to certain features of his work but were never really members of the inner circle. It was young men whom Socrates chiefly
sought, those who would be the future leaders of Athens.

Aeschines and Xenophon wrote about Socrates, but Antisthenes,
Aristippus, Phaedo, and Euclides—and Plato, of course—not only
wrote but also founded schools or fresh lines of Socratic work. Along
with Plato, Antisthenes was the most influential: he taught Diogenes
of Sinope, the first true Cynic and one of the most remarkable figures from ancient Greece; Diogenes then taught Crates, and Crates
taught Zeno of Citium, the founder of Stoicism, so it was because
of Antisthenes that the Cynics and the Stoics, throughout their long
histories, thought of themselves as descendants of Socrates. When
Aristippus returned to his native Cyrene, in North Africa, he founded
a school that promoted moderate pleasure as the goal of life, combined with skepticism about the possibility of objective knowledge
of anything, owing either to the limitations of the human mind or
to things being too indeterminate for us to get a proper grasp on
them. And Euclides founded the Megarian school, members of which
did important work in logic and the philosophy of language, as well
as Socratically inspired ethics; the school went through changes but
lasted until the end of the fourth century. We know too little about
Phaedo's school in Elis to be sure how to characterize it, but he seems,
like Antisthenes, to have promoted philosophy as a way of life and a

form of therapy rather than just a way of tackling abstract concepts. These were not "schools" in the sense that members had to toe the party line; they may not even have had a school building. They were simply groups of like-minded people.

The differences between these lines of Socratic work are telling, and they deserve a short digression. We happen to know the philosophical positions on pleasure attributed to Socrates by various Socratics. In *Protagoras*, Plato makes Socrates state a hedonist thesis. Wherever the word "good" is used with human reference, "pleasant" could be substituted, and every occurrence of "bad" could be replaced by "unpleasant." This looks like out-and-out hedonism, but a less indiscriminate kind is not ruled out, if we attribute to Socrates the belief that a thinking person will always find that his true long-term pleasure (as opposed to the short-term satisfaction of desire) coincides with the practice and performance of virtue. Socrates's position on pleasure would then dovetail with his position in Xenophon, where he holds that there are both good and bad pleasures—good pleasures being those that accompany moral behavior and bad pleasures being dangerous to one's moral self. On this view the value of pleasure depends on the value of the thing or activity we find pleasant; pleasure is not an out-and-out good. Hedonism is also attributed to Socrates in a papyrus fragment of a dialogue[33]—could it have been written by Aristippus?—but the text is too disjointed for us to be certain what kind of hedonism is involved. Antisthenes, however, appears to have been firmly anti-hedonistic. He comes close to Xenophon's Socrates when he says that his asceticism affords him greater pleasure than indulgence does—but he immediately goes on to say that he could wish that this were not so, since so much pleasure cannot be good for one.[34] Later sources report that Antisthenes claimed that only the pleasures of hard work are worthwhile, or even that he would rather

33. *PKöln* 205.
34. Xenophon, *Symposium* 4.39.

go mad than feel pleasure. Meanwhile, Aristippus held that avoidance of trouble of any kind is pleasant and is the goal of life.

What is important about this for Plato's biography is its demonstration that Plato was not, nor did he take himself to be, the only "true" Socratic. He had worked with and alongside other Socratics, and after Socrates's death, when the group dispersed and some of them started writing and lecturing, he read their work and kept in contact with them. They were not writing only dialogues. Antisthenes, for example, who had studied with Gorgias, also wrote speeches, systematic philosophical treatises, and a commentary on Homer. As well as his Socratic works, Xenophon wrote history, biography, essays and treatises on various topics, and a fictional account of the education of an ideal prince. As for their Socratic works, none of them was writing the history of philosophy; all of them were using Socrates as a literary device to express their own thoughts and puzzles.

In fact, where pleasure is concerned, they might *all* be true Socratics, if Socrates's position on pleasure was that pleasure or its lack is a natural or God-given guide as to what is beneficial for a person. All the views I sketched in this section are compatible with that. Suppose, then, that Socrates's role was to formulate generalizations such as this one, and then leave it up to his students to develop particular theories from them. Later, we will find Plato doing much the same in the Academy. No Socratic was just a spokesman for Socrates; there was no such thing as Socratic orthodoxy.

Even with our scant evidence, we can trace other disagreements among the Socratics, about more than just pleasure. The ancient biographies exaggerated these disagreements into rivalry and personal enmity. Socratic conversation, as I have said, involved people bouncing ideas off one another; through their books, the Socratics were, in effect, having just such conversations with one another and with their readers. And I imagine that among the key questions they asked themselves and one another were: "Would Socrates approve? Is this notion consistent with his principles?" We actually have a trace of this. Aristotle preserves a response by Aristippus to a "rather dogmatic assertion" by Plato: "But our mutual friend would never have spoken like that."[35]

On the whole, dialogue seems a better explanation than hostility, though it is possible that there were some clashes of personality. Aeschines and Aristippus were particular friends, and perhaps others were particular enemies. Antisthenes the ascetic might have found Aristippus's hedonism so distasteful that there was genuine rancor. Xenophon might have been thinking of Aristippus when he accused some people of gaining a few scraps of wisdom from Socrates for free and then selling them to others at a high price,[36] because Aristippus was reportedly the first of the Socratics to charge for a course of lectures. The title of Antisthenes's dialogue *Sathōn* was said to be a vulgar pun on Plato's name (*Platōn*): *sathōn* means "prick." In a sense, then, Plato was a rival of his fellow Socratic writers. This was not a sordid rivalry, seeking to attract students for monetary gain: like Socrates, Plato did not charge for his teaching. It is just that it is typically ancient Greek to proclaim your superiority to others in your field. Artists did it, and so did historians and comic poets; why not philosophers?

But, despite their differences, the Socratics were involved in a common enterprise, the importance of which outweighed any disagreements. They wanted to defend Socrates's memory and write good literature, but above all, they showed Socrates doing philosophy. They refused to let philosophy die with the physical death of their mentor.

Not surprisingly, given their common Socratic background, there are common themes to their work. Above all, they denied that the things that people usually take to be good, such as wealth and social status, were truly good, and held that only virtue truly fulfills a person's potential as a human being (procures them *eudaimonia*, happiness or well-being). Like everyone else, I aim in all I do for my own happiness; so the Socratics are saying that, properly understood and properly

35. Aristotle, *Rhetoric* 1398b32.
36. Xenophon, *Memorabilia* 1.2.60.

practiced, the virtues are my salvation. In fact (according to Plato, at any rate), to be virtuous is to align oneself, as microcosm, with the universe, the macrocosm: "Wise men say that cooperation, love, order, discipline, and justice bind heaven and earth, gods and men."[37] I suspect that these "wise men" are Plato himself and his fellow Socratics. They were so well known for their extraordinary emphasis on virtue that an outsider, the Athenian speechwriter Lysias, could arouse hostility toward Aeschines simply by saying how odd it was that a Socratic could have become involved in financial irregularities.[38]

So the Socratics were in pursuit of the truth, especially in the field of ethics, in the belief that knowledge of the truth about the world and its principles improves one's life and makes one a better person; they understood that respect for the truth is the foundation of all morality, and they sought rational and valid arguments that stood a chance of yielding the truth of any matter; they explored the relationship between body and soul (insisting that soul is the highest and noblest part of a human being), and the nature of soul; they discussed pleasure, the lure that binds us to the material world. They were not just inventing the discipline that we now call philosophy but also making sure that it took a Socratic direction. We can trace this process in some detail in Plato, but we do not have enough of the work of his colleagues to be sure of their contributions. We have the complete Socratic works of Xenophon, but, although the furrow that he plowed was certainly Socratic, it does not have the philosophical depth of Plato's work; nor, apparently, did Aeschines's publications.

Even lacking the details, however, it is safe to claim that the invention of philosophy was what Plato and his peers were up to. They went about it quite aggressively, as we shall see in Plato's case. They flooded the market with their books, writing scores of philosophical works in the forty or so years after Socrates's death. They were attempting to sweep aside anyone else's claim to be an educator, and so we see Plato's Socrates taking on sophists, rhetoricians, poets, and

37. *Gorgias* 507e–508a.
38. Lysias, Fragment 1 Carey (i.e., Fragment 1 in Carey's edition of Lysias's works).

anyone who was held to be an expert in anything—anyone who offered a different set of goals for people than those he held to be important. Even in the next generation, members of Plato's school, such as Aristotle and Heraclides of Pontus, wrote dialogues (though they did not feature Socrates): it had become one of the main ways to present philosophy. There are traces of the writing of dialogues, or bits of dialogue, by some of the sophists, but the Socratics made the genre their own.

Plato began writing in the 390s. He was probably not the first of the Socratics to write dialogues, but it is not certain which of his colleagues deserves the credit. Nor was Plato the inventor of the dialogue form: in a lost early work, *On the Poets*, Aristotle, a fairly close witness and a good researcher, attributes that to someone who was not a Socratic, a certain Alexamenus of Teos.[39] We can be reasonably certain that neither Plato nor anyone else started to write Socratic dialogues until after Socrates's death in 399: why would they bother when Socrates was still alive?[40] Why would they mythologize someone whose reality was available for all to see? Part of the point of the Socratics' dialogues was to make the Athenians wonder why they had ever put him to death. Apart from the obvious ways of doing this, by portraying him as a good and god-fearing man, they were also exploiting the tragic and ironic possibilities of including Socrates as a character in their works, and often the lead character, when every reader knew that this was a man who had been put to death by the authorities. To take the plainest example: in Plato's *Euthyphro* we (tragically) see Socrates discussing piety while waiting to be indicted for impiety, and we (ironically) hear Euthyphro's confidence that Socrates will win his case. The shadow of Socrates's trial and death looms over stretches of several dialogues.[41]

39. Aristotle, Fragment 72 Rose.
40. A tenuous indication of this is that at *Apology of Socrates* 39c–d Plato has Socrates tell the assembled Athenians that *after his death* his young followers would continue his work of reproaching them for living wrongly.
41. See, e.g., *Republic* 516e–517e, *Gorgias* 486a–b, *Gorgias* 521e–522a, *Meno* 94e, *Theaetetus* 172c–d.

Plato exploited these possibilities with more than just his Socrates character, and never more than when including the murderous oligarchs Critias and Charmides in a dialogue (*Charmides*) discussing self-restraint and self-knowledge, or when having Socrates talk to two Athenian generals, Nicias and Laches, about courage, when both had been responsible for setbacks that had helped seal Athens's defeat in the Peloponnesian War. Other Platonic characters had earned public opprobrium or met with unpleasant deaths, or both: Alcibiades, Polemarchus, Aristotle of Thorae, Phaedrus, Eryximachus. Plato's original readers would have read the dialogues with the fates of these people in the forefront of their minds. So at the end of *First Alcibiades*, for instance, when Alcibiades has promised to devote himself to justice, Socrates doubts whether he will manage to do so—because Plato and his readers knew perfectly well that he did not.

Aristotle recognized the books Plato and the rest were writing as a new genre of literature, which he called *Sōkratikoi logoi*, "Socratic discourses," and he compared them to the mimes of Sophron because they, too, were fictional representations of lifelike characters, written in prose, unaccompanied by music, and involving dialogue. The Sophron connection is highlighted by Aristotle and the biographical tradition, but arguably Athenian drama was just as great an influence on the dialogues, which are, after all, dramatized conversations by an invisible author. They include "stage directions" to help readers visualize the scene, characters entering and exiting, debate (a standard element of Athenian tragedy), changes of scenery, and so on. *Euthydemus* has five "acts" like an Athenian comedy and often ventures into the realm of the absurd.

At any rate, even Aristotle, writing perhaps sixty years after Socrates's death and drawing on what he had been told during his years in the Academy, believed that the dialogues were a kind of fiction, except that they were usually populated by actual historical people. They were, if you like, mimes of Socrates's life and conversations; so a Platonic dialogue does not just portray Socrates, but is written in the spirit of Socrates. The *Sōkratikoi logoi* shared themes and scenarios, confirming that the writers kept in touch with one another and were engaged in a common enterprise. For example, in addition to the two dialogues named *Alcibiades* that are included in the Platonic corpus, four other Socratics wrote dialogues with the same name, featuring Socrates in conversation with (and trying to tame) his beloved. Both Xenophon and Plato wrote a *Symposium*; both Euclides and Plato wrote a *Crito*; both Antisthenes and Aeschines wrote an *Aspasia*, featuring larger-than-life versions of the intellectual former courtesan who became the wife of Pericles, the leading Athenian statesman in the third quarter of the fifth century. For all that Plato's great fame has eclipsed the others, we should remember, as we track his career as a Socratic writer, that he was not alone.

3

From Politics to Philosophy

Early in *Letter 7*, Plato tells us of his expectation that, when he came of age, he would immediately "enter public life," or in other words, embark on a political career. From the age of thirty, he could make himself available for selection for senior office, but from the age of twenty he could begin to attend and address the popular Assembly, the legislative body of Athens. The system was that the Council (five hundred men) prepared motions for the Assembly (up to six thousand men), and once the Assembly had come to a decision, the Council then instructed the senior officers to carry it out or formed subcommittees to do the work. It was normal for aspiring young politicians to give speeches in the Assembly; hence the importance of the rhetorical training supplied by the sophists.

Plato's expectation was perfectly plausible because the Athenian democracy relied on members of the wealth elite to hold high office. Rich men were the only ones with the leisure (and, they were inclined to add, the expertise) to play a political role, for which they received no stipend. They were happy to do so—to trade monetary capital for political capital. Moreover, aristocratic families tended to have networks of friendships with their peers in other Greek city-states, which made them the natural choice to conduct foreign policy. Under the democracy, many official positions were subject to sortition—that is, to a lottery that was applied to a long list of volunteer candidates from each of the ten tribes. Such positions were often prestigious rather than powerful, but in both the military and financial fields there were posts that were filled by annual election because it was believed that these posts required expertise, not just loyalty to the democracy. So there was a whole range of possibilities for a rich and ambitious young man, from treating politics as an occasional occupation to making it a profession.

Several times in Socratic works, we see Socrates advising young men about their future political careers. They are always scions of wealthy houses: Plato's brother Glaucon, his uncle Charmides, Euthydemus (owner of one of the first libraries in Athens), Alcibiades, Theages.[1] In *Republic*, Plato imagines the corruption of a politically ambitious young man "from a wealthy and noble family."[2] Aristophanes, the writer of comedies, vulgarly confirms the point when he describes politicians as "stretch-arsed":[3] it was the kind of elite boy who had an older male lover in his teens who might later become a politician. Plato's interest in politics was sustained by Socrates's desire to change the amateurism of Athenian politics. Socrates played a normal citizen's part in Athenian politics, but he never sought high office because he believed, according to Plato, that society was too corrupt for effective political action.[4] But Plato felt himself destined for a political career; he thought he could do Athens good.

The Thirty Tyrants

Plato came of age at a time when even the most optimistic of his fellow citizens could no longer doubt that they were going to lose the war. The blame game was in full swing between rich and poor. The oligarchs of 411 had wanted to negotiate an end to the war even then, and since the city now, seven years later, had to surrender

1. Xenophon, *Memorabilia* 3.6, 3.7, and 4.2; Plato, *First Alcibiades*; [Plato], *Theages*.
2. *Republic* 494c–e.
3. Aristophanes, *Acharnians* 716, *Clouds* 1088–94.
4. *Apology of Socrates* 31c–32e.

unconditionally, they felt that they held the moral high ground. The stage was set for the regime of the Thirty Tyrants.

It was a shattered Athens that was besieged and starved into surrender in 404. Land had been devastated, overseas properties lost, livelihoods destroyed or undermined, families decimated, the state's revenues reduced to almost nothing. In August, several months after the city had fallen and around the time that Plato came of age, the ten democratically elected generals were deposed on Spartan orders, and a temporary board was formed of five "Overseers" to act as an interim administration; Critias, Plato's mother's cousin, was one of the five. In September the Spartans imposed the oligarchy of thirty men. A council of five hundred was appointed, which was to be permanent rather than annually chosen (as the democratic Council had been), and its members came from a select list of only a thousand men, rather than from the entire citizen body. Its job was to ratify the measures proposed by the Thirty, and the Thirty also gave this council supreme judicial power, removing it from the popular courts. Piraeus received, for the first time, its own administration, not least because it was known as a democratic bastion: it was placed in the hands of a board of ten. The Eleven (the Athenian officers responsible, with the aid of public slaves, for arrests, prisons, and executions) were freshly chosen henchmen, supported by a volunteer police force of three hundred armed horsemen, and all other offices were distributed to oligarchic sympathizers. All but three thousand men were denied full citizenship and residence in the city itself, and disarmed. Once the new regime seemed reasonably stable, the Spartan army departed.

Having restructured the administration to their liking, the Thirty set about their program of the moral rearmament of Athens. It is Plato, in *Letter 7*, who tells us that this is what the Thirty were up to: "I thought they would govern the state by leading it from an unjust way of life into the path of justice." This is surprisingly confirmed by the speechwriter Lysias, who was unremittingly hostile to the oligarchs—not just because he was a democrat, but also because he only just escaped arrest and execution by the Thirty, while his brother was imprisoned

and killed. Nevertheless, he acknowledges that the original intention of Critias and the Thirty was "to purge the state of unjust men
and turn the rest of the citizens over to goodness and justice."[5] It is
no wonder that this attracted Plato because it was Socrates's political
program as well, to see that good men and true were in charge of the
state. However, Socrates's definition of "good men and true" turned
out to differ from that of the Thirty, and toward the end of their brief
regime, he seems to have fallen afoul of the Thirty.[6]

Money was critically short, however. The Thirty chose to raise it by
killing or banishing the men of property among their opponents and
then reselling their property to other Athenians—an ugly program.
Inevitably, as soon as they embarked on this course, they were less
concerned with constitutional reform than with maintaining their
position in the face of escalating abhorrence and resistance. They go
down in Greek history as the first to make fellow citizens live in fear
of the pre-dawn raid.[7] Fifteen hundred people were killed in just a
few weeks, while others fled into exile.

The silver lining of every dictatorial regime throughout history
is that there is always a resistance. Athenian resistance to the Thirty
proved almost miraculously effective. After only a few months, the rebels were able to take over Piraeus, the port of Athens, and turn it into
a democratic stronghold. The Thirty marched against the harbor town
but were defeated in a gruesome little battle. Among the seventy or
so casualties on the oligarchs' side were Plato's cousin Critias and his
uncle Charmides. The rest of the Thirty fled. In late September 403,
the democrats processed in splendor and solemnity from Piraeus back
to Athens to sacrifice in gratitude to Athena on the Acropolis. The
state returned to democracy after little more than a year.

Plato tells us in *Letter 7* that he was disgusted and disappointed
by the Thirty. He clearly valued decency over family. He may have

5. *Letter 7* 324d; Lysias, *Against Eratosthenes* 5.
6. Plato, *Apology of Socrates* 32c–e; Xenophon, *Memorabilia* 1.2.31–38.
7. Or the first in the history of mainland Greece, anyway: Dionysius I had done much the
   same a couple of years earlier in Syracuse.

approved of the Thirty's intentions, but not the means they employed. He was particularly angry at their attempt to involve Socrates in their schemes by getting him to arrest a man called Leon of Salamis, a prominent democrat whom they wanted to execute. Socrates refused, but Leon was still killed. "I recoiled from the abuses of the time," Plato says.[8] He was still attracted to a political career, however; perhaps he could work within the restored democracy.

Socrates's Trial and Death

When democracy was restored, Plato says, his desire to take part in public life revived. Perhaps he even made a tentative start in that direction. But four years later this hope was dashed as well. "It so happened that certain powerful men took the friend of mine I've already mentioned, Socrates, to court, having brought against him an utterly iniquitous charge and one that he deserved less than anyone else. They charged him with impiety, and the Athenians condemned him and put him to death."[9] We have the actual wording of the charges against Socrates: "Socrates is guilty of not acknowledging the gods the city acknowledges, and of introducing other new deities. He is also guilty of subverting the young men of the city. The penalty demanded is death."[10]

The charge of irreligion would have been hard to make stick; the meat of the charge was the third bit, about corrupting the youth of Athens. As we have seen, from about 440 onward, Socrates had surrounded himself with a circle of wealthy young men. It was known that politics played a part in these groups. Xenophon, for instance, includes among the primary subjects Socrates investigated "what is a state, and who is a statesman; what it is to wield political power

8. *Letter 7* 325a.
9. *Letter 7* 325b–c.
10. Diogenes Laertius, *Lives of the Eminent Philosophers* 2.40. Diogenes was drawing on a reliable source who had seen a copy of the indictment in the Athenian Public Records Office.

and who is capable of doing so."[11] Since many of his followers were known for their oligarchic and pro-Spartan sympathies, and since it is commonly believed that students gain their ideas from their teachers, Socrates became tarred with the same brush.

Here the prosecutors had a good case, even if a circumstantial one. This is what they would have reminded the jurors. Socrates was known to be unsympathetic to democracy and its egalitarian values. Above all, he wanted to see the state run by experts, not by more or less random people chosen by sortition, or men who wielded power only because they were rich. It was not difficult for the prosecutors to present Socrates as an anti-democrat. Add to this the fact that, for a few years in the late 430s and early 420s, Socrates had been close to and probably the lover of the unscrupulous Alcibiades, who had been publicly cursed for sacrilege, had defected for a few years to Sparta, and had been suspected of harboring hopes of making himself the sole ruler of Athens. Add, again, the facts that several of the Thirty or their henchmen—Critias, Charmides, Aristotle of Thorae—had been in Socrates's circle, and that since Socrates was not, as many were, expelled from the city during their regime, he was probably one of the select Three Thousand who were permitted citizenship. The prosecutors might even have made him out to be the éminence grise of the Thirty. It is true that Socrates had also risked the wrath of the Thirty by refusing to obey the order to arrest Leon of Salamis, but his links to the Thirty must still have seemed overwhelmingly strong. Even where Leon was concerned, Socrates simply refused to take part in his arrest and went home; he did not actively try to prevent it.

But why take the elderly philosopher to court just then, in 399, when he had been known as a teacher of upper-class young men since the 430s? As had happened to other intellectuals in Athens before him, Socrates became a target only after he was perceived as a threat to public order. His links to the Thirty changed his status from harmless eccentric to undesirable. Some fifty years later, in 345, the

11. Xenophon, *Memorabilia* 1.1.16.

Figure 3.1 Socrates in prison. In this 1787 painting by Jacques-Louis David, Socrates is poised to drink the poison hemlock. Metropolitan Museum of Art, New York.

politician Aeschines said: "Athenians, you had the sophist Socrates put to death because he was thought to have been the teacher of Critias, one of the Thirty who overturned the democracy."[12]

Socrates had been living on borrowed time ever since the defeat of the Thirty in 403. This is not to say that the charge of impiety was, in some Stalinist sense, just a cover for a political show trial. Religion and society were so intertwined that to charge Socrates with impiety was already to accuse him of being an uncommitted citizen, and to charge him with corrupting Athenian youth was to accuse him of undermining the next generation of democratic statesmen. The three prosecutors who made up the team against Socrates were all prominent democrats. The leader, a man called Anytus, had even been one of the heroes of the resistance to the Thirty. Socrates was an undemocratic stain on the new Athens (see figure 3.1).

12. Aeschines, *Against Timarchus* 173.

The judicial murder of Socrates shocked not only his followers but intelligent Athenians in general: Lysias, the foremost speechwriter of the day, composed a pamphlet in the form of a defense speech for Socrates in which he attacked the motives of the prosecutors. But Plato was hit particularly hard. He had been one of Socrates's favorites. When Xenophon wrote an imaginary conversation between Socrates and Plato's brother Glaucon, he said that Socrates was kindly disposed toward Glaucon because of two of his relatives: Charmides and Plato. In his writing, Plato reflected several times on the trial. In *Gorgias*, for instance, he imagined Socrates looking ahead and saying:[13]

> My trial will be equivalent to a doctor being prosecuted by a confectioner before a jury of young children. How do you think a doctor would defend himself if he were up before that kind of court? The prosecutor would argue, "Children, the defendant has committed numerous crimes against your honored selves. He has ruined the youngest among you with his surgery and cautery and baffled you with compresses and nauseants; he gives you harsh potions and forces you to go without food and drink. He's not like me: I'm always giving you all kinds of delicious treats."

So Plato withdrew not only from Athenian politics but from practical politics altogether. He became, in Athenian terms, an "idiot"—an *idiōtēs*, one who is concerned solely with his own affairs. It was not an easy decision. The dialogue *Gorgias* essentially concerns the choice between a life in philosophy or a life in politics—a life dedicated to virtue or a life dedicated to worldly success. Philosophy wins the day, but politics is given some passionate and powerful arguments as well. But their effects on an individual's character are radically different:[14] "If you compare people who have spent their lives hanging around law courts and places like that with those who have been trained in philosophical pursuits, it's like comparing the upbringing of slaves with that of free men." Anyone who chooses to play a political role in his city is effectively a slave because he has to kowtow to the powers

13. *Gorgias* 521e–522a.
14. *Theaetetus* 172c–d.

that be, who in democratic Athens were the people. At the same time, anyone who enters politics with a desire to do good soon realizes that he is on his own, faced with a hopeless task, and so:[15]

> Once he has grasped all this with his rational mind, he lies low and does only what he's meant to do. It's as if he's taken shelter under a wall during a storm, with the wind whipping up the dust and rain pelting down; lawlessness infects everyone else he sees, so he is content if he can find a way to live his life here on earth without becoming tainted by immoral or unjust deeds, and to depart from life without anger and bitterness.

There may have been a practical, sensible aspect to Plato's quietism. He was tarred with the brush of being a relative of some of the Thirty and their henchmen, and with being close to Socrates, a convicted anti-democrat. He was likely to encounter hostility on this score. In *Apology*, he has Socrates say, "No one will be safe who genuinely opposes you or any other popular assembly and tries to put an end to the many injustices and wrongs that take place in the city."[16] One cannot help thinking that he was speaking as much for himself as for Socrates. He came to the embittered conclusion that the governments of all contemporary states, not just Athens, were corrupt and in need of reformation. He retreated from the real world into the alluring realms of contemplation and pure theory, developing Socrates's work in all fields, including political theory. And after a few years he began to take part in the enterprise of commemorating Socrates by writing dialogues showing him doing philosophy. His withdrawal from practical politics would last many years, and it generated many bitter comments in the dialogues.

After Socrates's Death

Immediately after Socrates's execution, according to the biographical tradition, Plato and other Socratics fled, finding Athens an

---

15. *Republic* 496d–e.
16. *Apology of Socrates* 31e–32a.

uncomfortable place to stay. This adventure story is yet another of the biographers' fantasies. It was not as if Socrates was universally reviled. The outcome of the trial was by no means certain. If a mere thirty votes had changed sides, out of a jury of 501, Socrates would have been acquitted, a swing of only 6 percent.[17] Athenians, on the whole, were not that concerned about Socrates.

Moreover, as Plato himself admits,[18] the restored democracy in general exercised considerable moderation. In the short term, immediately after the fall of the Thirty, they allowed any of the Thirty or their sympathizers who had not already left the city to do so; it was only if they chose to stay that they would be put on trial for their actions, and then only the most egregious crimes such as murder would come to court. Over the following decades, this amnesty seems to have worked: surviving courtroom speeches demonstrate that while prosecutors not infrequently denounced defendants during the trial for collaborating with the Thirty (as Socrates's prosecutors surely did), it was never part of any formal charge. Writing some decades later, Xenophon said, "To this day they live together as fellow citizens and the Athenian people abide by the oaths they swore."[19] Peace had been restored to Athens, and it is very unlikely that Plato or any of the Socratics felt themselves to be in danger.

Plato did leave Athens for a while, however, even if not out of fear of suffering the same fate as Socrates. Diogenes Laertius tells us: "At the age of twenty-eight, according to Hermodorus, he withdrew to Euclides in Megara, along with some other Socratics."[20] This statement by Hermodorus of Syracuse is presumably the origin of the idea that he fled in fear because anyone who accepted that the year of Plato's birth was 428/7 would conclude that Plato was twenty-eight in 399, the year of Socrates's trial and death. In fact, however, Plato would turn twenty-eight in 396/5. So, assuming Hermodorus, who

---

17. *Apology of Socrates* 36a.
18. *Letter 7* 325b.
19. Xenophon, *Hellenica* 2.4.43.
20. Diogenes Laertius, *Lives of the Eminent Philosophers* 3.6.

was a scholar of Plato's Academy, got the age right, Plato remained in Athens for a few years after Socrates's death before accompanying others on a visit to his friend Euclides in Megara.

The anecdotal tradition actually has Plato traveling for a dozen years before returning to Athens and founding the Academy in 387. He spent these years, they say, seeking out the wise men of the Greek world and of foreign lands to broaden his knowledge and enrich his mind. The places he is supposed to have visited are Cyrene in North Africa (northeast Libya, in modern terms), to stay with the mathematician Theodorus; southern Italy, to learn from the Pythagoreans; Egypt, to study with learned priests; and Phoenicia, to study with the Magi, the Zoroastrian priesthood. He did visit Pythagoreans in southern Italy, and we will come to that trip in its proper place, but otherwise there is, I believe, no truth to these tales.[21] Wanderjahre are commonly attributed to famous thinkers in anecdotal traditions, and the fact that no two sources give Plato the same itinerary shows that they are basically making it all up.

A constant facet of Greek orientalism was the idea that the priestly traditions of "the East" were the source of all wisdom. Plato was not the only Greek thinker to be credited with a sojourn in Egypt; the list includes Orpheus, Homer, Solon, and Pythagoras. According to Christian writers, who admired and learned from Plato, he went there to study the books of Moses. The historically minded geographer Strabo of Amasea visited Egypt late in the first century BCE and was shown the house where Plato had stayed.[22] Even this does not make Plato's sojourn there plausible because tales of clever Greeks gaining wisdom in Egypt worked both ways, enhancing the reputation of the Egyptian priests as well as the Greek visitor. Once Plato was famous all over the Mediterranean, it was in the priests' interest to perpetuate the myth, and so we can accept Strabo's account while still refusing

---

21. The earliest of the ancient biographies of Plato, the one written by Philodemus of Gadara, has Plato going *only* to southern Italy and Sicily, with no mention (at least, in the extant fragments) of more fanciful and far-flung journeys.
22. Strabo, *Geography* 17.1.29; see also Diodorus of Sicily, *The Library* 1.96–98.

to believe that Plato ever went there. In the dialogues, Egypt and things Egyptian are mentioned quite a few times, but the information is always trivial and of the kind that was common belief or hearsay: the dignity of their music, the antiquity of their legends, the place of mathematics in their educational system, their unwelcoming attitude to strangers, their opposition to cultural change. None of this has the depth that a personal visit would have provided.

So Plato stayed in Megara with Euclides for a while, but he was soon back in Athens, and this is when he would have seen military service. Any adult male in Athens was liable to be called up until the age of fifty-nine, but only in the direst emergencies would an older man have to serve. Plato was in his prime, however, and Athens was again at war. The Corinthian War, as it is called, lasted from 395 until 386 and was an attempt by several Greek states—Boeotia, Corinth, Argos, and Athens—to curb the dominance of Sparta. It achieved exactly the opposite: at the end Sparta was more dominant than ever, having gained the backing of the Persian king.

Aristoxenus of Taras, writing about thirty years after Plato's death, seems to have claimed that Plato fought in three engagements, at Tanagra, Corinth, and Delium.[23] The fighting in the Corinthian War was bogged down around Corinth for some time (hence the name of the war), so that much is plausible, but there were no battles at Tanagra or Delium during this war. However, there was fighting at those three places, in the order given by Aristoxenus, in the years 426 to 424, during the Peloponnesian War. And when we are told that at Delium Plato was awarded the prize for valor, we can recognize Aristoxenus's confusion. In *Symposium*, we read that Socrates fought at Delium in 424, and just a few lines earlier Plato had mentioned that Alcibiades won the prize for valor in a battle in northern Greece, despite feeling that it should have gone to Socrates.[24] So we have no way of knowing which specific battles Plato was involved in—given his wealth, he

23. Diogenes Laertius, *Lives of the Eminent Philosophers* 3.8.
24. *Symposium* 220d–221b. See also *Laches* 181b.

would have served as a cavalryman—but it is likely that he did see action in the mid to late 390s or early 380s.

The Order of the Dialogues: Preliminary Considerations

Sometime in the 390s Plato began to write. This was the start of a writing career that was to last about fifty years. For the life of a writer, we want to know the order in which he wrote his books. It is not easy to do this in Plato's case. There is no way of telling just when he began to write, and while we might be able to detect clusters of dialogues, we often cannot tell in what order dialogues within each group were written. Plato was in any case a great reviser, so there may have been earlier and later drafts of dialogues in circulation. There is nothing strange about this either in its time (Aristophanes wrote a second edition of his play *Clouds*; orators were publishing revised versions of delivered speeches) or in any time; it is no different from the contemporary practice of producing second editions of books. The canonical versions of the dialogues are the result of the Academy's preserving the works after his death—in some cases probably after having edited them to a certain extent—and keeping them unchanged out of reverence.

It was possible for more than one version of a dialogue to exist because of what passed for "publication" of a work in Plato's time. It is likely that the dialogues, or the majority of them, were written in the first instance to be read out to small groups of friends, students, and admirers, just as Zeno, at the start of *Parmenides*, reads aloud a piece of his work for discussion by those present. That was the normal first step toward getting one's work known. If anyone wanted a copy of this draft, he asked permission to transcribe it or have it transcribed. In one anecdote, Plato gives his associate Hermodorus permission to copy some of his dialogues and take them to Sicily. Gradually the text reached a wider audience—not that literacy was widespread at the time—and if it proved popular enough, an enterprising shopkeeper might make copies and offer them for sale. Proof that Plato's works achieved a reasonably wide circulation is the frequency with which comic poets refer to them: they could assume that enough people in the audience would recognize the allusions and greet them with a chuckle, perhaps of a bemused kind.

There was no copyright, nor was Plato paid for writing his books, and copies were undoubtedly made without his permission. Even centuries later, Arrian complained that his transcript of the Stoic philosopher Epictetus's *Discourses* had ended up in the public domain "without my consent or knowledge."[25] But in many cases, this leaked text would still be only a draft. The shorter dialogues would perhaps undergo fewer changes, but longer works would leak out bit by bit, even while the author was still working on the book as a whole and revising what he had already written in the light of its reception when he read it out to friends. Some stylometric tests indicate considerable variety among individual chapters of longer works such as *Republic* and *Laws*, which suggests gradual accretion. And it is easy to conjecture something similar in the case of several other dialogues: the two parts of *Parmenides* look as though they were originally separate compositions; the early pages of *Philebus* use the terms "limit" and "unlimited" in a sense that is incompatible with their subsequent use; some scholars detect signs of revision and accretion in *Gorgias* and *Protagoras*. All this obviously spoils the attempt to determine the order of the publication of the dialogues, since the longer dialogues, at any rate, grew over many years.

There is solid evidence that Plato revised at least some of his work. First, on the two occasions when he describes the editorial process, he talks of "cutting and pasting the various parts [of the work] into different relations with one another," and, in an analogy with painting,

25. Arrian, Preface to *Discourses*, writing early in the second century CE. See also Cicero, *Letters to Atticus* 13.21a, and Diodorus of Sicily, *The Library* 40.8, both writing in the first century BCE.

of "erasing things and painting them in again."[26] Second, we are told that Plato was constantly working on the opening of *Republic*.[27] But we do not have to rely only on the later writers who supply this information. By an incredible stroke of good luck, we actually have hard evidence for revision in the case of two dialogues. Two incompatible versions of a passage of *Cratylus* have survived, and another passage also seems to be a carryover from an earlier version.[28] And an anonymous commentary on *Theaetetus*, dating perhaps from the first century BCE, reveals that there was originally an alternate version of the opening frame of the dialogue, starting not with Euclides greeting Terpsion but with someone asking a slave whether he has fetched the transcript of the dialogue.[29]

In 392 or 391 the Athenians were treated at one of their annual dramatic festivals to a comedy by Aristophanes called *Assemblywomen*. There is a long episode in the play where the heroine, Praxagora, outlines her plans for reforming Athens. They include the communistic sharing of property and the abolishment of marriage so that men can sleep with any woman they like and children will be brought up to regard all older men as their fathers—all sketched with great humor, of course. With Praxagora's "innovations," there will be concord in the city, and the whole nest of ideas is said to require a shrewd and "philosophical" intelligence. These are exactly some of the suggestions that Plato makes in the second to fifth books of *Republic* for the Guardians of his imaginary city. The fit is so exact that it cannot be coincidence. And we can be pretty certain that Aristophanes was not getting the ideas from someone else, or from his own fertile imagination, because

---

26. *Phaedrus* 278d–e, *Republic* 501b.
27. Riginos, *Platonica* 185–86.
28. The first passage starts at 437d10; the second is 385b2–d1.
29. When Plato wrote *Sophist* and *Statesman* (which form a pair) he assumed this alternate opening of *Theaetetus*, rather than the one we read nowadays. For the conversations of *Sophist* and *Statesman* are supposed to take place the day after that of *Theaetetus*, but they are set in Athens, whereas the existing frame of *Theaetetus* sets the conversation in Megara.

Aristotle tells us that Plato was the first to think along such radical lines.[30] This means that some bits of the work that later became *Republic* were in circulation by the late 390s, even though the whole work, as we have it now, was certainly completed later. There are signs that *Republic* is a patchwork: the two assaults on the value of poetry, in the second-to-third and tenth books, are somewhat incompatible, for instance, and few scholars doubt that the first book of *Republic* was originally written as a stand-alone dialogue. It was probably called *Thrasymachus*, and it was one of the series of works in which Socrates confronts sophists: *Hippias Major, Hippias Minor, Euthydemus, Protagoras*, and *Gorgias*.

Another factor is the opening of *Timaeus*. The dialogue begins with what it claims is a summary of *Republic* (because the conversation of *Timaeus* is supposed to be taking place the day after the conversation of *Republic*), but it omits a great deal of *Republic* as we have it and the discussants are not those of *Republic* as we have it. Could it be a description of the proto-*Republic*? Yet another factor is that the Roman writer Aulus Gellius says that Xenophon wrote his *The Education of Cyrus* in response to a version of *Republic* that was short enough to occupy only two papyrus rolls;[31] at about ninety thousand words, the work as we have it would occupy three rolls. But on what authority does Gellius say this? He was writing in the second century CE, five hundred years later than Plato.

Plato's habit of revision is not the only impediment to ordering the dialogues. They are so multifaceted that the question of the order of their composition or publication could be approached from many

---

30. *Politics* 1266a, 1274b. The brief mention by Herodotus (*Histories* 4.104) of a Scythian tribe who hold their women in common is not detailed enough to form the background of Aristophanes's or Plato's proposals. There also seems to be parody of certain features of *Republic* in Isocrates's *Busiris* (especially 15–17 and 23), but the date of *Busiris* is uncertain. It could be around 390, but it could be much later. In either case, it is probably still a parody of *Republic*, but in the latter case it tells us nothing about a proto-*Republic* in the 390s.
31. Gellius, *Attic Nights* 14.3.3.

angles, and each angle would give us a different ordering.[32] So how far can we go toward determining the order of the dialogues? There are some clues. First, there are occasional mentions of one dialogue in another, proving that the one mentioned is earlier. Second, we can roughly date a few dialogues from the anachronisms that I mentioned in the introduction—places where a dialogue, despite being set in the fifth century BCE, references an event from the subsequent fourth century. Third, there may be passages in some dialogues that are incomprehensible or make little sense without taking into account something from another dialogue, which is therefore earlier. Fourth, if we find a passage where a valid insight from another dialogue would have enabled Plato to clarify some point or other, we can assume that the dialogue without the insight is earlier than the one with it. But Plato's words are often hard to interpret, and doctrinal considerations such as those on which these last two criteria rely may fail to yield objective results rather than different readers' opinions. It is best to rely on stylometry (the statistical analysis of variations in literary style), anachronisms, and uncontroversial cross-references within the dialogues, and on doctrinal considerations only when they are plain and obvious, requiring no interpretation.

Doctrine and Development

There are two dominant approaches to interpreting Plato's works: unitarianism and developmentalism. My tent is pitched in the latter camp. Unitarians come in various forms but essentially believe that Plato never changed his mind; he had worked out his total philosophy, at least in its broad outlines, before he started writing, and the dialogues are simply successive elaborations of aspects of this philosophy. Plato's writing career spanned about fifty years, and the idea that his

32. One scholar, writing in 1982, listed 132 competing dialogue sequences (Thesleff, *Studies in Platonic Chronology*, reprinted in his *Platonic Patterns*). By now, the number has probably doubled.

thought underwent no development seems implausible. We accept evolution and even changes of mind in the case of other philosophers who began their careers at a relatively young age, such as Immanuel Kant, George Berkeley, and Ludwig Wittgenstein. Why not Plato as well?

However, there is one respect in which unitarianism is correct. There are certain basic principles—together they make up what has been called Ur-Platonism—that underlie all of Plato's metaphysical and epistemological work. First, he was always opposed to materialism, the doctrine that only bodies exist, and equally opposed to the kind of mechanistic explanations on which materialists rely. In a famous passage, Plato has Socrates pour scorn on the idea that the fact that he is sitting in prison is better explained by talking of his body's bones and joints than by the decisions he made that led to his being there.[33] The ultimate cause is God, or soul, which has the power to initiate movement. Second, and relatedly, he was always opposed to nominalism, the idea that there are no such things as universals but that only particular things exist and their properties are no more than ways of thinking about these particulars. Plato succinctly pours scorn on this idea, too: "So does someone whose horizon is limited to beautiful things, with no conception of beauty itself [the universal], . . . strike you as living in a dream-world or in the real world?"[34] He gets the answer he expected. Third, he was always opposed to relativism, the denial of absolute values; if something is true, it is not just true *for me*, but for all time and all people, like $2 + 2 = 4$. Plato's metaphysics is essentially an inquiry into what is true and real. Fourth, he was always opposed to skepticism, the idea that it is impossible to attain knowledge of anything.

There are also ethical principles that are common to all the dialogues. A human being must try to fulfill the divine, rational part of his nature, not his bestial side, that will attach him via pleasure, the

33. *Phaedo* 98b–99b.
34. *Republic* 476c.

satisfaction of desire, to the things of this world. Everyone aims for happiness or fulfillment, but that is not a product of satisfying the bodily appetites. Virtue is not of minor relevance to happiness, as most people might think, but the sine qua non of happiness, and virtue is knowledge, which makes cultivation of the rational aspect of the soul imperative. At the very least, we have to understand what is truly valuable to us as human beings and try consistently to put that into practice. Actions are not good unless the person performing those actions is good; goodness is primarily a condition of the soul.

The doctrinal edifice that Plato built on these foundations, however, did change; they were the foundations for developments in various directions. The critical point here is that the dialogues do contain substantive doctrinal points; they are not just provocative documents that express ideas that were interesting Plato at the time of writing, or teaching tools intended to solicit reflection rather than give answers, or dramas written to entertain as well as instruct. Nor does the fact that quite a few of the arguments, especially in the shorter dialogues, are tailored for the particular interlocutor with whom Socrates is speaking mean that the arguments, or most of them, do not contain ideas that can be generalized. It is true that each dialogue is, in the first instance, a self-contained product because that is how its original audience got to know it.[35] Each of the dialogues has independent dramatic unity. This is one of the main factors that makes attractive the idea that their function is no more than to inquire, provoke, inspire, or teach. And it is true that the dialogue form is more suited to these objectives than to systematic philosophy. But Plato was not writing systematic philosophy. He did not write treatises; he dramatized arguments.

The extent of the drama in the dialogues should not be overestimated. A dialogue could be properly described as a drama only if the action is carried forward by the idiosyncratic characters of the dialogue,

35. Educated members of the audience or readers, however, would be able to make connections between what they were hearing and previous works by Plato that they had heard or read.

as in a play. But that is not the case here: the action of the dialogues is carried forward more by ideas and arguments than by personalities. The dramatic message of *Phaedo* is conveyed by Socrates's calmness in the face of his imminent death, but that is not the main philosophical point of the dialogue, which is to air a sequence of arguments about the immortality of the soul. The arguments of the dialogues naturally are often affected by the character of Socrates's interlocutor: Callicles in *Gorgias* is too identified with his worldly desires to understand what Socrates is saying; Ion is too stupid, Euthyphro too blinkered, Hippias too self-important, Thrasymachus too irritable. One of the messages of *Meno* is that, although virtue may be teachable since it is a form of knowledge, it is not teachable to a Meno. The introduction of a new character in a dialogue to confront Socrates generally signals an increase in the sophistication of the argument, or at least a change of direction.

But Plato was seeking philosophical truth. He shows us conversations between particular people, but he is attempting to develop ideas that are valid for more than those particular people. The message conveyed by the characterization of Callicles and others is that the truth is not attainable unless we shed the constraints of our personalities. This is not to say that the dialogues, or some of them, are not performable (though they would be rather dull). They do seem to have been performed at pretentious occasions in Roman times,[36] but I very much doubt that Plato intended them to be performed. The meaning one finds in a play depends on the characters, their speeches, and their interactions; the meaning of a Platonic dialogue lies in the philosophy and in the attempt to get us, the readers, to think about things for ourselves.

A dialogue conveys information both directly and indirectly. The dramatic elements of a dialogue make the philosophy more palatable and engage our emotions. The glorious myths with which Plato sprinkled the dialogues serve, in part, the same purpose, though they are also Plato's way of communicating ideas that are not liable to

36. Plutarch, *Table Talk* 711b–c; Athenaeus, *Savants at Dinner* 9.381f–382b.

rational, argumentative exposition. Philosophical writing did not occupy a single register for Plato. Where a point could be made by reasoned argument, he used reasoned argument, but when he wanted to talk about things that could not be demonstrated in this way, or perhaps simply for the sake of variety, he wrote a myth, appealing to the imagination as much as reason.[37] Sometimes, even the reasoned arguments are poor, as though, as with the myths, Plato was more concerned to persuade his readers of the importance of an idea than anchor it in valid argumentation.

A related question is which, if any, of the dialogues were intended for a wide audience and which were written initially for a more erudite audience. Many of the latter dialogues would have leaked out anyway, especially as Plato's fame increased, but wide publication was not their original purpose. Here we are in the realm of guesswork. My guess is that few of the dialogues are accessible enough to have been intended for general publication in the first instance: *Apology of Socrates* and *Crito* because of their readability and their message to the Athenian public, defending Socrates as the moral conscience of the city; *Menexenus* because of its survey of Athenian history, even though the tone of the survey is lightly satirical; *Euthydemus* because of its knockabout fun, its distinction of Socrates from the worst kind of logic-chopping sophist, and its quiet introduction of some fundamental Platonic ideas; *Laches* because of its extended scene-setting, featuring famous Athenian generals from the Peloponnesian War, and the accessibility of its arguments; *Protagoras*, for its humorous scene-setting, for its succinct portraits of various sophists, and for the way it shows Socrates tying Protagoras in knots; and *Symposium* because of the richness of its characterization and scene-setting, its defense of Socrates against the charge (which played a part at his trial) of having corrupted the notorious traitor

37. There are extended myths in *Protagoras* (the origin of virtue), *Gorgias* (the postmortem judgment of souls), *Symposium* (the androgyne; the birth of Love), *Phaedo* (the alternate world), *Republic* (Er's afterlife journey), *Phaedrus* (the winged soul; the discovery of writing), *Statesman* (the two cosmic eras), and *Timaeus/Critias* (Atlantis and antediluvian Athens).

Alcibiades (and so we might add *First Alcibiades* to the list), and the lightness with which it introduces the theory of Forms. Presumably the proto-*Republic* should also be on the list, since it seems to have been known, and Aristophanes, at any rate, thought some of its content worth parodying before a popular audience.

These are the only dialogues whose wide public appeal I feel confident about; as far as the others are concerned, even where Plato has taken care over the scene-setting and other dramatic elements, most of them are too philosophical (some are very dry) or too long or both. In later centuries, it seems that *Phaedrus*, *Republic*, and *Symposium* were the most widely read dialogues outside philosophical circles. *Laws*, Plato's most down-to-earth work, was certainly written for a less philosophical audience than many of the dialogues, but it is very long, often rather unclear and allusive, and even rather tedious in places.[38] Many of the dialogues would simply be incomprehensible or strike an audience as odd, unless they already had a background in this kind of thinking.[39] Of course, the dialogues will have circulated among more philosophically inclined readers, but not, I think, to a wide public.

Reading Plato

Plato, then, did use his books to raise points of doctrine. Some of these ideas might be theories rather than doctrines. Nevertheless, whatever they are, we are obliged to take seriously some ideas that occur in the

---

38. In *Icaromenippus*, written in the second century CE, the belletrist Lucian of Samosata has Zeus complain that his altars have become "more frigid than Plato's *Laws*." At much the same time, Plutarch, who called himself a Platonist, admitted that "few people read *Laws*" (*Moralia* 328e [*On the Fortune of Alexander*]).

39. There is some evidence for the restriction of at least some of the dialogues to a scholarly audience. Galen, writing in the second century CE, says that Plato let "only very few people, those capable of following a scientific discussion" have access to *Timaeus* (*On the Natural Faculties* [4.758 Kühn]). At *Parmenides* 136d–e Plato says how difficult "ordinary people" find philosophical argumentation, and at *Statesman* 286d–287a he claims, rightly, that most people would be bored by the long-winded methodology he is employing.

dialogues—those that are endorsed by the protagonist of the dialogue and are supported by vigorous (not necessarily rigorous) argument. The obligation only increases when we find certain ideas recurring across the dialogues and forming a coherent set. For instance, the notion (which we have already met) that human happiness and fulfillment requires our assimilation to God occurs in *Theaetetus, Timaeus, Republic,* and *Laws,* and is hinted at in *Symposium* and elsewhere; and it dovetails perfectly with ideas such as the one proposed in *Phaedo* that philosophy is "practicing dying and being dead," or the frequent suggestion that our true self is our rational mind, which is the divine part of us.

However, the dialogue form is not just a fancy way of presenting doctrine that could otherwise have been presented in the form of a treatise; it is a more effective way of getting readers to think for themselves than a treatise. At the end of the conversation with the young slave in *Meno,* Plato insists that the slave now has to work to understand the results of the conversation—to convert belief into knowledge. An idea, a thesis, a piece of doctrine is not owned by readers of a dialogue—it remains an idea of Plato's alone—until they have argued it through for themselves. Each dialogue should certainly be interpreted in the first instance on its own, without reference to other dialogues. But when related ideas crop up in more than one dialogue, we are entitled to put them together, and when a dialogue is clearly dogmatic—one thinks especially of *Sophist,* but of others, too—we are entitled to find doctrine in it. Plato may not have intended these ideas to be carved in stone for all time, but at the same time he was not the skeptic that, for a while, the later Academy made him out to be.[40] Moreover, when Aristotle, who was with Plato in the Academy for twenty years, refers to the dialogues, he says "Plato believes that . . . ," not "Plato floats the idea that. . . ."[41] Or he also often says "Socrates

---

40. They read the dialogues as "peirastic" (testing) rather than dogmatic.
41. See also Diogenes Laertius, *Lives of the Eminent Philosophers* 3.52: "Plato presents his own views through four characters: Socrates, Timaeus [*Timaeus*], the Athenian Visitor

believes that . . . ," recognizing that Socrates is Plato's spokesman in many dialogues. In fact, attributing doctrine to Plato was as normal in the fourth century as it has been for the rest of time.

If we attribute doctrine to Plato, we are bound to recognize Socrates as Plato's usual spokesman, as Aristotle does. There are scholars who deny that Plato has any spokesman in the dialogues. But the dominance of Socrates tells very strongly against this thesis. He is more fully characterized than anyone else; it is he who steers the discussions, criticizes others' views, generates doctrine, and so on; he refutes others but is never refuted (except occasionally by himself); he answers all objections; his interlocutors are not his equals. We are bound to *respond* to Socrates's interlocutors, but he is the only one with whom Plato encourages us to *identify*. Plato is not silent in the dialogues but a ventriloquist.

And if there is doctrine, there is likely to be development. There are, to begin with, inconsistencies among the dialogues, some of which may be the result of Plato's changing his mind. However, it remains unclear how much help developmentalism affords the attempt to arrange the dialogues in chronological order. As I have already said, scholars' interpretations of Plato's thought vary so greatly that almost every possible arrangement based on doctrine has been proposed. Interpretation can even be completely polarized. In *Parmenides* Plato levels a series of well-argued criticisms against his emblematic metaphysical theory, the theory of Forms. He argues that there are formidable weaknesses in the way that Forms themselves had been described (in dialogues such as *Phaedo* and *Republic*) and in the way that they had been said to interact with the things of this world. Did Plato see these criticisms as so devastating that he abandoned the theory of Forms or certain aspects of it? If that is so, we can take *Parmenides* to be a watershed, such that any dialogues that contain the theory of transcendent Forms must be earlier than it. On the other

[*Laws*], and the Eleatic Visitor [*Sophist, Statesman*]." He might have added Parmenides in *Parmenides*, though that would have been controversial.

hand, if we find transcendent Forms in later dialogues, then perhaps *Parmenides* was designed to expose misunderstandings of the theory, or as a teaching tool within the Academy. It is an aspect of Plato's brilliance and perennial fascination that we are still arguing about such things. He sometimes leaves it up to us to make up our minds; that is part of the joy of reading his books.

Two Clusters and a Group

Doctrinal considerations, then, are unhelpful in ordering the dialogues, unless, as I said, they require no interpretation.[42] It is best to rely on other criteria. Stylometry does not rely on readers' vague and differing impressions of a writer's style but instead on carefully chosen criteria that stand a chance of delivering objective results. Features of style that can reasonably be regarded as unconscious are therefore better than those that the writer has deliberately chosen. Early stylometric studies of Plato were spoiled above all by a failure to realize that skillful writers are aware of the weight of every word they put on the page.

For instance, whenever Plato avoided what phoneticists call "hiatus," he chose to do so—and therefore could have chosen to do so at any point in his writing career. It is a feature of the Greek language that many words end or begin with a vowel, so that when a word ending with a vowel is followed by one that begins with a vowel, the words run together when spoken. This is what makes Greek (the modern version too) such a fluent language. In the fourth century, when books were still usually being read aloud rather than to oneself, writers aspiring to a mannered and elevated style tried to avoid such hiatuses, even at the cost of distortion of the normal word order of a sentence.

---

42. Perhaps the easiest process of development to track in Plato's dialogues is his political thought, and in the rest of the book I shall sometimes focus on that, because an individual's political views tell us more about him as a person than, say, his views on metaphysics or epistemology.

Plato's contemporary Isocrates was the master of hiatus avoidance, and in some of his dialogues Plato followed suit, although not with as much rigor as Isocrates.

Happily, however, more recent stylometric tests, chosen to avoid circularity (often a danger in stylometry) and drawing on unconscious features of style[43] revealed that the hiatus-avoiding dialogues do in fact belong together stylistically. They are *Sophist*, *Statesman*, *Timaeus*, *Critias*, *Philebus*, and *Laws*. The same series of tests also revealed another stylistic cluster, consisting of *First Alcibiades*, *Charmides*, *Gorgias*, *Meno*, *Phaedo*, *Phaedrus*, *Protagoras*, *Republic*, *Symposium*, and *Theaetetus*. That leaves twelve dialogues unaccounted for: *Apology of Socrates*, *Cratylus*, *Crito*, *Euthydemus*, *Euthyphro*, *Hippias Major*, *Hippias Minor*, *Ion*, *Laches*, *Lysis*, *Menexenus*, and *Parmenides*. We can call this the "loose" group because they do not form a cluster: they have fewer stylistic affinities than the members of the two clusters.

This is a start, but without other criteria it would be illegitimate to infer that the clusters have any chronological significance. There are, however, indications that *Laws* was a work of Plato's old age. Aristotle tells us that it was later than *Republic*, which we could have guessed anyway, because in *Laws* Plato makes unmistakable references to *Republic*.[44] There is an anachronistic reference in the first book of *Laws* to the re-annexation of the southern Italian town of Locri by Dionysius II of Syracuse, which happened in 356 after he had been driven from Syracuse by Plato's friend and student, Dion. Plutarch tells us that it was a work of Plato's old age,[45] and in the dialogue Plato himself stresses more than once the old age of the three participants in the conversation. Moreover, there was a rumor that some

---

43. Especially Ledger's *Re-Counting Plato*; see "Further Reading" at the back of the book, in the section "Ordering the Dialogues." This is really the only satisfactory stylometric analysis of Plato because it is the only one to employ multivariate analysis. However, as well as identifying clusters of dialogues, he goes on to use the data to order the dialogues sequentially within clusters, which is asking too much of the data.
44. *Laws* 739b–e, 807b, 875c–d. The Aristotle reference is *Politics* 1264b26.
45. *Laws* 638b1–2; Plutarch, *Moralia* 370f (*On Isis and Osiris*).

of the book was still in draft form on Plato's death, and that these draft passages were transcribed onto papyrus by Plato's colleague, the mathematician Philip of Opus.[46] This seems to be confirmed by the long-recognized fact that the dialogue shows signs of incomplete revision, especially in the last two of its chapters (or "books") and possibly also of the involvement of more than one writer.[47] Finally, the three Letters that I accept as authentic all date from the 350s, the last full decade of Plato's life, and they are stylistically on a par with *Laws* and the rest of the members of this cluster. *Laws*, then, was one of the last books Plato wrote. That does not mean he sat down and wrote it from beginning to end in one go, so to speak, but it seems likely that it was occupying him in his last decade. So we have a fixed point.

We can go some way toward sequencing the *Laws* cluster. *Sophist* and *Statesman* are the first two books of a projected trilogy; Plato intended to define first a sophist, then a statesman, and finally a philosopher, but *Philosopher* was never written.[48] The opening of *Sophist* connects the dialogue with *Theaetetus*: the conversation of *Sophist* is supposed to take place the day after the conversation of *Theaetetus*. Moreover, *Sophist* clarifies some of the arguments of *Theaetetus*. So *Theaetetus* is earlier than *Sophist* and *Statesman*. Next, both *Theaetetus* and *Sophist* refer to *Parmenides*, so that was an earlier work.[49] It is possible that Plato could have written these references separately and

---

46. Diogenes Laertius, *Lives of the Eminent Philosophers* 3.37: "Some say that Philip of Opus transcribed Plato's *Laws*, which was on wax." But *Laws* is far too long to have all been written on wax tablets, which were small and used only for short and temporary work. Either this is a garbling of a report that a few passages were still on wax tablets, or the phrase "on wax" is a metaphorical way of saying "in draft form," not necessarily on wax tablets at all.

47. See also the *Anonymous Prolegomena to Platonic Philosophy* 24.10–15 and 25.5–7, which also infers from the dialogue's unfinished state that it was Plato's last work.

48. If we think that it was never written because Plato died before he could write it, that could be another argument for the lateness of these dialogues. The sequence *Sophist—Statesman* is secure anyway, but there is also a back reference to *Sophist* at *Statesman* 284b.

49. Trilogy: *Sophist* 217a. References to *Parmenides*: *Theaetetus* 183e and *Sophist* 217c.

inserted them into the texts, but there is no point in being overly skeptical. We can accept this evidence at face value.

So we have a sequence of dialogues: *Sophist—Statesman—Laws*. The other three members of this group, *Philebus*, *Timaeus*, and *Critias*,[50] should be slotted somewhere into this sequence. And, with as much confidence as almost anything in Plato's biography warrants, we can call these dialogues the late group. Furthermore, it is plausible to add *Parmenides* and *Theaetetus* to the beginning of the sequence, and we know that all these dialogues postdate *Republic*, not least because *Parmenides* criticizes or reflects on the theory of Forms that is found in *Republic*, and *Theaetetus* problematizes the account of knowledge given in *Republic*. These are solid gains.

What about the other cluster and the loose group? There are, interestingly, some similarities in each case. The cluster (*First Alcibiades*, *Charmides*, *Gorgias*, *Meno*, *Phaedo*, *Phaedrus*, *Protagoras*, *Republic*, *Symposium*, and *Theaetetus*) contains all the doctrine-building dialogues that develop the views that are generally considered most typical of Platonism, such as the three-part soul, utopian politics, the existence of immaterial Forms thanks to which we identify the things of the world and think in concepts, and the notion—the theory of Recollection—that we do not *get to know* Forms; what we do, when we identify something in the world as, say, good, is *remember* or *recognize* the Form of goodness from a past disembodied existence, between incarnations, when we glimpsed the Plain of Truth, the homeland of Forms. Since we have already placed *Republic* and *Theaetetus* before the late dialogues, and since they appear in a cluster with stylistic affinity, it looks as though this cluster belongs en masse before the late cluster.

---

50. *Timaeus* and *Critias* form a pair, and Plato might have intended them to be the first two of a trilogy. Not only did he never write the third piece, however, which would have been called *Hermocrates* (see *Critias* 108a–b), but *Critias* is unfinished (it ends literally in the middle of a sentence), and since it was one of Plato's later works, we are bound to wonder if he died before completing it. Plutarch (*Life of Solon* 32) certainly thought that was the case.

And the final group (*Apology of Socrates, Cratylus, Crito, Euthydemus, Euthyphro, Hippias Major, Hippias Minor, Ion, Laches, Lysis, Menexenus*), especially now that I have removed the maverick *Parmenides* from it,[51] contains most of the dialogues that show Socrates confronting experts and demonstrating that they cannot come up with a universal definition of the core concept about which they claim expertise. Since our guiding assumption is that stylistic affinity has chronological significance, it follows that if any of these dialogues belonged to either of the clusters, they would share stylistic affinity with other members of the cluster. So we are bound to think that these works were written early. If Plato's style had not yet settled into a groove, that might explain the stylistic dissimilarities among the group.

We have ended up with three clumps of dialogues that can be called "early," "middle," and "late." And curiously, although I made no prior assumptions and have adopted a fresh approach to the problem, the three clumps we have arrived at coincide to a large extent with the three groups the majority of recent scholars have identified. There is, then, a broad scholarly consensus, at least as far as the grouping of the dialogues is concerned. But can we be more precise?

A Partial Chronology

Further help is afforded by the anachronisms that I mentioned in the introduction. *Menexenus* contains a concise and partial history of Athens that goes down to the Peace of Antalcidas in 387/6. *Symposium* refers to the Spartan destruction of the city of Mantinea in 385/4, but more importantly, in an obviously ex post facto passage, one of the speakers recommends the establishment of a homosexual battalion,

51. Quite a bit of *Parmenides* consists of very simple vocabulary on which Plato builds abstract arguments concerned with unity and being. This narrow focus, with its repetitive vocabulary, is likely the reason why stylometry does not include *Parmenides* in the cluster where, along with other scholars, I am sure it belongs. I also think that *Cratylus* was slightly later, with its stylometric analysis distorted by the dialogue's frequent etymologizing.

as the Thebans did in 378.[52] So *Menexenus* was written in or around
386 (assuming that Plato was referring to an event that was fresh in
his mind), and *Symposium* after 378. The anachronistic reference in
Theaetetus to a battle at Corinth in 391 is not much help, since it is in
any case certain that the dialogue was written later than that.

Plato's rival in education, Isocrates of Athens, refers to ideas that are
found in the dialogues. Since we can date some of Isocrates's speeches
with some certainty, they might help us date some of the dialogues.[53]
Erring on the side of caution, because it is possible to get carried
away with finding such references, we are left with two.[54] First, *Helen*
refers to the Platonic idea, developed in *Protagoras*, that all five car-
dinal virtues (justice, self-control, courage, piety, and wisdom) are one,
or at least mutually entailing, because they are all forms of knowledge; *Helen* was written sometime in the 380s or 370s. Second, *To
Nicocles* responds to what Isocrates perceived as personal attacks by
Plato in *Gorgias* and *Euthydemus*; *To Nicocles* was written around 370.[55]
And the *On the Sophists* of another speechwriter, Alcidamas, written
around 390, seems to have been on Plato's mind when he composed
Phaedrus.[56] These parameters are too broad to be of much help.

There are only a few more certainties. A comedy by Theopompus
of Athens called *The Pleasure Lover*, that survives only in fragments,

---

52. *Menexenus* 244d–246a; *Symposium* 179a and 193a.
53. Isocrates had a long career as a writer, and some of his references to Platonic dialogues
    were written late in Plato's life, or even after his death, so they do not help us date
    them with any precision.
54. In note 30 to this chapter, I already rejected any possible help that Isocrates's *Busiris*
    might offer toward dating *Republic*.
55. Isocrates had good reason to refer to Plato, since they were debating various issues,
    but attempts to find echoes of Plato in other fourth-century speeches, by Aeschines
    and Lycurgus, are not convincing.
56. At *On the Sophists* 27–28, Alcidamas wrote: "In my opinion, it's wrong to even use the
    term 'speeches' for the written versions. They should rather be thought of as images,
    representations, and imitations of speeches.... Just as real bodies have far less attractive
    forms than beautiful statues, but are many times more useful in the real world, so a
    speech that is spoken spontaneously from one's mind is ensouled and living." This
    echoes, or is echoed by, *Phaedrus* 276a, where Plato has Phaedrus say, "You're talking
    about the living, ensouled speech of a man of knowledge. We'd be right to describe
    the written word as a mere image of this."

can be dated with some assurance to the late 380s or early 370s, and alludes to a passage in *Phaedo*.[57] We can be sure that *Meno* precedes *Phaedo* because it introduces, explains, and illustrates at length the idea that Forms, the essences of things, are recollected from an earlier existence, which *Phaedo* takes for granted. The theory of the three-part soul is expounded in *Republic* and *Phaedrus* and then taken for granted in *Timaeus*, *Statesman*, and *Laws*. Early in *Meno* there is a clear reference back to *Gorgias*.[58] *Cratylus* probably precedes *Phaedo*, *Symposium*, and *Republic*. In the latter three dialogues, Plato assumes that the flux and instability of the world preclude our having *knowledge* about it; at best we can have *beliefs* about it. This doctrine depends on an argument from the end of *Cratylus*.[59] And since *Phaedrus* announces a new method for defining things—the method of collection and division— which Plato then puts to use in *Sophist*, *Statesman*, and *Philebus*, I think that *Phaedrus* was probably written around the time of *Theaetetus*, another dialogue that we have found to precede *Sophist* and *Statesman*. In *Phaedrus* Plato began to toy with avoiding hiatus in his writing, and that perhaps entitles us to place it immediately before the dialogues of the late cluster, where hiatus avoidance is more prominent.

Here is another consideration. There are two main ways in which Plato presents the dialogues. He himself gives a clear description of the alternatives close to the start of *Theaetetus*:

> [Euclides speaking] Here's what I wrote, Terpsion. I didn't write the discussion down in the form in which Socrates repeated it to me, with him doing all the talking, but as a dialogue between him and those who he said took part in the discussion—who, he told me, were the geometer Theodorus and Theaetetus. I wanted to avoid the nuisance of all the bits that Socrates had to insert about himself for clarification, like "And I said" or "And I remarked," or about the interlocutor, like "He

---

57. Theopompus, Fragment 16 Kassel/Austin. The fragment reads: "Since one isn't even one, and two is barely one, as Plato says." This looks like a reference to *Phaedo* 96e– 97a, but, just possibly, it might refer to something from the second part of *Parmenides*.
58. *Meno* 71c.
59. The argument beginning at *Cratylus* 438a.

agreed" or "He disagreed." So I omitted all that kind of stuff and wrote it down as a dialogue between them.

Presumably, then, any dialogues which are narrated by a single character, with the necessity of all the "nuisance" additions, rather than being in the dramatic mode (scripted like a play: SOCRATES: Am I talking nonsense, then? THEAETETUS: Not at all), must predate *Theaetetus*. Earlier dialogues could be either narrated or dramatic, or a mixture of both, but now Plato seems to be setting his face against narration, and so any dialogues that by other criteria we find to be later than *Theaetetus* should be in dramatic mode.

It seems very likely to me, and I am far from alone, that *Apology of Socrates*, which is not a dialogue as such but an alleged transcript of the speeches delivered by Socrates at his trial in 399, is an early production. It was one of the Socratics' purposes to defend their beloved teacher's memory, and it is hard to imagine a better way of doing that than the superb, ironic, and profound *Apology*. It gives us an undying portrait of an extraordinary person. At the heart of the work is a question that occupied Plato throughout his life: how should a philosopher react to the corrupt society in which he lives? The work should have been published quite soon after the trial, while the event was still fresh in people's minds, and therefore probably dates from earlyish in the 390s.

There is one final factor to mention. In some of the shorter dialogues (mostly included in our "loose" group), Plato has Socrates question interlocutors and expose inconsistencies in their belief-sets. The argumentative methods he uses for eliciting the truth of some issue and refuting his interlocutors are bundled together by scholars under the label "the elenchus." The word implies testing or challenging, but since Socrates's interlocutors frequently fail to give coherent answers to his challenge, it often implies refutation as well. In these shorter dialogues, Plato puts the elenchus to use, but he does not reflect on it. In *Gorgias* and *Protagoras* he does just that, chiefly by getting Socrates to respond to his interlocutors' criticisms of it. Plato denies that the elenchus merely exposes inconsistencies in a person's views and insists that it is a way of achieving results in which one can have complete confidence and that deserve to be called true. *Gorgias* and *Protagoras* are therefore probably later than at least some of the short dialogues.

Putting together all the scattered results from the foregoing discussion, and remembering that Plato would have gone on tweaking his texts, we have: *Apology of Socrates* [c. 396]—*Proto-Republic* [c. 393]—*Cratylus*—*Menexenus* [c. 386]—*Phaedo* [c. 380]—*Symposium* [c. 377]—*Republic* (the bulk of it)—*Parmenides*—*Theaetetus*—*Phaedrus*—*Sophist*—*Statesman*—*Timaeus*—*Critias*—*Philebus*—*Laws*—Plato's death in 348/7. The remaining five dialogues from the second cluster (*First Alcibiades, Charmides, Gorgias, Meno, Protagoras*) were written, let's say, between 390 and 375, with *Gorgias* and *Meno* preceding *Phaedo*. *Gorgias* and *Euthydemus* were published before 370, and *Protagoras* perhaps before 375. In chapter 6, we will find reasons to date *Gorgias, Meno, Phaedo,* and the rewritten *Republic* after 383. The remaining dialogues from the loose group could have been written at any time, but they are probably the first of Plato's productions. And, apart from the dialogues, we have the three genuine letters, which are more or less precisely datable: *Letter 3* [between 358 and 356]—*Letter 7* [late 353 or early 352]—*Letter 8* [later in 352].

This is, I think, as far as one can go with the chronology of Plato's writing. These conclusions have emerged from a rather dry and scholarly exercise, especially since many readers will not yet know much about the content of the dialogues; but it is important that we have a sense of the progress of Plato's career as a writer, not just for the obvious biographical reasons but as a foundation for considering questions such as whether Plato's thinking remained the same throughout his life, or whether development and changes of mind are features of his work. It is unsafe to use doctrinal considerations to trace the chronology of the dialogues, but it is legitimate to trace doctrinal development once we have even a partial chronology in which we can have confidence.

4

Writing and Research in the
390s and 380s

B y the end of the 390s and into the 380s, Plato was well launched
on his career as a writer. Unexpectedly, we are in a position to
know what he thought about writing. Toward the end of *Phaedrus*, he
tells one of his shorter myths, in which he imagines that the clever
god Theuth invented writing and boasted of it to the Egyptian god-
king Thamous.[1]

> Theuth said, "Your highness, this science will increase the wisdom of
> the people of Egypt and improve their memories." But Thamous re-
> plied, "The loyalty you feel for writing, as its originator, has just seduced
> you into telling me the opposite of its true effect. It will atrophy peo-
> ple's memories. Trust in writing will make them remember things by
> relying on marks made by others, from outside themselves, not on their
> own inner resources, and so writing will make the things they have
> learned disappear from their minds. Your invention is merely a potion
> for jogging the memory. You provide your students with the appearance
> of wisdom, not true wisdom."

A nice anecdote arose at some point in the biographical tradition
and is preserved by a Neoplatonist of the fifth century CE.[2] One of
Plato's students had taken notes from all his lectures but lost them
at sea. When he returned to Plato, he said that he now knew from

1. Extracts from *Phaedrus* 274e–275a.
2. Hermias, *Commentary on Phaedrus*, on 275c.

Figure 4.1 A papyrus fragment, dating from the second century CE, of part of Plato's *Phaedrus. The Oxyrhynchus Papyri* vol. XVII no. 2102.

experience the truth of this passage of *Phaedrus*: he could not remember anything that he had written in his notebook.

A little later, Plato has Socrates continue:[3]

> There's a peculiar feature of writing, Phaedrus, that makes it exactly like painting. The offspring of painting stand there as if alive, but if you ask them a question, they maintain an aloof silence. It's the same with written words: you might think they were speaking as if they had some intelligence, but if you want an explanation of any of the things they're saying and you ask them about it, they just go on and on forever giving the same single piece of information.[4]

And he concludes that anyone who wanted to "sow seeds" by means of the written word would not take writing seriously, compared to the living conversation of a true philosopher, who can sow the right kind of seeds in a student's mind. The trouble with books (which were usually read out loud in Plato's day, so the contrast is not between the written and the spoken word) is that they encourage passivity rather than active participation.

---

3. *Phaedrus* 275d.
4. See also *Protagoras* 329a: "If someone were to ask one of these people a question, they'd behave like a book and could neither answer nor ask a question themselves."

These are hard words, but they should not be exaggerated, as they often are, into a blanket condemnation of writing. That would be a paradox indeed—to condemn writing in a written work. There is an escape clause, and it is repeated three times in this part of *Phaedrus*.[5] The use of writing, Plato says, and in fact the only thing it can do, is to remind people of things they have forgotten. And we know exactly what kind of forgetting and remembering Plato is talking about because his language here echoes a passage earlier in the dialogue. In the course of the great myth of the winged soul, he explains that all souls have risen up on their wings and gained a glimpse of the Plain of Truth, a "place" beyond the heavens, where the gods dwell in contemplation of Forms:

> But not every soul is readily prompted by things here on earth to recall those things that are real. This is not easy for souls that caught only a brief glimpse of things there, nor for those which, after falling to earth, have suffered the misfortune of being perverted and made immoral by the company they keep and have forgotten the holy things they saw then. When the remaining few, whose memories are good enough, see a likeness here that reminds them of things there, they are amazed and beside themselves.[6]

It is important that Plato says that *all* human souls have had at least a glimpse of the Plain of Truth; he excludes only animals. So writing, "if written by one who has knowledge of the truth,"[7] can act as a reminder to all of us. It can do no more than remind us—it cannot give us knowledge of Forms—but in some cases that will be enough to motivate a person to try to recover that lost knowledge. This may take finding a teacher, such as Socrates, who can elicit knowledge in a person by his living conversation—that is, steer the student's soul back toward the Plain of Truth. The student will first be reminded of what latently he already knows, and then: "At the moment, these

5. *Phaedrus* 275a, 275c–d, 276d.
6. *Phaedrus* 250a. That sense data here on earth can remind us of Forms is a constant thread in the dialogues.
7. *Phaedrus* 278c.

beliefs have only just been stirred up in him and it all feels like a dream, but if he were repeatedly to be asked the same questions in a number of different ways, he'd assuredly end up with knowledge of these matters."[8] And, since thinking is just internal conversation and self-questioning, he can even progress toward knowledge on his own "by long acquaintance with the matter and by being embedded in it," when "suddenly, like a light that is kindled by a leaping spark, it is born in the soul and at once becomes self-sustaining."[9]

Nor is the usefulness of the written word limited to philosophical texts. In a passage of *Laws* Plato points out that "once what the laws ordain has been set down in writing, it remains unchanged and ready to submit to examination for all time."[10] He would presumably say the same about, for example, the text of a play that one wanted to study. There are some things that should not lightly be altered—laws and texts—and writing perfectly suits them. The function of jogging the memory is far inferior to live conversation or internal dialogue, especially in a philosophical context, but it still serves a purpose.

It is typical of Plato's high-mindedness that he would belittle his writing, even though he must have recognized his talent for it. In Plato's opinion, his writing was greatly inferior to his work as a live teacher, but, for all that, it did serve a useful philosophical purpose. Plato was keenly aware of the power of words: hence his banishment of all poetry that could warp a child's character from the ideal state he constructs in *Republic*. A reminder may not be the truth itself, but it is still a reminder of truth.

Plato did not confine himself to live teaching because he could reach a wider audience through his books. He wrote to perpetuate the memory of Socrates, and he wrote to engage readers in their own

---

8. *Meno* 85c–d.
9. *Letter* 7 341c–d, a passage I quoted also in the introduction. It is a clever piece of writing, because the bit that I have translated "by long acquaintance with the matter and by being embedded in it" could also be translated "after much conversation about the matter and a life lived together." Knowledge can be kindled either by one's own deep reflection or by long acquaintance with a teacher such as Socrates.
10. *Laws* 890e–891a.

internal dialogue. He wrote dialogues because many of Socrates's ideas, and those that he later would put into Socrates's mouth, are radical; it helps if we can see the thinking behind them, spelled out in conversations with interlocutors who are in relevant ways like ourselves. Plato and other Socratics may even have felt that it was their duty to write books. Many of them did become authors, though hardly anything of their work survives. But I feel sure that Plato also wrote because he had no choice: some people can fulfill their potential only by writing. The many-layered artistry of the dialogues (in the best of them there always seems to be more going on than one can quite catch), the combination of hard argument, bold philosophy, and myth, with a leavening of dramatic scene-setting and characterization—all this speaks of someone who wrote for the sheer joy of it.

The Early Dialogues

By the middle of the 380s, Plato was well known as a philosopher. But what was he famous for? What kinds of works had he been writing? In other words, what are the chief features of the group of dialogues that were probably his earliest works? This group, we found, was made up of *Apology of Socrates, Cratylus, Crito, Euthydemus, Euthyphro, Hippias Major, Hippias Minor, Ion, Laches, Lysis,* and *Menexenus.* Some of these, possibly most of them (none of them is long), had been written by the mid-380s. Several of these dialogues explore a moral concept, but *Crito* focuses on a moral issue: would it be right for Socrates to avoid execution by escaping from prison?

Menexenus is an acknowledged maverick, and perhaps no more than a jeu d'esprit. It consists largely of a jingoistic and occasionally willfully distorted account of Athenian history, delivered as a parody of the funeral speeches that were spoken every year in Athens over the war dead.[11] If it is not clear from the speech itself, the opening

11. Most famously, the speech delivered by Pericles in 431 and preserved or paraphrased by Thucydides, *The Peloponnesian War* 2.34–46.

conversation clearly indicates the parodic nature of what follows. The point is probably to support the claims that political rhetoric panders to the views of the masses and is designed to give its audience pleasure rather than knowledge, though it is not clear how many of Plato's immediate audience would have grasped the point.

Apology serves as a kind of introduction to these dialogues, in that Plato has Socrates use his defense speeches to explain what he does and why he does it. But since Plato was not writing Socrates's biography, he is really explaining what *he* does and why he does it. In *Apology* Socrates says that his friend Chaerephon asked the oracle at Delphi whether there was anyone wiser than Socrates, and the oracle said that there was not. Socrates was puzzled, because he did not think he was wise, so the oracle triggered his mission. He tested it by going around and questioning people who had a reputation for wisdom, and he consistently found that they did not know what they were talking about; so he concluded that the oracle was right in that he at least knew that he was ignorant, whereas the people he tested believed themselves wise.

But this oracle story is almost certainly a fiction.[12] This is so even though Xenophon, too, includes a version of the story in his *Apology of Socrates*. This is simply the phenomenon known to literary critics as "intertextuality," whereby one author borrows and transforms something from another author. We can occasionally detect Xenophon's nods toward Plato, and if we had more of the work of other Socratics, there is no doubt that we would find many more cases where one author's text was shaped to a certain extent by another's. The reason the story is fiction is that Socrates was only ever known as the person who went around questioning others; that was how he had gained a reputation for wisdom. So the oracle cannot have triggered his mission because his mission must have been well launched for Chaerephon to want to ask the oracle that question in the first place. It was Plato's way of explaining what he was going to have his character Socrates do

12. It was doubted even in antiquity: Plutarch, *Moralia* 1116e–f (*Against Colotes*).

in these early dialogues—that is, test the wisdom of alleged experts. Another factor suggesting the story's fictionality is that it is never mentioned anywhere else than in these two *Apologies*, Plato's and Xenophon's. But it would have been a famous incident, were it true.

Most of these dialogues are quite short—similar in length to the works that, as far as we can tell, the other Socratics were writing as well. Several of them belong to a series that scholars call the dialogues of search. They are also commonly called the "Socratic dialogues," the assumption being that in these dialogues Plato was more concerned than he was later to portray the historical Socrates at work. However, as I have already indicated, I regard them as largely fictional accounts of Socrates. It does not seem likely that Plato would have spent a good ten years of his life doing little more than writing pen portraits. However devoted he was to Socrates, his homage to his teacher consisted in developing philosophy along Socratic lines, not in parroting versions of Socrates's actual conversations. No philosopher worthy of the name simply takes over another's beliefs or arguments; others' ideas are at most a base camp for future expeditions.

Typically, in one of these dialogues, Plato has Socrates seek the definition of a moral term: piety in *Euthyphro*, fineness in *Hippias Major*, courage in *Laches*, friendship in *Lysis*, justice in *Thrasymachus*, which became the first book of *Republic*.[13] Typically, the search fails.[14] A number of definitions or pseudo-definitions are tried out, but in the end none satisfies the participants in the conversation. Plato gives examples of the kind of definition he is after: "Speed is the ability to get a lot done in a little time"; "Shape is the limit of a solid body"; "Color is an emanation emitted by shapes that is commensurate with sight"; "Mud is earth mixed with water"; "Even number is number that is divisible into two equal parts."[15] But it is much more difficult

13. Later dialogues continue this kind of quest: *Charmides*: What is self-control? *Meno*: What is virtue? *Theaetetus*: What is knowledge? The quest fails in all three cases.
14. Definitions are finally given of several of these moral terms in the fourth book or chapter of the later *Republic*.
15. *Laches* 192a–b, *Meno* 76a, *Meno* 76d, *Theaetetus* 147c, *Euthyphro* 12d.

to come up with definitions of moral terms that will cover all cases, and these dialogues often end in *aporia*, an impasse or dead end (and so they are also commonly called the "aporetic" dialogues). *Hippias Minor*, an investigation into lying and truth-telling, also ends with an impasse—the unacceptable paradox that it is a good person who is the best liar and worst criminal (because people are good if they have knowledge, and knowledge can be used for good or ill: the best doctor is also the best poisoner). *Ion* ends with an implicit impasse, in the sense that Ion's claims for his area of expertise, the Homeric poems, become increasingly absurd, until he goes so far as to claim that his knowledge of Homer would make him the best possible commander at a time of war.

Impasse is reached because every idea entertained by Socrates's various interlocutors proves, under his sometimes ruthless questioning, either simply to be inadequate as a definition or to contradict another of the interlocutor's fundamental beliefs. For instance, Laches suggests that courage is to be defined as mental persistence—until Socrates demonstrates that mental persistence is not always a good thing, while Laches believes that courage is always good. *Cratylus*, an evaluation of two opposing theories about the correctness of names (whether, for instance, we say "horse" just because that is the conventional name for a horse, or whether the name is somehow a natural reflection of what it is to be a horse) is also an aporetic dialogue, in that Socrates ends up casting doubt on both theories. Throughout all the dialogues, Plato consistently thought that the worst intellectual error, with appalling moral consequences as well, was the conceit of knowledge—being sure that you know something when you really do not. These early dialogues are exercises in exposing such conceits and in suggesting a cure: keep searching for the elusive truth by self-examination and critical reasoning.

If a dialogue ends inconclusively, readers are bound to ask themselves why. And so they will be doing philosophy. At the least, they will be sharpening their appreciation for good argumentation, but it may also lead them to come up with a solution. If it is courage that the interlocutors of a dialogue have failed to define, readers may come up with a definition themselves, based on what Plato says. Many readers search in this way within the arguments of these aporetic dialogues for clues that allow them to escape the impasse. Their conclusions may or may not be right, but they are doing what Plato wanted: thinking and searching for the truth.

In these dialogues, Socrates disclaims knowledge and claims not to be steering the conversations but simply following the logic of the arguments. He often merely interrogates his interlocutors, acting (the image comes from *Theaetetus*, a later dialogue) as a midwife of others' ideas—that is, he draws ideas out of them and tests them to make sure they are not "stillborn." But the interrogation is guided by certain dubious assumptions: that the kind of precise knowledge that is possible in the arts and crafts is possible in ethical inquiry too; and that a single word such as "justice" corresponds to a single reality, so we should be able to come up with a single definition that covers all cases where we apply the term. In the phrases "a good man" and "a good pianist," does "good" mean the same thing? The assumption that a single term should have a single definition leads to so many difficulties in *Charmides*, written some years later, that one is tempted to think that Plato was actually challenging it in this dialogue.

Another typical feature of these dialogues is that Socrates's interlocutors are people who might be considered experts in the matters under investigation—or Socrates teasingly assigns them expertise: "You two are friends, so you must know what friendship is." Socrates, by contrast, is presented as an ignorant amateur, wielding no more than common sense. Plato assumes (another dubious assumption) that an expert must be able to come up with a proper definition, and that failure to do so indicates lack of knowledge of the subject. This is where the questioning gets personal and adversarial, as under the spotlight of Socrates's questions the interlocutor is shown to be no expert after all. People as well as propositions are tested by Socratic questioning; if definition is at issue, for instance, it is not just the pseudo-definitions themselves that are refuted but also the

interlocutor's belief in the correctness of the pseudo-definitions and
the way of life that he bases on these beliefs:[16]

> I don't think you appreciate what happens when you come into close
> proximity to Socrates and strike up a conversation with him. Whatever
> the original topic of your conversation, eventually he's bound to head
> you off and trap you into trying to explain your own way of life and
> how you've lived up to now. And once you're caught in the trap,
> Socrates won't let you go until he's subjected every detail to a thor-
> ough, rigorous test.

The interlocutors, not surprisingly, often react with anger or exas-
peration to Socrates's questioning. The people to whom he talks feel
pain, as if they had been bitten by a viper or a gadfly, or stung by a
stingray.[17] In dramatic terms, these early dialogues are some of Plato's
best creations. Characters are delineated with economy and wit; we
see their pomposity and other qualities, and we watch them wriggle
as they try to escape the force of Socrates's arguments. Socrates's job
as a gadfly was to stir people from their complacency, forcing them to
rethink what they thought they knew.

These dialogues show a philosopher—*the* philosopher—working
through problems, and they encourage us to do the same. The implicit claim is that it is worth engaging in philosophical conversation, even when no satisfactory solution to the problem is found,
because by tackling the issues we become engaged at an emotional
level with the quest. Moreover, as Plato states in a late dialogue, awareness of ignorance clears the ground for the pursuit of knowledge.[18]
Philosophical inquiry may be difficult and frustrating, but it is essential. Hence, perhaps, the strong emphasis in these dialogues on methodology. There are often pauses as the interlocutors consider the best
way to go forward.

There is more to the early dialogues than just a ground-clearing exercise, however. Positive views also crop up. They are essentially those

16. *Laches* 187e–188a, Nicias talking to Lysimachus.
17. Viper: *Symposium* 217e–218a. Gadfly: *Apology of Socrates* 30e–31a. Stingray: *Meno* 80a.
18. *Sophist* 230b–e.

views whose negations are invariably refuted in the dialogues; Plato takes this to be enough to establish their worth. The most important are those that infused his thinking forever: that virtue is knowledge, so that we are probably meant to think of courage, for example, as knowledge of what is and is not genuinely fearful; that a good person's body may be harmed, but not their soul; that it is never right to do wrong, or even to repay wrongdoing in kind; that it is better to suffer injustice than to commit injustice; that no one does wrong willingly (that is, everyone thinks that what they are doing is good for them, even though some people are objectively wrong about this); that if one does wrong, it is better to be punished (by re-education) than to escape punishment; that virtue and knowledge are necessary, and possibly also sufficient for human well-being; that conventional "goods" such as wealth and prestige are matters of indifference in themselves and are only good and non-injurious if they are put to virtuous and intelligent use. These are startling claims, pointing to a way of life far removed from what has been normal in every generation of human existence; this is brought out especially well in *First Alcibiades*. Plato was always a radical in ethical matters. One of the reasons for the negative conclusion of many of these dialogues is that, each time, it hints at the incommensurability between a philosophical and an ordinary way of life.

Knowledge and Belief

Perhaps the most important lesson Plato teaches with these early dialogues is that knowledge and belief are different, and that the difference is of fundamental importance in all walks of life. This was a topic to which he returned with vigor in later dialogues as well, especially in *Meno*, *Republic*, and *Theaetetus*. One of the main things Plato has Socrates do in the early dialogues, as we have just seen, is ask, "What is X?" where "X" is usually a moral concept such as courage or justice. He insists that interlocutors who cannot satisfactorily answer this question do not *know* what they are talking about. A true expert in any topic must be able to explain that topic, with an explanation that survives in-terrogation. He might think he has knowledge, but it turns out that he has only beliefs. Knowledge is certain, knowledge is of the truth, and knowledge is irrefutable. Beliefs are commonly based on persuasive agents—such as common sense, popular opinion, emotion, advertise-ments, talking heads, eloquent speakers—and are therefore unstable, in that they can alter under the influence of a more persuasive agent. This is most obvious—and most alarming—in a jury trial: the rival teams of prosecution and defense are each trying to persuade the members of the jury to believe what they want them to believe; the jury ends up not with knowledge but with belief.[19] We are all familiar with this phe-nomenon, wherein an idea we hear or read seems persuasive—until a more convincing take on the same subject makes us change our minds (or, if we are inflexible, dismiss the new notion as "fake news").

The difference between belief and knowledge is not just a nice piece of philosophical theory. The trouble, as Plato saw it, is that we go ahead and act on the basis of our beliefs, not realizing that they are only beliefs, not knowledge. We perpetuate beliefs by our actions and our statements. Since no one does wrong willingly (because to do wrong is to self-harm), only knowledge can be a reliable guide to living. Without knowledge, there is no guarantee that anything we do will turn out well or will be good for us; conversely, acting with knowledge is a guarantee of success. Virtue is knowledge, so that the reformation of character is the necessary foundation of moral be-havior. Moreover, beliefs may well be false; the very fact that we can change our minds shows that we think our new belief is more sound than the one we have shed. We should discipline ourselves by testing our beliefs with Socratic self-questioning.

Beliefs, however, may be true as well as false, and Plato acknow-ledges that true belief may, in practical terms, be as good a guide as knowledge. Someone who correctly believes (because they trust a map, say) that I-95 will take a person to Miami is just as good a guide

19. Compare *Theaetetus* 201a–c.

as someone who knows it; it is just that the person with belief always has to consult a map, whereas the person with knowledge consults their experience rather than a map. But the trouble still remains: persuasion can alter even a true belief (by casting doubt on the reliability of the map), since it is just a belief and not knowledge. Since both true and false beliefs are generated by persuasion, there is no way for us to know whether a belief we have is true or false; only knowledge provides a reliable foundation for action: "The problem is that true beliefs tend not to stay for long; they escape from our minds and this reduces their value, unless they're anchored by working out the reason."[20] If you work out why your true belief is true, you understand it and convert it into knowledge, and then no one can change your mind. Many modern philosophers, too, would agree that "well-grounded true belief" is a workable definition of knowledge.

So in the early dialogues Plato urges us to think for ourselves and to argue with ourselves, rather than accept what we have taken in from an outside source. The source may be something as reputable as a trusted teacher or decades of convention, but we still should not blindly accept it. And this, as I have already said, is certainly one of the reasons that Plato wrote dialogues in the first place while not affirming or denying anything in his own name. We are forced to think for ourselves rather than merely be persuaded by what we read. The distinction between belief and knowledge is one of Plato's lasting legacies.

The Demarcation of Philosophy

Taken as a whole, the early dialogues tell us quite a lot about one important strand of Plato's agenda. In most of them, he has Socrates converse with people who either think of themselves as experts of some kind or who could reasonably be thought to be experts. He converses with educational experts (*Hippias Major, Hippias Minor, Thrasymachus*),

20. *Meno* 98a.

an expert in the Homeric poems (*Ion*), a self-proclaimed religious expert (*Euthyphro*), friends, who therefore, according to Plato, should know what friendship is (*Lysis*), two famous Athenian generals (*Laches*), and two alleged experts in names (*Cratylus*).

On occasion, Plato might make sure that we are aware of Socrates's targets by having them boast of their expertise, as Euthyphro does: "Socrates, if I didn't have precise knowledge [about the gods, and what is holy and unholy], I'd be worthless. Euthyphro would be no different from any ordinary person."[21] But the outcome of every conversation is the demonstration that the alleged expert does not know what he claims to know and should know. In *Euthydemus* the brother sophists Euthydemus and Dionysodorus of Chios are not shown up in quite the same way but are simply exposed as fools who have no interest in benefiting the people to whom they talk, only in scoring points (with often ridiculous arguments) and attracting acclaim. They claim to teach virtue, and indeed to be "the best and quickest teachers of virtue alive,"[22] but in fact they teach litigation rather than justice, martial arts instead of courage, and disputation rather than wisdom.

At a personal level, these dialogues encourage readers to think, and they clear the ground for them to arrive at a more coherent set of beliefs, one that can withstand scrutiny and enable them to live a life based on a more stable foundation. But there is more to these dialogues than that. Plato used them for no less a purpose than to stake the claim of Socratic philosophy to be the only true education. By proving that others' claims to wisdom were spurious, Plato was claiming victory for Socratic education. The thrust of Socrates's arguments in these dialogues is to challenge the authority of others, and especially the authority of conventional beliefs, and thereby to boost the authority of philosophy. Socrates's particular skill in these dialogues is to meet his interlocutors on their ground and to gradually

21. *Euthyphro* 4e.
22. *Euthydemus* 273d,

lead them away from the conventional views that they unthinkingly repeat and toward a more Platonic position.

Plato's focus in these early dialogues is on people's ordinary moral and political assumptions; since these assumptions turn out to be incoherent, there is something wrong with the educational system that supplied them, because an authentic education would make people knowledgeable rather than stuffed with incoherent beliefs. Wealthy Alcibiades must have received the best possible education that Athens and the sophists had to offer, yet as far as Plato's Socrates was concerned, he was "completely uneducated."[23] Society does not function with knowledge of the values on which it is supposed to be based. Ignorant orators and sophists give speeches to ignorant audiences. An orator might praise a donkey as a fine horse, and the audience would not know the difference.[24] Society condemns people for injustice, cowardice, and impiety when no one knows what justice, courage, and piety are. Thinking something through and identifying underlying assumptions are always preferable to the unthinking and uncritical acceptance of society's norms and injunctions. The critical thinking that Plato encouraged is the foundation of the humanities, the study of the human world and society: stepping back, identifying a problem, applying rationality to developing a solution to the problem—and then having the courage to do something about it, even if that involves dissenting from a majority opinion.

One of Plato's guiding principles was that philosophy is incompatible with base self-interest. It is not philosophy if you want to get rich or famous from it. So insofar as poets, sophists, and politicians were public figures, competing with one another for acclaim, Plato felt he had to distinguish philosophy from what they did. To get ahead, poets and politicians have to please their audiences. They are not concerned with truth or education, properly understood, but only with giving pleasure; yet education should hurt, since it should reform a person's

23. *First Alcibiades* 123d.
24. *Phaedrus* 260b–d.

character, which Plato saw as the foundation for true philosophical work. Poets of all stripes, including writers of satirical comedies, were considered (and considered themselves) to be advisers of the state, so Plato has to dismiss them as unknowledgeable. They are traffickers in pleasure and therefore necessarily perpetuating worldly values rather than trying to improve their audiences. The Presocratic philosopher Heraclitus of Ephesus had made the same point: "What intelligence or insight do they have? They trust the people's bards and take for their teacher the mob, not realizing that 'Most people are bad, few good.'"[25]

What all these people do is in effect a form of flattery, and the same goes for sophists too. When Plato famously said that there was "an ancient quarrel between poetry and philosophy,"[26] he was referring to no historical fact, no long debate about the relative values of poetry and philosophy: he was driving a wedge between the two occupations for the same purpose—to distinguish philosophy from all rival claims to wisdom. By "poetry" he did not mean what would first come to our minds—reading Dylan Thomas or Emily Dickinson to ourselves—but the public performance of plays and epic poems in front of large audiences, the ancient equivalent of movies and television today. We may admire the surviving plays of ancient Greeks such as those of Euripides and Aristophanes, but Plato thought that they were educationally perilous. His hostility toward poetry is an aspect of his hostility toward rhetoric. Ideas have an effect on character, and so the only ideas that should be perpetuated are those that have a positive effect. In chapter 5, we will see Plato driving the same wedge between his Academy and rival schools in Athens.

This dismissal of other pursuits in favor of philosophy was not something that occupied Plato only in the earliest phase of his writing. *Symposium*, for instance, consists of a sequence of speeches in praise of love. Each of these speeches is meant to be authoritative in

25. Heraclitus, Fragment D10 Laks/Most.
26. *Republic* 607b.

its own way, from an erotic or traditional religious perspective, or as spoken by a doctor, a comedian, or a tragedian. All the earlier speeches are then shown to be deficient when Socrates begins to speak. In *Meno*, Plato makes sure that we know that Meno had studied with the sophist Gorgias, with the result that we are inclined to attribute Meno's pathetic attempts at defining virtue to the deficiencies of sophistic education.

In this way, philosophy was born in the fourth century BCE. Before Plato, the word *philosophia* (literally, "love of wisdom") and its cognates had been rare and had referred largely to intellectual curiosity or advanced education in general, not to any narrower aspect of it; it had possibly even started life as a term of opprobrium for someone who aspired to the wisdom of the sages. But Plato and the Socratics tried to restrict the term to Socratic philosophy, which is to say to philosophy as we still understand it today. The Socratics, and especially Plato, gave the term a specialist meaning in order to distinguish philosophy from other pursuits and occupations. It was a study in contrasts: philosophers seek knowledge and truth through conversation, while others seek to give pleasure and perpetuate beliefs that have not been properly examined; philosophy pursues virtue and has nothing to do with self-interest, but that is the raison d'être of the anti-philosophical pursuits; philosophy persuades by argumentation, while others rely on rhetorical strategies. One of the consequences of Plato's demarcation of philosophy is that Socrates, who by any reasonable criteria would have been classified as a sophist in his lifetime, is distinguished from the sophists as much as possible.

In the previous century, the Hippocratics had, in their own ways, begun to differentiate their medical practices, which they reckoned to be based on scientific fact, from quackery and folk medicine. Plato was following a general trend toward specialization—toward separating insiders from outsiders. The outcome was the plain declaration that Socratic philosophy was the one true and effective educational system and the only occupant of the moral high ground. This was the conviction that motivated Plato and the other Socratics, and a way of advertising their wares and attracting students.

Southern Italy and the Pythagoreans

Taking a break from writing, Plato set off, probably in 385, on a research trip to Greek southern Italy and Sicily. Because Plato says that he was about forty years old,[27] those who believe that he was born in 428/7 date this trip to 388/7; but this is unlikely, because the Corinthian War was still in progress, and Syracuse, the chief city in Sicily, was sympathetic to Sparta, the enemy of Athens. It would have been dangerous for anyone to set sail on non-military business, and even more so for an Athenian to go to Syracuse, as Plato did. The year 385 was the earliest Plato could have set sail, after peace had been restored the previous year. It almost looks as though he had been waiting for the war to end so that he could leave.

In southern Italy he seems to have been interested above all in meeting Pythagoreans, and specifically Archytas of Taras (Tarentum to the Romans, modern Taranto). Within a few years Archytas would become the leading man of Taras, which had a quasi-democratic constitution at the time and was the head of a league of local city-states, so it is likely that by the time of Plato's journey Archytas was already famous enough as a scientist and philosopher—and perhaps as a rising star in Tarentine politics—for Plato to have arranged to meet him. Besides, there were other Pythagoreans in Taras.

Plato was already acquainted with Pythagoreanism from his reading, and he had Pythagorean friends from the inner circle of the Socratics: Simmias and Cebes of Thebes, who were with Socrates in prison on the last day of his life. But now it seems that he wanted to learn more; perhaps he also needed a break from writing, and time to mull his increasing conviction that he would have to start a school. Isocrates,

---

27. *Letter 7* 324a.

whom Plato considered an heir of the fifth-century sophists, started his school in Athens around 390. In a pamphlet *Against the Sophists*, written to advertise the school's principles and methods and attract future political thinkers and leaders, he had criticized the Socratics, among others. Plato wanted to stake out the educational claim of Socratic philosophy in rivalry with Isocrates.

Pythagoras was born on the island of Samos, but he fell out with the tyrant of the island, the far-famed Polycrates, who made the island for a while the most powerful and glorious state in the Greek world, and around 530 he fled to southern Italy. Settled by Greeks from the second half of the eighth century onward, the city-states of southern Italy and Sicily were known collectively as Magna Graecia, Greater Greece, and were famous for their prosperity and comfortable lifestyle. We still use the word "sybarite" for someone who indulges in sensuous luxury; it refers to the southern Italian town of Sybaris. But Pythagoras was far from being the only philosopher or scientist to come from Magna Graecia; the roll call includes some of the greatest names: Parmenides and Zeno of Elea, Empedocles of Acragas, Philolaus of Croton, Archimedes of Syracuse.

Quite what Pythagoras taught is lost in the mists of time, shrouded by the facts that he wrote nothing and that later thinkers who called themselves Pythagoreans cast their discoveries back as discoveries of Pythagoras himself, the founder of the school. In any case, Pythagoreanism may not have been altogether a unified system of thought. Minimally, we can say that he taught that the soul was immortal and was forever reincarnated in other bodies, unless an aspirant purified it by ascetic practices until, godlike, he could break free of the cycle of reincarnations. These ideas had reached the Greek world from India. Later Pythagoras became famous as a mathematician, though he did not discover the theorem that we still call "Pythagorean," which was known in Babylon centuries earlier.

In fact, we have no idea to what extent Pythagoras himself was a mathematician; the Pythagorean interest in mathematics and arithmology (the study of the properties of numbers)[28] was largely a development of the fifth century, especially by Philolaus of Croton. By Plato's time, the Pythagoreans were teaching that the orderliness of the universe is because of its being informed by number and in particular by the primary musical ratios (the discovery of which probably goes back to Pythagoras himself), and Pythagoras had become the figure that is still familiar to us today—a combination of religious prophet and natural scientist.

In southern Italy, Pythagoras established groups that, over the subsequent decades, followed the rules of living that he laid down, which included vegetarianism and other dietary regulations. Vegetarianism was a logical consequence of belief in reincarnation: you do not want to run the risk of eating your reincarnated grandmother. Pythagoreans were famous for living a frugal, god-oriented, disciplined, and mindful way of life, and the single mention of Pythagoras by Plato describes him only as the founder of a way of life.[29] Uniquely for the time, women might be full members of the Pythagorean groups.

In Croton, the followers that Pythagoras gained came to win political power and were responsible for the revival of the city's fortunes, and eventually for its dominance of the region, from about 510 until 450. The Pythagoreans spread from Croton until they were the chief political power throughout southern Italy. They did not instigate revolutions or form new governments, but people recognized their integrity and allowed them gradually to infiltrate existing institutions, whether the city they lived in was democratic or oligarchic in constitution. But anything that looks like a cult is liable to retaliation, and around 450 there was an uprising in the course of which many Pythagoreans lost their lives, and subsequently they focused more on philosophy and science than on politics. It is clear from Archytas's career, however, that Pythagoreans could still win respect and political power.

28. See especially the late Pythagorean text *The Theology of Arithmetic*.
29. *Republic* 600b.

This was the sect that Plato wanted to visit and learn more about; later we will see the effect on his written work. From Athens, he would have gone down to Piraeus, sailed across the Saronic Gulf to Cenchreae, the southern port of Corinth, and walked or been driven across the narrow isthmus (the site of the modern Corinth Canal) to Lechaeum, the city's northern port. From there he would have caught another boat along the Gulf of Corinth and sailed across the Ionian Sea to Italy.

Plato in Southern Italy and Sicily

In Taras, Plato made the acquaintance of Archytas, and they entered into the formal relationship known as *xenia*. The word literally means just "the condition of being a host or a guest" and is usually translated "guest-friendship." It was a sacralized and ritualized relationship, and particular to members of the Mediterranean wealth elite. Once it had been initiated by ritual means and the exchange of gifts of equal value, it was perpetuated by means of hospitality when either party visited the other's city and by the free and generous donation of goods or services as and when called on between such visits. No doubt some *xenoi* were fond of one another—that is, were friends as well as guest-friends—but that was not essential to the relationship, which was formed by a ritual act rather than by affection.

Plato's relationship with Archytas was somewhat ambivalent. He greatly respected the mathematician's work in both pure and applied mathematics, but he seems to have thought that Archytas himself had not seen its philosophical importance. For a philosopher, Plato believed or came to believe, the study of the mathematical sciences is not just an end in itself but a way of shifting a person's gaze from the mutable, perceptible world to the immutable world of Forms, which resemble mathematical entities in being immaterial and unchanging. Moreover, as we will see later, Plato was angry with Archytas at one point for encouraging Dionysius II in the belief that Platonism was a matter of doctrine alone, rather than also including practical work designed to reform character. Dionysius, like the rest of us, had first to cleanse his soul of impurities such as the conceit of knowledge, the unconscious lie, and immoral thoughts and behavior. Like the rest of us, Dionysius was sick without realizing it, and without understanding that philosophy was the cure.

Plato also quickly became disillusioned by the political prospects of the Greek cities of Greater Greece. In *Letter 7* he ends his account of his disappointment with Athenian politics by making one of his most striking political statements, which echoes a famous cry in *Republic*: "The human race will never be free of trouble until either those who go about philosophy in the right way and with sincerity gain political power, or the rulers of our cities, by some dispensation of providence, take up authentic philosophy."[30] And he says that when he went to Italy and Sicily for the first time, he was already convinced of the rightness of this position. But his first impressions of Greater Greece were not favorable. He found that people there were largely preoccupied with the distinctly unphilosophical pursuits of filling their bellies with fine food and wine and indulging their sexual proclivities, and he held out little hope that, under such circumstances, the cities could ever have "a just and equitable form of government."

If Plato did not already know about Pythagorean rule in southern Italy in the sixth and fifth centuries, he would have heard details from his new friends. However else one describes Pythagorean politics, they were clearly attempting to see that intelligent people with principles were responsible for the administration of the cities in their charge. This could have been an aha moment for Plato: Did he begin to think that Socrates's proposals about leadership could actually be realized? Did he begin to contemplate a return to practical politics?

After a stay presumably of some weeks, Plato moved on from Taras to Locri, on the toe of Italy, where he met more Pythagoreans. Perhaps in both Taras and Locri he read some of his work to them, although

---

30. *Letter 7* 326a–b; see *Republic* 473c–d, 487e, 499b, 501e.

it was undoubtedly already known in Magna Graecia. From Locri he crossed over to Sicily. He wanted to meet more Pythagoreans, such as Archedemus of Syracuse, but he also went just as a tourist; we are told that he wanted to visit and explore Mount Etna. The visit paid dividends in the fantastical myth of the "true earth" and the soul's afterlife fate with which he ended *Phaedo*; the myth is based on Sicilian geography (with an explicit reference to the island's volcanic properties) and Pythagorean ideas.

It was especially easy to move between Locri and eastern Sicily because, though rebellion was looming, Locri was at the time part of the realm of Dionysius I, the tyrant of Syracuse and ruler of central and eastern Sicily (see figure 4.2). Dionysius had come to power in

Figure 4.2 A silver ten-drachma piece from the time of the Syracusan tyrant Dionysius I. The head is that of Arethusa, the personification of the freshwater spring on the island of Ortygia, where Syracuse was founded.
Found in the area of Lyon; Giraud Collection, 1911.

Syracuse in the last few years of the fifth century, when he was only twenty-five or so years old, and held his position until his death in 367. He was a remarkable man. He had one of the best military minds the Greeks produced; he restored Syracusan supremacy in Sicily and managed to confine the Carthaginians (originally from Carthage in what is now Tunisia), resurgent for the first time in many decades, to the west of the island,[31] depriving them of much territory that they had held at the start of his tyranny; by conquest and diplomacy he developed the Syracusan empire into the most powerful state in Europe, with possessions not just in Sicily but also in the toe of Italy and up the southeastern coast of Italy in the Adriatic; he won first prize at an Athenian dramatic festival with one of his own plays (though that may be more because of the Athenian need to flatter him, rather than the excellence of the work: we cannot tell because none of his plays has survived); he had one of the longest reigns of any ancient monarch; and he managed the rare feat of dying in his bed (possibly as a result of prolonged celebration of the victory of his tragedy) rather than on the battlefield or by assassination. At the time of Plato's visit he was preparing for war against the Carthaginians and their allies; the war ended in 375 with slight gains for the Carthaginians in Sicily, while in Italy Dionysius recovered Locri and gained the city of Croton. Taras, however, despite having been another of the Carthaginians' Italian allies, managed to preserve its independence by negotiating with Dionysius.

Plato tells us very little about this first visit to Syracuse, presumably because there was little to tell.[32] The most important thing that happened is that he met Dion, Dionysius's future brother-in-law and trusted adviser (see figure 4.3). Dion, Plato assures us, was cut from a different cloth than the majority of the power possessors of Magna

31. When Plato says that Dionysius made a single polity out of the entirety of Sicily (*Letter 7* 332c), he means Greek Sicily.
32. *Letter 7* 324a–b, 326b–327b, followed by Plutarch, *Life of Dion* 4.3–5.7.

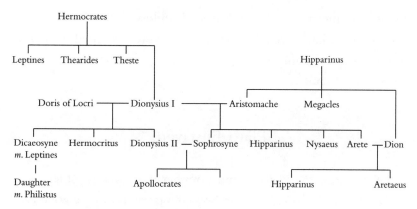

Figure 4.3 The Families of the Dionysii and Dion

Graecia: he was interested in philosophy, he chose virtue over pleasure, and he wanted to convert at least some of his fellow Syracusans to the philosophical life. It was likely, given his interest in philosophy and Plato's fame, that he had heard of the Athenian philosopher before he arrived on the island, and before long he was a convert to Plato's way of thinking, especially about political matters. It is clear that Plato was very taken with Dion, who was aged about twenty, and saw him as an ideal student. It may not be going too far to say that Plato loved him, but not in an overtly sexual way. At any rate, he must have spent quite a few weeks in Syracuse at this time, over the winter of 385/4, to cement the relationship with Dion and to capitalize on the young man's attraction to philosophy. There may have been a circle around Plato in Syracuse, but his focus was on Dion.

Most of the ancient biographers say that Plato met Dionysius I, and was even invited to Syracuse by the tyrant, at Dion's urging. Some of them claim that Plato tried to persuade Dionysius to change his tyranny into an oligarchy of the best men. But there is no indication in the best sources, starting with *Letter 7*, that Plato spent time in Dionysius I's court or even met him. Nevertheless, I have no doubt that they met: there is no way that Dionysius, who liked to pose as a patron of culture, as most monarchs do, would have passed up the opportunity to meet a famous writer and thinker. I doubt they met regularly, or discussed philosophy and politics; it is possible that Plato gave a lecture that the tyrant attended. Somehow, Dionysius got the impression, no doubt rightly, that Plato was hostile toward tyranny.

Plato Enslaved?

In the spring of 384 Plato set out from Syracuse back to Athens, leaving Dion as a confirmed disciple. Something seems to have gone badly wrong on the return voyage. At any rate, several of our later sources, starting with Diodorus of Sicily and Philodemus of Gadara in the first century BCE, tell an odd tale, or some version of it. A Spartan ambassador called Pollis was returning from Syracuse to the Greek mainland as well, so Plato took ship with him. But Dionysius was so angry with Plato for his belittlement of his majesty that he ordered Pollis to either kill the philosopher during the voyage or sell him into slavery.

So, on returning to Greece, Pollis went to the island of Aegina because he knew that the Aeginetans had been staunchly pro-Spartan in the recently ended Corinthian War; they had fought the Athenians with some intensity in the last two years of the war, and they still had a law in place that any Athenian who set foot on the island was to be summarily put to death. The hostility between Aegina and Athens was by then at least 150 years old. Plato's fame, however, was such that the sentence was commuted, and a Libyan Greek called Anniceris, who happened to be on the island, paid the large fine or ransom that was required to win Plato's freedom. Anniceris was a member of the Cyrenaic school, founded in Greek Libya by the Socratic Aristippus. He had stopped off in Aegina on his way to Elis to take part in the Olympic Games, which confirms the date, because 384 was an Olympic year. On his return to Athens, Plato and his friends offered to repay Anniceris (perhaps with Dion's help), but he refused, and the money was instead put toward the purchase of some land near the Academy park, where before long Plato established his school.

No ancient author doubted the story,[33] and it was persistent enough to attract variants. Perhaps Plato was put up for sale in Syracuse, not Aegina; perhaps Dionysius entrusted his fate to some merchants, not to Pollis; perhaps neither merchants nor Pollis were involved, but Plato was captured and sold by pirates; perhaps Plato was bought not by Anniceris but by an ordinary Aeginetan of no standing (which implies, rightly, that Plato would have made a terrible slave).

Plato himself is completely silent about the story,[34] but that may not be enough to entitle us to dismiss it: he may have wanted to suppress a painful memory. Could this be why he so studiously avoids mentioning his interactions with Dionysius? The story seems to have good fourth-century origins: the account in Philodemus names Philiscus, an Aeginetan writer of the later fourth century, as the ultimate source, and there may be a reference to it in Aristotle, when he writes, in the course of a discussion of chance, "as when we say that it was by chance that the foreigner came and paid the ransom before leaving."[35] I think we should accept the story in some form. I believe that Dionysius's involvement is a later accretion—tyrants of Dionysius's stature attracted hostile tales—as probably is that of Pollis as well: after all, if he was returning to Sparta, why would he have gone so far out of his way and taken Plato to Aegina? That would have involved rounding Cape Malea, which no ancient ship's captain liked to do.

So here is what might have happened, if we are inclined to give the story any credence. Plato took ship with some merchants from Syracuse (as in the earliest version, that of Philodemus), not with Pollis. The ship was attacked by pirates, who were a constant problem throughout Mediterranean history until relatively recently. In the

33. Though Olympiodorus assigns it to Plato's second visit to Syracuse and the younger Dionysius, and Philodemus seems to date the episode to around 399, since he says that Plato was frightened of being taken off to King Archelaus in Macedon, who died in 399. But this makes no sense: Plato did not travel to Sicily in 399.

34. The issue is relevant to the question of the authenticity of *Letter 7*: it is hardly likely that a forger would have omitted such a sensational and well-known story, assuming it was known in his day.

35. Aristotle, *Physics* 199b20–21.

fourth century, piracy was a recognized way of making a living, and one of their principal sources of income was ransoming or selling as slaves those they captured. Or perhaps Plato's ship was intercepted for some reason by the Aeginetan navy. Plato ended up in the slave market on Aegina, and when the authorities found out that he was an Athenian they condemned him to death. But the sentence was commuted, Anniceris paid his fine, and Plato was able to return to Athens. Not long after he returned, he founded the Academy, the ancient world's most successful institute of higher education and research.

5

The Academy

In 383 BCE, shortly after Plato's return to Athens from Magna Graecia, he founded his school, the Academy. The least muddled account of the location comes from one of the ancient biographies of Plato, the *Anonymous Prolegomena to Platonic Philosophy*: "He then returned to Athens and founded a school near the residence of Timon the misanthrope. . . . Part of the school grounds Plato dedicated to the Muses as a sacred precinct." Timon, known as a misanthrope for his solitary ways and contempt for humankind (and famous to us for having inspired William Shakespeare's play *Timon of Athens*), was an older contemporary of Plato. Other writers pinpoint the location in another way: Plato founded his school in the suburban district of Athens that was named after the local hero Hecademus or Academus, who in legend had once saved the city from destruction. And so we know the school as the Academy.

Plato had certainly been teaching before this time.[1] He would have been old enough and well enough known to attract students by the end of the 390s, at the latest, but apart from Dion in Syracuse, we largely lack their names. Theaetetus, an Athenian who died of battle wounds in 391 while still in his twenties but had already made significant contributions to mathematics (he more or less invented the field of solid geometry), seems to have associated with Plato, but whether he was a student is not so clear. We also hear of Plato's relationship

---

1. For what it is worth, in *Letter 2*, the author, pretending to be Plato writing in 363, says that people have been "receiving instruction" from him for thirty years.

with another mathematician, Leodamas of Thasos, but we know too little to be able to say with confidence that he and Plato were associates in the 390s.

The only other early student we can be sure of is Speusippus, who was of an age to start studying with his uncle by about 390. But apparently he was not at first inclined toward philosophy:[2]

> Plato redirected his nephew Speusippus away from a life of considerable self-indulgence and debauchery, not by saying or doing anything that would hurt him, but when the young man was avoiding his parents, who were always pointing out the error of his ways and telling him off, Plato presented himself as a friend and displayed no anger, and hence instilled in him a high degree of respect and admiration for Plato himself and for philosophy.

There must have been other young men as well, besides Speusippus. Since many people thought of philosophy as no more than the final stage of their higher education, Plato would not have been short of students. Chabrias and Phocion, later famous Athenian generals, were said to have studied with Plato,[3] and that would probably have been in the 390s and 380s, since they were born, respectively, around 420 and around 402. Their studying with Plato for a while is perfectly plausible, just as in the previous century aspiring public servants studied with the sophists. Generalship in Athens was both a military and a political position.

So the significant moment in 383 was not that Plato started teaching in Athens but that he bought property in which his school would be housed. The cost was either twenty or thirty minas.[4] That is quite a lot of money, so we should assume that the house was well appointed and the garden sizeable. From then on, his teaching had a more recognizable existence, a fixed location as a school. In fact, the Academy combined teaching with research, so it would be just as accurate to

2. Plutarch, *Moralia* 491f–492a (*On Brotherly Love*); *Moralia* 71e (*How to Distinguish a Flatterer from a Friend*).
3. Plutarch, *Moralia* 1126c (*Reply to Colotes*).
4. Diogenes Laertius, *Lives of the Eminent Philosophers* 3.20.

describe it as a research college. Scholars were called not just "students," but "friends" and "intimates"—or, rather, beginners were "students," and a more advanced group, members of the inner circle, were "friends."

The atmosphere was convivial. For the inner circle, it was as much a society of friends who dined, conversed, and discussed ideas as a hierarchical institute of teachers and students. The Academy went through many changes, but it survived in some form until the sixth century CE. The school was dedicated to the Muses, the goddesses of culture and education, and Plato was venerated as the founder. Dedication of the Academy to the Muses dovetailed nicely with Plato's attempt, described in chapter 4, to claim that Socratic philosophy was the only valid educational system: he was claiming the Muses for the Socratic work of the Academy and implicitly denying it to anyone else. They may have their Muses, but Plato had "the true Muse, with her companions Reason and Philosophy."[5] The Muse of Philosophy embraces all other Muses. Plato derived the word "Muse" from a verb meaning "eager desire," which is spelled out as "eager desire for research and philosophy."[6]

The Academy Park

By Plato's time, the term "Academy" referred in the first instance to a park a short distance beyond the city walls of Athens to the northwest (see figure 5.1). It and two other parks, the Lyceum to the east of the city and the Cynosarges to the southeast, on the river Ilissus, were popular haunts, famous for their shady groves—the ancient Athenian equivalents of the Parisian Bois de Boulogne and Bois de Vincennes. Hecademus had long been worshipped in the district named after him, and it was in other respects, too, a sacred site. There was a grove of dedicated olive trees there, under the protection of Zeus, the oil

5. *Republic* 548b.
6. *Cratylus* 406a.

Figure 5.1 The Academy park in Athens. The Academy's shady walkways remain today. These steps, of uncertain age, lead down to the site of the ancient gymnasium, of which very little remains.
Photo by David Fideler.

from which was used for festival purposes. One comic poet imagined Plato illegally taking some of these olives for himself.[7] There were several greater or lesser shrines and altars, including an altar of Eros, which was the starting point for races, held on festive days, in which the runners carried blazing torches (hence, perhaps, the road that ran between the Dipylon Gate and the Academy was exceptionally wide).

7. Anaxandrides, Fragment 20 Kassel/Austin.

In the sixth century, gymnasia were built in these locations, to take advantage of the space and the shade. Around 520 a substantial one was built in the Academy by Hipparchus, who was then the junior co-tyrant of Athens with his brother Hippias; they were the sons of Peisistratus, the first tyrant of Athens. At the same time, Hipparchus commissioned a precinct wall to create a park, but the wall was never completed, and the phrase "Hipparchus's Wall" became proverbial for a futile and expensive building project. Nevertheless, it was effectively Hipparchus who, with the idea of a surrounding wall, designated part of the Academy district as a park.

In the middle of the fifth century, the statesman and general Cimon continued this process by spending some of his great personal wealth on a thorough refurbishment of the park: "He transformed the Academy from a dry, unirrigated spot into a well-watered grove, and he equipped it with stone-free running tracks and shady walks."[8] Lines from poets writing later in the fifth century show that it was a pleasant and popular place for people to meet (see figure 5.1).[9] Reviews of the Athenian cavalry in all its splendor were held there. If you walked out of Athens through the Dipylon Gate and the potters' quarter, and past the monuments that lined the road, after about a kilometer and a half (just under a mile) you would come first to the Academy gymnasium and then beyond the gymnasium the well-wooded park, which reached the banks of the Cephisus River. Apart from the various altars and shrines, and a few other buildings of uncertain function, there were also a few dilapidated buildings dating from past centuries. It must have been a delightful spot, but there are elements of the biographical tradition that describe it as unhealthy— because they want to say that Plato chose it in the belief that suffering is good for the soul.

In the fifth century, philosophers and other intellectuals began to use these parks and rooms in the gymnasia for teaching. A gymnasium

8. Plutarch, *Life of Cimon* 13.8. A short stretch of the terracotta pipeline that channeled water to the park has been found.
9. Aristophanes, *Clouds* 1005–1008; Eupolis, Fragment 36 Kassel/Austin.

was a multi-use, homosocial facility. Typically, as well as a running track, it would have a large, square central court, called a "palaestra," a wrestling-ground. This court was surrounded by a colonnade with viewing benches, off which there were rooms for all the various functions of a gymnasium: changing, training, bathing, massage, meeting friends, attending lectures and discussions. The Academy gymnasium, however (or at least the scant surviving remains, which may date from a later period), seems to have had fewer rooms and always to have been as much a place of education as a place for exercise.

At first, teachers went wherever they might find an audience; we hear of Socrates, for instance, at both the Lyceum and the Academy, as well as at lesser palaestras and in the Agora, the central square of Athens. Eventually, however, as philosophers founded schools or at least gained a stable group of students, particular people became associated with particular park-and-gymnasium complexes: Antisthenes taught in the Cynosarges, Plato in the Academy, Aristotle in the Lyceum. Philosophers were moving out of central Athens to the relative peace of the suburbs, but not too far to be out of reach of potential students. They were still public figures—that is why the comic poets were able to raise a laugh by caricaturing them—but they were a bit less public than before.

The Academy School

When Plato started acquiring a following in the 390s and 380s, before the first visit to Magna Graecia, he may have rotated among the available gymnasia; but in 383 he bought property near the Academy park and moved out of Athens to live there. His property was not *in* the park, as is often said. As public ground, the park was not available for private ownership. The confusion stems from the fact that by the fourth century "the Academy" may refer to the park, the gymnasium, or the school that met in Plato's nearby property. The house lay to the northeast of the park, toward the Colonus hill. The district was well known for its suburban houses and commercial vegetable plots.

From this time onward, then, research and the teaching of committed students mainly took place in this house and the large attached garden—large enough for Plato to establish a small shrine to the Muses in it[10]—but his and other Academicians' public lectures and courses for beginners were still held in the nearby gymnasium, and strolling together along the paths of the park also continued. Hence a fragment of the comic poet Alexis talks of a woman "pacing up and down like Plato"—that is, deep in thought or conversation—and getting nothing for it but tired legs.[11] It must have seemed like a kind of graduation to be invited to attend the discussions in Plato's house, rather than be one of a crowd listening to lectures in the gymnasium. The public nature of some of the Academic lectures and discussions is confirmed by the fact that once in a while we hear of hecklers: in a fragment of the contemporaneous comic playwright Epicrates (translated later in the chapter in the section "The Curriculum"), a passerby is so disgusted by the nonsense he hears some of the scholars talking that he comments on it with a derisive fart. Moreover, comic poets even referred to specific aspects of Plato's teaching: the immortality of the soul; the difficulty of defining unities; the difference between knowledge and belief; the method of definition by division.[12] In his tellingly entitled play *Phaedrus*, Alexis drew on Plato's *Symposium*, and elsewhere he made fun of Plato's use of homely analogies;[13] Amphis and Alexis both wrote plays called *Women in Charge*, perhaps with reference to *Republic*; around 350 the playwright Aristophon wrote a whole play called *Plato*. None of this work survives except in a very few fragments.

10. Speusippus later added a statue group of the Graces (Diogenes Laertius, *Lives of the Eminent Philosophers* 4.1).

11. Alexis, Fragment 151 Kassel/Austin.

12. Respectively, Alexis, Fragment 163 Kassel/Austin; Theopompus, Fragment 16 Kassel/Austin; Cratinus Junior, Fragment 10 Kassel/Austin; Epicrates, Fragment 10 Kassel/Austin.

13. Alexis, Fragment 247 Kassel/Austin; Fragment 1 Kassel/Austin.

Plato's house was presumably a regular Greek house, but more spacious than most. It had a colonnade-surrounded courtyard (for cooking, sitting, strolling) and various rooms off the colonnade.[14] There was no indoor accommodation for students. Not many years later, during Polemo's time as head of the school (314–269), a few students who had nowhere else to stay built little huts in the garden of the Academy "near the shrine of the Muses and the veranda."[15] We should imagine the same happening in Plato's day as well, though most students will have commuted from Athens.

Scholars were expected to fend for themselves in other ways too. Apart from occasions when they met and dined together (usually the official feast days of gods), all their living expenses were their own. Keeping costs down meant that Plato did not have to charge fees; he did not see the Academy as a means of accumulating wealth. The majority of the scholars would have had little difficulty in meeting their expenses. Most of the people who were interested in education were wealthy and capable of maintaining themselves.[16] But it does seem as though some of the expenses of the Academy were paid by patrons such as Dion. Patronage was perfectly normal in the fourth century. When money became tight, in the 340s after Dion's and Plato's deaths, Speusippus looked around for a new patron and wrote to Philip II of Macedon, the greatest monarch in Europe, obsequiously seeking his patronage by blackening the reputation of Isocrates, his rival for Philip's money. Possibly Dion's endowment was used to support less well-off students, but we also hear of their expenses being covered by

---

14. After Plato's death, Xenocrates and Polemo, the third and fourth heads of the school, lived in this house (Plutarch, *Moralia* 603b [*On Exile*]), but Speusippus, who headed the school after Plato, seems not to have. He probably already had property nearby, specifically the house owned by Dion when he was living in Athens, that he bequeathed to Speusippus when he returned to Sicily (Plutarch, *Life of Dion* 17.2-3).
15. Diogenes Laertius, *Lives of the Eminent Philosophers* 4.19.
16. Comic poets occasionally poked fun at Academicians for their elegance: Antiphanes, Fragment 35 Kassel/Austin; Ephippus, Fragment 14 Kassel/Austin. Aristotle and Heraclides in particular liked to dress well.

their better-off fellows, and of their finding paid work to keep them going.[17]

Dining together was an important aspect of the communal life of the Academy. The shared meals were famously modest. The Athenian statesman and general Timotheus once dined at the school and remarked that afterward he had slept well, had no hangover, and could remember the erudite talk that had taken place during and after the meal.[18] Plato scorned those who needed to hire entertainers for their symposia, rather than making conversation among themselves, and an anecdote has Plato saying that the only appropriate occasion for drunkenness was at feasts in honor of Dionysus, the god of wine.[19]

Rules were drawn up that governed behavior during meals; presumably, as in Plato's *Symposium*, they regulated how much one ate, drank, and talked. A passage in *Laws* suggests that each meal might have been supervised by someone chosen to see that the regulations were followed.[20] The purpose of the communal dining in the Academy was for the diners "to honor the gods, enjoy one another's companionship, and refresh themselves with learned discussion."[21]

The communal meals were paid for out of Plato's pocket or the endowment fund, as was everything else, such as the maintenance of the buildings and the acquisition of books. A library is of course essential for a research institute. There are plenty of stories in the biographical tradition about the lengths to which Plato went to get hold of books—and how much he was prepared to pay. He once sent one

17. Diogenes Laertius, *Lives of the Eminent Philosophers* 4.38; Athenaeus, *Savants at Dinner* 4.168a–b. That the Academy had an endowment fund at least later in its history is proved by Olympiodorus, *Commentary on Plato's First Alcibiades* 141.1–3: "Perhaps Plato made a practice of taking no fees because he was well off. That is why the endowments have lasted until now, despite many confiscations."

18. Plutarch, *Moralia* 686a–c (*Table Talk*).

19. Scorn: *Protagoras* 347c–d. Anecdote: Diogenes Laertius, *Lives of the Eminent Philosophers* 3.39.

20. *Laws* 639c–641a; see also 671c–672d.

21. Antigonus of Carystus (writing in the third century BCE), quoted by Athenaeus, *Savants at Dinner* 12.547f–548a. Communal dining is envisaged by Plato for the Guardians of Callipolis at *Republic* 458c.

of the Academy scholars all the way to Colophon in western Asia
Minor to collect a copy of a book of poems.[22] He seems to have been
especially keen to acquire Pythagorean treatises. But we should not
imagine a well-stocked modern library, shelves bulging with books.
Plato would have done well to have acquired a thousand papyrus
rolls in addition to those that contained his own works. But soon the
scholars of the Academy would generate another explosion of philosophical writing, just as the Socratics had in the early decades of the
century. In addition to the library, we should probably also imagine
walls adorned with charts, maps, diagrams, and other teaching tools.

Prospective students were attracted to the Academy by Plato's
fame and by his writings, which were beginning to circulate widely.
Menedemus of Eretria in Euboea, later a famous philosopher in his
own right, was converted to philosophy after listening to a reading
of some of Plato's work. A Corinthian was converted after reading
Gorgias. After reading *Republic* a woman called Axiothea traveled to
Athens from Phleious in the northeastern Peloponnese and became
a follower of Plato, disguising the fact that she was a woman. After
she was found out, she was allowed to stay on. Axiothea is one of
two women who seem to have been scholars of the Academy during
Plato's lifetime; the other was called Lastheneia, and she too was from
the Peloponnese.[23] We know nothing of their work, and all the rest of
Plato's students seem to have been male. This is not surprising, given
the relatively repressed lives women lived in fourth-century Greece; it
is more surprising that there were any women there at all, but we hear
about these two on fairly good authority.[24] However, they would not
have been able to attend all the school's functions: no women were
allowed into a gymnasium, where men and boys exercised naked.

22. Proclus, *Commentary on Plato's Timaeus* 1.90.20–24 Diehl.
23. Athenaeus, describing Lastheneia as a courtesan, says that she had an affair with
    Speusippus (*Savants at Dinner* 7.279e, 12.546d). This is not impossible, since courtesans
    were often more highly educated than other women of their day.
24. Diogenes Laertius (*Lives of the Eminent Philosophers* 3.46) cites Dicaearchus of Messana,
    who was writing about fifty years after Plato's death.

Many of Plato's casual students were Athenians, but some of the inner circle came from far afield. For them, just as for Menedemus and others, reading Plato's dialogues was the lure. Eudoxus of Cnidus came from Cyzicus on the Sea of Marmara; Xenocrates came from Chalcedon, a town on the Asian shoreline opposite Byzantium (so that it is now a district of the sprawling city of Istanbul); Aristotle came from Stagira in Macedon; Heraclides from Heraclea Pontica on the southwest coast of the Black Sea; Hermodorus from Syracuse.[25] In the fifth century, well-born young Athenians sat at the feet of visiting foreigners, the sophists; in the fourth, foreigners came to sit at the feet of Athenians. But the Academy was slow to pick up; most of our references to it come from the 360s and later, after the arrival of Aristotle and Eudoxus, its two most famous alumni.

Plato was critical of those who allowed just anyone, or at least anyone who could afford the fees, to undertake a course of education, so presumably there was some kind of test before a candidate was allowed to join the school—as much an assessment of character, perhaps, as a test of intellectual ability. He tested, as he once put it, for "affinity to philosophy," taking account of age and lifestyle.[26] The basic qualities required were "a good memory, quickness at learning, broadness of vision, elegance, and love of and affiliation to truth, justice, courage, and self-discipline."[27] An implausible anecdote claims that Plato used to test prospective students by getting them drunk, on the principle of "in vino veritas"—that under the influence of alcohol, they would

25. We should probably take with a grain of salt the tales that Plato's reputation reached farther east, such that "Mithridates of Persia" commissioned a statue of Plato for the Academy park (Diogenes Laertius, *Lives of the Eminent Philosophers* 3.25), or that "Pythagoras traveled to Persia when he wanted to learn the wisdom of the Magi, but the Magi came to Athens because of Plato, eager to be initiated into his philosophy" (*Anonymous Prolegomena to Platonic Philosophy* 6.19–22). The stories probably arose not long after Plato's death, at a time when some Academicians (Eudoxus, Aristotle, Hermodorus of Syracuse, and Heraclides of Pontus) were proposing that Persian thought anticipated some of Plato's central ideas.

26. *Letter 7* 344a. Olympiodorus, *Introduction to Logic* 11.31–32 says that Plato tested prospective students for their suitability for studying the mathematical sciences.

27. *Republic* 487a.

tell the truth. When Plato wanted to test Dionysius II of Syracuse, he laid out for him all the work he would have to undertake to make progress in philosophy. He believed that, while this would deter people whose interest was no more than superficial, a glimpse of the work involved would actually encourage those who had a genuine attraction to philosophy.[28] The advantages of the Academy were those of any educational establishment with voluntary scholars: most of them were committed students. It was fertile ground for the development of philosophical, scientific, and political theories.

Isocrates's Rival School

Plato's school was unique in many respects, but there were prior models to which he could have looked. There were plenty of precedents for communal dining, which had been a feature of temple life for centuries (consuming the meat after a sacrifice), and social clubs had added learned and elegant conversation while eating and drinking. In southern Italy, the Pythagoreans had practiced a communal way of life that Plato would have heard of, and possibly encountered, during his visits to Taras and Locri. This precedent would have reinforced the importance of communal dining and sacrifices as a way to bind a group together and form its identity. Two other Socratics, Euclides in Megara and Antisthenes in Athens, had attracted enough followers to be considered "schools," but we know too little about them to be able to guess whether they influenced the Academy.

More immediately, in Athens there were the schools of Alcidamas and Isocrates. They were rhetoricians and both had studied with Gorgias, but they came from opposite ends of a spectrum, in that Alcidamas championed spontaneous public speaking, while Isocrates recommended adherence to prepared speeches, with plenty of technical polish. Their aim was to turn out the intellectual elite that they

28. *Letter* 7 340b–341a.

felt Athens sorely needed, who would be effective political speech-makers and sound decision-makers. In Plato's *Phaedrus*, Phaedrus first reads out a prepared speech of Lysias, and then Socrates spontaneously composes two more speeches in response. The hint to prospective students is that in the Academy they will learn how to string words together in a persuasive fashion better than they would from either Isocrates or Alcidamas. In both *Apology of Socrates* and *Menexenus* Plato has Socrates deliver extemporized speeches.

Isocrates founded his school seven or eight years before the birth of the Academy; he used the Lyceum gymnasium for his lessons. He expressly distinguished himself from and set himself up as a rival to the sophists and the Socratics, but above all to Plato and the Academy. His works contain many implicit attacks on Plato. Antisthenes the Socratic and Speusippus the Academician responded with tracts against Isocrates. There was little malice involved (or at least there was little in the first generation: Speusippus's *Letter to Philip* has some bitter words for both Isocrates and his pupil Theopompus of Chios). Quite a few people attended both schools. This is not surprising, see-ing that for most people—those who had not comprehended Plato's message—studying philosophy was a way to round off their educa-tion, not something to which they might devote their entire lives. But Isocrates thought Plato was wasting his own and his students' time with hairsplitting arguments, and with abstract and impractical stud-ies. He allowed the kind of philosophical training that Plato and oth-ers provided only insofar as it sharpened the wits in preparation for the training *he* offered.[29] Isocrates wanted his students to be successful, while Plato wanted his to be knowledgeable.[30] A course of study at Isocrates's school lasted three or four years and cost a thousand

---

29. Isocrates, *Antidosis* 261–269.
30. Plato refers to Isocrates twice in his written works, once implicitly (*Euthydemus* 304d–306d) and once by name (*Phaedrus* 278e–279b), where he hints that, with his talent, Isocrates might have developed a truly philosophical rhetoric. The rivalry is reflected in the anecdotal tradition in a plausible story that Plato criticized Isocrates for taking money for his teaching.

drachmas, so it was designed only for the rich, and indeed it would be only the rich who would be interested in a course designed to prepare them for moral leadership in public life.[31]

What remains of Isocrates's speech *Against the Sophists* is an announcement of his program and an advertisement for prospective students, while *Antidosis*, a kind of autobiographical defense of his life, written in 354/3 when he was in his eighties (he died at the age of ninety-eight in 338), also tells us a lot about his aims as a teacher.[32] His students studied grammar, elocution, and the composition of speeches, but also whatever subjects were needed for them to give their speeches social, ethical, and political content. He employed a "rules and models" teaching method: his students learned, say, the rules of grammar and studied past masters of the art, and were then drilled until they had everything thoroughly rehearsed and understood. The emphasis was squarely on teaching rather than research. If Plato's Academy is the ancestor of our research institutions, Isocrates's school is the ancestor of our wider, humanistic educational systems.

We have already seen, in chapter 4, how Plato worked to claim the title of "philosophy" for what he wrote and taught, and to deny it to everyone else, perhaps especially rhetoricians such as Isocrates. Rhetoric he saw as intrinsically harmful because it perpetuates corrupt values and works with belief rather than knowledge; his most sustained assault on rhetoric, in *Gorgias*, may have been written in part as a kind of anti-Isocratean manifesto for the Academy. Isocrates and Alcidamas were particular targets because, just like Plato, they wanted to deny the label "philosophy" to any educational system except their own. Plato won this battle: what we nowadays call "philosophy" is his version, not theirs.

A critical difference is that Plato established the position of "scholarch," head of the school, so that whereas the other Athenian schools

---

31. Isocrates, *Antidosis* 86–88.
32. In *Antidosis*, Isocrates pretends to have to defend himself against the same charges that
    Socrates faced in Plato's *Apology of Socrates*.

died with the founder's death, the Academy was able to continue, and it did so for centuries. So Plato won in terms of longevity as well—but whether he won at the time, in the sense that he was able to attract more students to the Academy than Isocrates did to his school, is less certain. And in one respect, Isocrates certainly came off best: although he had foreign students, he was in a position not just to claim that he himself had benefited Athens with his own wise counsel but also to reel off the names of a number of his students who had done the city good as politicians.[33] Many of the scholars of the Academy, however, were foreigners, and the cities they benefited were foreign states, as we shall see.

A Diverse Academy

We have little direct information about the teaching curriculum of the Academy, but more about the kind of research that scholars were doing. We can perhaps to a certain extent infer the former from the latter. We know the names of many Academicians from the first forty years of the school, but we more rarely know details of their scholarly interests. Five men in particular stand out: Speusippus, Xenocrates, Heraclides, Eudoxus, and of course Aristotle, Plato's greatest colleague.

That these five were the leading lights of the Academy is a fair inference from the fact that we know far more about them than we do about the rest. We are told that Plato used to dine with twenty-eight of the scholars.[34] If we assume that they constituted the senior scholars, the inner circle, on that basis we might guess that there were at any given time, once the Academy was thriving, about fifty scholars in total, made up of the inner circle and the younger students, chiefly Athenians, who came and went year by year.[35] The senior scholars,

---

33. Isocrates, *Antidosis* 93–94, 101–139.
34. Athenaeus, *Savants at Dinner* 1.4e.
35. The Academy scholars are often indiscriminately called "youngsters" by our sources; this is presumably because over the course of the years, the younger students, most of

the researchers, stayed for years, even decades, and did some teaching themselves; the younger students came and went, and yet others only attended the public lectures. Their names are largely lost to history. In the 370s and 360s, three young men who later became political leaders of Athens—Demosthenes, Hyperides, and Lycurgus—attended lectures at the Academy; but, like most of Plato's students, they were not wanting to become philosophers themselves, just to tune and hone their minds on philosophy. Men of literature were attracted to the school as well, the most famous being Theodectes, one of the leading Athenian intellectuals of the fourth century, who wrote fifty tragedies, speeches for delivery, and a book on the theory of rhetoric as well. Hardly any of his work survives, and only in fragments.

A survey of the work of the principal five Academicians, and of others whose work we know something about, reveals certain common trends. The mathematical sciences, especially geometry and astronomy, loomed large.[36] An apocryphal story arose later that Plato had inscribed over the entrance to the school, "Let no one ignorant of geometry enter here."[37] Eudoxus in particular made important contributions to mathematics and astronomy, but we know the names of a good dozen other mathematician scholars, several of whom Eudoxus brought with him from Cyzicus when he merged his school with the Academy. Following his arrival in or shortly after 370, the Academy became the center of mathematical research in the Greek world. Another aspect of mathematical work is reflected in the Pythagorized and mathematized versions of Plato's metaphysics and cosmogony (theorizing about the origin of the universe) that were developed by Speusippus and Xenocrates.

whom came and went within a year or two, greatly outnumbered the older ones who stayed on to do research.

36. All these subjects counted as parts of "philosophy" until separation gradually took place between the seventeenth and nineteenth centuries. So, for instance, in *Gulliver's Travels* (1726) Jonathan Swift says, "The King [of Brobdingnag] . . . had been educated in the study of Philosophy, and particularly Mathematicks."

37. Olympiodorus, *Introduction to Logic* 9.1–2.

A second trend is polymathy—that is, wide-ranging knowledge or learning. Scholars, including the principal five, wrote on every scientific and philosophical topic imaginable, from optics to ethics, from physics to politics, and from logic to rhetoric. Several of them wrote on religious topics. Aristotle did fundamental work in every field of human intellectual endeavor that then existed. And these Academicians wrote voluminously: Aristotle is credited with more than 150 books (of which about 30 survive), Xenocrates with more than 70, Heraclides with about 50, Speusippus with about 30. Hardly anything of the work of these last three survives, and then only in the reports of others, such as Aristotle.

And a third and final trend is that the scholars of the Academy commonly disagreed not just with one another but with Plato. A great deal of their work was developed in response to Plato's ideas. Sometimes they agreed with him, sometimes their work was a development of his work, but sometimes they disagreed. Aristotle and Eudoxus held that the properties of things reside in the things themselves: the whiteness that makes snow white is a physical ingredient of the snow and is not owing to its participation in a separable, transcendent Form of White. Speusippus retained Plato's idea that knowledge needs stable entities, but rejected the theory of Forms and took mathematical entities to be the objects of knowledge. Plato had left unsettled the question of what exactly there were Forms of,[38] and Xenocrates created Platonic orthodoxy in this field (as in others): he seems to have excluded Forms of man-made objects (where Plato had allowed Forms of Bed and Shuttle),[39] of bad things (such as injustice and crookedness), of individuals (such as you and me), and of parts of things. Following Plato,[40] he probably also excluded Forms

38. The most complete list is at *Letter 7* 342d, but at *Republic* 596a Plato overgeneralizes and says: "We customarily hypothesize a single Form in connection with each of the many things to which we apply the same name."
39. Bed: *Republic* 597a–b. Shuttle: *Cratylus* 389a–b.
40. *Statesman* 262c–e.

that correspond to no justifiable classification of reality, such as "non-Greeks," because there is nothing that unifies "non-Greeks" into a genuine whole.

Aristotle was already writing books that were critical of Plato's ideas while he was in the Academy and Plato was alive. His rejection of the theory of Forms is only the tip of an iceberg; he disagreed with Plato on many fundamental issues. He thought the world was eternal, not created; he was dismissive of the political provisions of *Republic* and thought that Plato's account of the Form of Good was seriously flawed by not taking account of different varieties of goodness; he agreed that the goal of human life was well-being (*eudaimonia*) but differed over what it is that procures well-being; he trusted the senses far more than Plato; for him, the soul was not separable from the body and could not be reincarnated. Aristotle brought philosophy down to earth.

This is all quite remarkable, and it shines a clear light on the Academy. It was not a school for the perpetuation of "Platonism." Plato's dialogues were read and studied, but they were not taken to be expressions of an orthodoxy. Plato was in any case still writing, so there was no fixed corpus of his works that could count as authoritative. There was no collective identity for the scholars apart from "scholars of the Academy." Philosophy was practiced in an open-ended, Socratic fashion; the discussion could go in any direction. The kind of cultic reverence for the teacher that was a feature of the Pythagorean communities was discouraged by Plato.[41] After Plato's death, but presumably with his blessing, Speusippus, who rejected Plato's emblematic theory of Forms, was made head of the school. Nothing could more clearly show that the Academy was not designed to perpetuate any kind of orthodoxy. Plato saw his job as attracting and fostering fine intellects and groundbreaking work, not as turning out clones of himself. Perhaps the only thing all the scholars agreed about was that, leaving aside all their theoretical disagreements, they should all be trying to live a philosophical life, which is to say, as we

41. Olympiodorus, *Commentary on Plato's Alcibiades* 2.154.

have seen, that they all in their various ways aimed to control their base appetites and become assimilated to God.[42]

The Curriculum

In *Republic* Plato outlines a formidable course of study designed for philosophers.[43] It starts, at the age of twenty, with a ten-year course in arithmetic, plane geometry, solid geometry, astronomy, and harmonics (in that order) and concludes with five years of dialectic, the acquisition of knowledge rather than belief, as the copestone. Actually, in a sense the course starts earlier, because Plato says that these studies are only suitable for someone who has already been educated in virtue by athletic and other forms of training; as usual for Plato, reformation of character comes first. Progress is impossible unless the moral slate has first been refreshed.

Clearly, it would be impractical for any such course to be applied in real life, but it still represents Plato's firmest higher educational convictions. Why the emphasis on mathematics? First, because of the practical benefits; second, because mathematical studies make a student quicker at other subjects and are a good test of character because of the difficulty of the work; third, and most importantly, "because it's particularly good at guiding the mind upwards," away from the physical world and toward the timeless realm of number and Forms.[44] An anecdote has Plato furious at Eudoxus and Archytas for relying on mechanical models to solve mathematical problems instead of abstract thought—for looking downward instead of upward.[45] This conversion of the direction of the mind's gaze was the function of a true education, according to Plato. So the emphasis on mathematical research in the Academy no doubt reflects the program of studies.

42. *Timaeus* 89d–90d.
43. *Republic* 521c–541b.
44. *Republic* 525d, 526b–c; see also 527b, 529a, and *Theaetetus* 173e–174a.
45. Plutarch, *Life of Marcellus* 14.5–6; *Moralia* 718e–f (*Table Talk*).

In the Academy, too, Plato felt that the mathematical sciences were good at turning minds in the right direction. As Aristotle remarked, Academicians treated mathematics as a means to an end, not as an end in itself.[46]

All this may sound very dry and intellectual, but Plato did not see it that way. The turning of one's mind away from the material world was simultaneously a reformation of character. One was no longer mired in the world and its values—especially in its unthinking assumption that pleasure is the criterion of goodness. No one can make progress in philosophy unless they are prepared to let go of their past assumptions and attachments; that, as we have seen, was one of the messages of the early dialogues, and it remained Plato's conviction forever. The intellectual work of the Academy was simultaneously transformative. Academicians understood that reformation of character was the foundation of all that followed. Without it no one could become a philosopher worthy of the name, and no one could presume to play a political role in the real world, because they would not know how to recognize goodness, and they would not act as role models for other members of their communities.

The mathematical sciences and politics seem to us remote from each other, but they were paired in Plato's mind. Another function of the mathematical sciences, according to Plato, is that they afford knowledge of important political values, such as unity, concord, order, and proportion. Reports of Plato's public lecture "On the Good" (on which more below) reveal, though unfortunately not in detail, the close relation Plato saw between mathematical concepts and goodness; the objective of the curriculum in *Republic* is that philosophers should gain knowledge of the good, and one reason for this is so that, as philosopher kings and queens, they can rule Callipolis, the imaginary city he is constructing, in a way that makes it the best community, one in which everyone is good to the best of their ability. And the reason they need to be conversant with the realm of Forms in general is so that they become so

46. *Metaphysics* 992a32–34.

accustomed to stability that they can see how to stabilize an intrinsically unstable entity, a city-state. So political theory will have been studied as well, and we shall soon see the fruits of this in some Academicians we have not yet met.

Natural science played a part in the curriculum of the Academy. The sensible world would always, for Plato, be ontologically inferior to the world of Forms, and was at best the object of belief, not knowledge, but the principles that governed the natural world were a fit subject for study. Epicrates, a contemporary comic poet, poked gentle fun at this facet of Academic work:[47]

SPEAKER A [*overexcitedly*]: What about Plato, Speusippus, and Menedemus? What are they occupying themselves with these days? What deep notion and what line of argument is being subjected to their investigations? Give me precise details, if you know anything. Tell me, in the name of Earth!

SPEAKER B: Why, yes, I can give you good, clear information, because at the time of the Panathenaea I saw a group of youngsters in the Academy gymnasium, and I heard some incredibly weird stuff. They were propounding definitions about nature, and separating into categories the way that animals live, the nature of trees, and the various kinds of vegetable. And in this context they were wondering to what genus the gourd should be assigned.

A: So what definition did they arrive at? What is the gourd's genus? Tell me, please—that is, if you know the answer.

B: Well, at first, they all stood over it without speaking, and with heads bowed they reflected for a long time. And then suddenly, while the youngsters' heads were still bent low in study, one of them said that it was a vegetable of the spherical kind, while another said it was a grass, and a third that it was a tree. And when a certain medical man from Sicily heard the nonsense they were talking, he let loose a fart.

47. Epicrates, Fragment 10 Kassel/Austin.

A: I suppose they got terribly angry and shouted at him for mocking
   them? It was scarcely a polite thing to do in the middle of
   such talk.
B: No, the lads weren't fazed at all. And Plato, who was there, very
   gently (he was entirely unruffled) told them to try once more
   to state to which genus it belonged. And so they set about their
   divisions.

Epicrates may mock,[48] but the scene shows us more or less the birth
of biology, which was to be greatly developed by Speusippus (who is
mentioned in the fragment) and Aristotle.

   Scholars gathered data and presented the results of their researches
and thinking to the assembled Academicians for discussion and
criticism. At one point in his *Metaphysics*, Aristotle attributes a particular account as having first been given by the Presocratic thinker
Anaxagoras of Clazomenae, "and later by Eudoxus in his discussions."[49] Some of Plato's dialogues were written for much the same
purpose. Two dialogues in particular stand out in this respect. *Philebus*
is, among other things, a repository of views of pleasure (including,
among those we can recognize, that of Eudoxus),[50] as *Theaetetus* is of
views of knowledge. They must have been written at least in part as
responses to discussion within the Academy and to stimulate further
thinking on their subjects. Eudoxus held that pleasure was the human
good, Speusippus denied this and argued in true Platonic fashion that
virtue and peace of mind were the appropriate goals for a human
being. Heraclides, too, was opposed to hedonism. Philip of Opus,
Xenocrates, and Aristotle also entered into the debate. Another major
debate was over Plato's *Timaeus*, with Speusippus and Xenocrates
claiming that Plato had written as if there were creation in time only

---

48. Plato himself was not averse to a little mockery of the definitional process, if it is
   right to read his alleged definition of a human being as a featherless biped (Diogenes
   Laertius, *Lives of the Eminent Philosophers* 6.40) as tongue-in-cheek.
49. Aristotle, *Metaphysics* 1079b21.
50. This helps us date the dialogue because Eudoxus did not arrive in the Academy until
   c. 370.

for pedagogical purposes, and Aristotle taking Plato literally at his word (and then criticizing him for it).

Even more interesting is the case of *Parmenides*. In the first half of this dialogue, the canonical theory of Forms is subjected to what appears to be pretty severe criticism, while the second half lays out a series of highly abstract logical exercises on metaphysical topics, such as (I paraphrase): "If one is, what follows for the one in relation to itself and in relation to other things?" The first half is not intended to annihilate the theory, because Plato has Parmenides say that Forms are necessary for thought; and the second half is expressly signaled as a training exercise.[51] *Parmenides* reflects discussions on metaphysical topics that were taking place among the scholars.[52] Along with many scholars, I do not believe that *Parmenides* represents a significant watershed in Plato's thinking, such that after it he abandoned the fully fledged, middle-period theory of Forms. The only real adjustment is that he allowed Forms to be related to one another (*Sophist*) and focused more on that than on their relationship with the things of this world. Despite the differences of emphases of the late dialogues, Forms appear in them, and I think the dramatic point of making Socrates very young in *Parmenides* is meant to indicate that the criticisms should be answerable by more mature minds.

These dialogues stand out, but any of Plato's works could have been used as a starting point for discussion within the Academy. Perhaps they were used to generate debates among the scholars, with one proposing that, for instance, virtue is teachable (the issue addressed in *Protagoras* and *Meno*) and someone else opposing the thesis. The dialogues contain doctrine in which Plato believed, as I argued earlier in the book, but at the same time they were also meant to suggest directions for future work by the scholars. The

51. Forms necessary for thought: *Parmenides* 135b–c. Training exercise: 135c–136c.
52. The theory of Forms is also subjected to (rather more gentle) criticism at *Sophist* 248a–249d, where Plato discusses the views of a group of people he calls "friends of the Forms." At 246a–248a, the views of another group, the "giants," are discussed; their position looks very like that of Eudoxus.

early aporetic dialogues—those that attempt to define a term but end inconclusively—would have made excellent discussion documents, as well as training students to spot hidden assumptions and to resist assenting too readily to arguments; they also served as repositories of multiple views of the topics discussed, such as friendship, courage, and justice. *Timaeus* launched Academic discussion of the natural world and cosmogony. In a telling remark in *Statesman*,[53] Plato says that the real purpose of the "method of division" (as scholars call it) that he is using to try to pin down the statesman is not so much to define the statesman as to make people who use the method "better at philosophical discussion." And at several points in the dialogue, the Visitor from Elea (the lead character in this dialogue, as in *Sophist*) deliberately gets his interlocutor, Young Socrates (so called to distinguish him from *the* Socrates), to reach mistaken conclusions so that he can correct him in a teacherly fashion.

Aristotle's many discussions of Platonic dialogues show the kind of treatment they were receiving in the Academy—intelligent and thoughtful, but by no means bowing to Plato's authority. If that is right, we can add to the list of areas of Academic study, because the following are all topics that occur and recur in the dialogues: definition, educational theory, ethics, moral psychology, metaphysics, epistemology, aesthetics, language, logic, sophistry, Presocratic thought, dialectical argumentation based on hypothetical premises, rhetoric, the natural sciences. The senior researchers, whose work I outlined earlier, ranged wider—into areas such as history, geography, and literary criticism—but this list probably accurately reflects the bulk of the Academy's teaching and research programs. As for methodologies, we are on safe ground in concluding that dialectical conversation,[54] critical thinking and discussion, writing, seminars, the reading of Plato's dialogues, and lecturing were the principal ways in which inquiry and instruction were carried on.

53. *Statesman* 286e–287a; see also 285c–d.
54. In the eighth book of his *Topics*, Aristotle formulated, in typically pedantic and thorough fashion, the rules for such conversations.

Plato's Role

If Plato's purposes in setting up the Academy were to teach and to foster important research, what was his role in the school on a day-to-day basis? Throughout the dialogues, he always evinces a keen interest in the education of young men, so no doubt he took on quite a bit of the elementary teaching, though senior scholars played a part in that as well. As for the research, the best description of Plato's role is that of Dicaearchus of Messana, whose words are preserved by Philodemus of Gadara. Dicaearchus describes Plato as the "architect" of the mathematical research, rather than being an active mathematician himself.[55] Just as builders follow an architect's plans, but the architect is no builder himself, so Plato initiated and supervised others' research (see figure 5.2). Without such supervision, Plato suggests at one point in *Republic*, no work would get done.[56]

Here is a good example. We hear that Plato set the astronomers of the Academy a particular task—to explain the movements of the heavenly bodies on the assumption that none of them are "wanderers" (*planētes*), but that each of them has a uniform and orderly motion.[57] In a geocentric universe, this was a hugely complex task because from the earth, the heavenly bodies appear to have all kinds of irregular motions. But Plato felt that there must be a solution that would be more in keeping with their divine status; divine beings should move in perfect circles. The result was the foundation of mathematical astronomy by Eudoxus, on whose model the universe consists of twenty-seven layers of transparent spheres, each of which carries a heavenly body or a group of heavenly bodies around with it at distinct speeds and inclinations. Heraclides's contribution was the hypothesis that the apparently

55. Philodemus, *Index Academicorum*, col. Y.
56. *Republic* 528b–c.
57. Simplicius, *Commentary on Aristotle's On the Heavens* 488.18–24 and 492.31–493.5 Heiberg.

Figure 5.2 Plato and his students. An 1807 copper engraving by Meno Haas, showing Plato and some scholars of the Academy in the garden of the school. Plato amongst his disciples.
Copper engraving, 1807, by Meno Haas (1752–1833) after a drawing by Johann David Schubert (1761–1822).
13.8 × 9.5cm.
Berlin, Sammlung Archiv für Kunst und Geschichte.
Akg-images

irregular movements of the heavenly bodies were attributable to the earth's rotation, rather than to their irregular movements. It was probably as part of his gathering of data for this program of study that Aristotle observed the eclipse of Mars by the moon on either March

20, 361, or May 4, 357.[58] Philip of Opus also studied the problem by observing the heavens. By the time Plato wrote *Laws*, he was confident that each of the heavenly bodies followed a circular path.[59] This astronomical program was an important part of a general Academic enterprise—following the Presocratics—to explain the world as a rational structure and as comprehensible by the human mind.

Another story—one with pretty good credentials[60]—also illustrates Plato's role as "architect." The people of the sacred island of Delos were suffering a plague, and Apollo had told them, through an oracle, that the plague would go away if they doubled the size of his altar on the island. The altar happened to be a cube, and doubling a cube is no elementary problem. They had tried to solve it themselves but had failed. So they approached Plato for a solution, and Plato told them that the mathematicians of the Academy (different mathematicians are named in different versions of the story) would sort it out for them. Menaechmus and Eudoxus came up with solutions, but the most elegant one was discovered outside the Academy, by Archytas.

There is also good evidence, following clues in *Republic*, that Plato encouraged the mathematicians of the Academy to take their subjects back to first principles—to make the mathematical sciences depend ultimately on axioms or definitions of their terms, such as "odd," "even," "point," "line," "angle," and so on—the kind of use of axioms that we find in Euclid's *Elements*, which was written a few decades later. And so Theudius of Magnesia, a scholar in the Academy, was a predecessor of Euclid in this respect: he too wrote an *Elements*. And we hear that the mathematician Philip of Opus "carried on his investigations according to Plato's instructions."[61] But Plato did not limit his supervisory role to mathematics. Even the fragment of the playwright Epicrates that I translated earlier in the chapter points in this

---

58. Aristotle, *On the Heavens* 292a3–6.
59. *Laws* 817e–822d.
60. It goes back to the third century and Eratosthenes of Cyrene, who had the resources of the library of Alexandria to draw on.
61. Proclus, *Commentary on the First Book of Euclid's Elements* 67.23–68.6 Friedlein.

direction, since Plato does not himself come up with a solution to the problem but encourages the Academicians to return to the drawing board. Given the extent of some Academicians' disagreements with Plato's ideas, it is clear that they were allowed considerable leeway in all fields.

So, as regards the research that went on in the Academy, Plato, following Socrates in this, saw his role as setting the agenda and then standing back and letting others get on with it. Just as we saw that one of the messages of the early dialogues was "Think for yourself," so he encouraged the scholars to do just that. He seems to have taken this role very seriously. In his written works, Aristotle frequently expresses dissatisfaction and irritation that Plato did not sufficiently clarify even central aspects of his thought. But Aristotle was in the Academy alongside Plato for twenty years. If he wanted clarification, why did he not consult Plato himself? It seems that was not an option; the scholars understood that they were not to interrogate Plato in this way. Or perhaps they gave up asking him such questions once it became clear that every time he would toss the ball back into their court.

So Plato, as head of the school, organized the school activities, set at least some of the agenda, supervised the research and the teaching, especially to ensure that scholars did not get lost in the details but maintained an overview,[62] and did some teaching himself. Many of his dialogues reveal a concern with methodology, making it likely that he suggested ways for researchers to go about their research and required rigor in the presentation of proofs. He also kept the Academy Socratic by encouraging a diversity of perspectives and discussion of alternative views. One good reason for his aloofness is that if he started to explain what he meant in the dialogues to students, there would be no end to it: he would have to do the same with every generation of students. There is doctrine in the dialogues, but Plato did not want it to become dogma.

62. *Republic* 537c.

"On the Good"

Plato was also to a certain extent the public face of the Academy. Everyone knew it was "Plato's Academy." And so, once in a while, he gave public lectures and readings. As a matter of fact, we hear of only one of each, but there may have been more. If the purpose of such public meetings was to attract members of the public to philosophy, neither was successful. The public reading was of the dialogue *Phaedo*, and we are told that the rest of the audience drifted away and only Aristotle remained to the end.[63] The dialogue is so wonderful, however, that I am sure this is just malicious gossip.

Even if this anecdote is untrue, the stories surrounding the occasion when Plato lectured in public on the good are certainly authentic.[64] A number of the Academy scholars attended the lecture, including Speusippus, Xenocrates, Aristotle, Heraclides, and Hestiaeus of Perinthus; they took notes during it and subsequently wrote up those notes for publication, along with their developments and criticisms of what Plato had said. None of these works survive, but they appear in the lists of works attributed to them as *On the Good*. The audience for the lecture came in the expectation that Plato would talk about human goods such as health, wealth, and status, and would give them a recipe for the good life; instead they were treated to abstract and perplexing talk about "mathematics, numbers, geometry, astronomy, and finally the argument that the good is one."[65] Plato was clearly treating the good not just as a moral concept but as the transcendent source of all value in the world, as the universal object of desire (and thus the cause of motion), and as the ultimate cause of all

---

63. Diogenes Laertius, *Lives of the Eminent Philosophers* 3.37.
64. Riginos, *Platonica*, 124–126.
65. Aristotle, fragment 28 Rose; Aristoxenus, *Elements of Harmony* 2.30–31. Aristoxenus is the source of the other accounts we have of the lecture, by Themistius (*Orations* 21.245c–d) and Proclus (*Commentary on the Parmenides*, on 127b [p. 688 Cousin]). Themistius has Plato lecturing in Piraeus, the port city of Athens, but the Academy gymnasium seems the more likely venue.

things. Naturally, this interpretation went over the heads of most of the audience. Nevertheless, the talk was famous enough to be mocked by comic poets; one came up with the ingenious suggestion that not marrying is good because in that way a man remains single, just like Plato's Good![66]

In the lecture, Plato apparently claimed that the ultimate principles of the universe, and the elements of Forms, were the One and the Indefinite Dyad, unity and duality. This notion came to have great influence within the Academy, especially on Speusippus and Xenocrates, but there is also some trace of it in *Philebus* (and so I think the lecture was delivered sometime in the 350s). We also have various other accounts of a mathematized view of Forms that corresponds to little or nothing in the dialogues.[67] In view of this information, some scholars, taking into account Plato's alleged repudiation of writing in *Phaedrus* and *Letter 7*,[68] borrow a phrase from Aristotle and talk of Plato's "unwritten doctrines"; they claim that these teachings were given systematically in a course of lectures in the Academy and constitute Plato's most mature thought and even his "esoteric" teaching, as though he reserved his most important ideas for senior scholars in the Academy. They say that this entire course was entitled "On the Good."

But it is clear from the sources that Plato's lecture was a one-off affair, and I side with those scholars who think that accounts of the so-called unwritten doctrines are derived from the notes taken by the Academicians who attended the lecture,[69] and from their speculations

---

66. Philippides, Fragment 6 Kassel/Austin. See also Alexis, Fragment 98 Kassel/Austin, and Amphis, Fragment 6 Kassel/Austin. These were all written after Plato's death, so the lecture left a lasting impression.

67. See especially Aristotle, *Metaphysics* A6 and M-N, though the ideas criticized in the latter books are those of Speusippus and Xenocrates as well as those of Plato. Then there are many other passages in Aristotle and later thinkers where some mention is made of these ideas; these texts can be found in translation at the end of J. Findlay's book *Plato*, listed in "Further Reading," in the section "Plato in General."

68. See pp. xxxii–xxxiii and 95–9.

69. This is exactly what Simplicius says in his *Commentary on Aristotle's Physics*, at 187a12–21. He was writing in the sixth century CE, but he was an excellent scholar.

about Plato's meaning. It is clear that Plato gave no more than an outline of his views in the lecture. If he was giving a regular series of lectures to senior scholars about these principles, it is hard to see why they all treated the lecture "On the Good" as so singular that they felt they should take notes. The One and Indefinite Dyad would have been perfectly familiar to them if they were being regularly lectured to by Plato on them. Moreover, the teachings can hardly count as "esoteric," since the talk was delivered to a general audience. On all the many occasions when Aristotle refers to Plato's dialogues, he never suggests that they may not contain Plato's true thoughts. The so-called unwritten doctrines are no more than traces of Plato's lecture and of other ideas he expressed within the Academy.

Practical Politics

Amid all this talk of metaphysics and theoretical speculation, there is a final aspect of Academic work that is surprisingly practical: the school turned out international political troubleshooters. In a few cases, Plato's role as "architect" is again clear: an appeal or request was sent from some ruler or state to the Academy, and Plato allocated the task to specific individuals and, I dare say, discussed strategy and tactics with those he had selected. This is plausible in itself and, for what it is worth, is backed up by the spurious *Letter 5*, in which "Plato" recommends his Academic colleague Euphraeus as a political troubleshooter to Perdiccas III of Macedon. I have already said that Academicians studied political theory, but that in itself would not have given them the credentials to do any practical work. Requests came from abroad partly just because the Academy had the reputation of harboring the cream of Greek intellectuals. But the scholars also studied various constitutions so that they could determine what makes for success or failure and adapt their advice or their actions to specific needs. To a certain extent, scholars could find guidelines as to how to act in Plato's published political works, especially the practically oriented

Laws, which draws on Athenian, Spartan, and Cretan institutions, and perhaps others that we cannot recognize.

Plato's interest in practical politics, which he had earlier renounced out of disenchantment, had revived. In this respect, at least, knowledge was not just an end in itself but was to be put to use. In the famous allegory of the Cave in *Republic*, even after throwing off their chains and leaving the gloom of the cave for the enlightenment of the outer world, philosophers are to be forced to return to the pit to help the other prisoners. So the training program for philosophers in *Republic* ends with fifteen years of practical politics, when they are required to "go back down into that cave and take charge of warfare and what- ever other areas young people should be responsible for, so that they gain as much practical experience as everyone else."[70]

Plato's objective was not the impractical one of *Republic*, to create a true "aristocracy," the rule of the best people (*aristoi*). Nor was he in a position to do anything about Athens; his most important students were foreigners, who could never have more than honorary status in Athens; and if it is right to describe the fictional city of *Laws* as an idealized Athens, that just proves that its reform remained for Plato at a theoretical level. But he might be able to do some good abroad. The Academy was, in this aspect, a kind of consultancy, offering advice to governments on a range of issues, and sometimes practical help. The idea was not to push a particular political agenda but to do what was right for the particular circumstances of whatever crisis they were being asked to address. And Academicians differed widely in their understanding of what was right.

As usual, assessing the reliability of the evidence for Academicians' enterprises is difficult, but, on the principle of "no smoke without fire," there is enough of it for us to be sure that practical political activity was an authentic feature of the Academy.[71] The dating of some of the events is uncertain, nor is it clear how long some of the

70. The allegory occurs at *Republic* 514a–518b; the quotation is from 539e.
71. In addition to the usual sources, there are relevant passages in Plutarch (*Moralia* 1126c–d [*Against Colotes*]) and Athenaeus (*Savants at Dinner* 504e–509e).

people involved had studied in the Academy or how much contact they had had with Plato himself. In some cases, the individuals may have been acting on their own and were not in any sense emissaries of the Academy. In any case, as we found with metaphysical and ethical speculation as well, there was no "party line" that Academicians were required to follow. Some killed tyrants, while others tried to set themselves up as tyrants. Some took action, while others merely offered advice.

Erastus and Coriscus came to study in the Academy from Scepsis in northwestern Asia Minor. They returned to the region at the invitation of Hermias, the ruler of nearby Atarneus, who was probably wanting to enhance his court with some philosophers. Under their influence, and thanks also to visits from Xenocrates and Aristotle (who married Hermias's daughter or niece), he began to rule less tyrannically, and as a result, other coastal city-states, including Assus, voluntarily joined his kingdom.[72] He then funded the school, perhaps modeled on the Academy, that Erastus and Coriscus set up in Assus. In the mid-360s, Euphraeus of Oreus managed to work his way into a position of some influence in Macedon during the rule of Perdiccas III and was even said to have brokered a power-sharing arrangement between Perdiccas and his brother Philip (later the great Philip II). Hence, in his letter to Philip, written in 342, Speusippus claimed that Philip owed his kingship to Plato. Aristotle dedicated his *Protrepticus* (which exists only in fragments) to Themison, the king of a Cypriot city, urging him to take up philosophy. Xenocrates wrote a book for Alexander the Great, the son of Philip II, on the nature of moral leadership. Aristotle accepted the post of tutor to Alexander, though there is no sign that the future career of the prince was at all influenced by philosophy.

72. Some of the evidence for this comes from [Plato], *Letter 6*. Isocrates's pupil Theopompus attacked Hermias in a fragmentary *Letter to Philip*: "Barbarian though he is, he philosophizes with the Platonists."

Dion, as we shall see in more detail later, brought down the tyranny of Dionysius II of Syracuse in 357; he was aided by Speusippus, who supplied him with information and "won renown for the Academy" by urging him in an open letter to rule with moderation and adherence to the laws.[73] Python of Aenus and his brother Heraclides assassinated Cotys, the king of much of Thrace, in 359, and were rewarded with Athenian citizenship. In 352, Chion of Heraclea returned from the Academy to his native city and killed Clearchus, who had established a tyranny; Clearchus himself had studied in Isocrates's school and attended a lecture or two at the Academy. With the support of Alexander the Great, Chaeron of Pallene made himself sole ruler, in 335, of his native city; he had been a student of both Plato and Xenocrates. Euaeon of Lampsacus and Timolaus of Cyzicus attempted but failed to seize power in their native cities.

Plato sent the scholars Aristonymus, Phormio, and Menedemus to create or reform the constitutions of their native cities: respectively, Megalopolis, Elis, and Pyrrha (on the island of Lesbos). All these interventions took place between the late 370s and early 360s. Phormio had to overthrow an oligarchy in Elis in order to gain the space for his reforms. Eudoxus of Cnidus and Aristotle of Stagira both drafted more democratic sets of laws for their native cities. Plato was asked by the Greek city of Cyrene in North Africa to rewrite their laws, but he refused on the grounds, it was said, that the people were too prosperous—which is to say that there were too many people with vested interests who would have objected to his proposals.[74] There was at least one precedent for a philosopher drafting the laws of a city-state: Protagoras had done so in 443 for the new foundation of Thurii in southern Italy.

So Academicians seem to have engaged in practical politics whether that involved regime change, consultation, or legislation. In some cases, to repeat, they were not acting as scholars of the Academy, but

73. Plutarch, *Moralia* 70a (*How to Tell a Flatterer from a Friend*).
74. Plutarch, *Moralia* 779d (*To an Uneducated Ruler*).

in other cases there is good evidence for contact between the state or ruler and the Academy. Would Plato or his successors have connived at political murder? It would be too easy to project our modern values back and answer no. But the answer is not so certain. Epaminondas of Thebes was a Pythagorean, but he connived at political murder during the liberation of Thebes from Spartan control in 379, and he was aided in this effort by Simmias, a Pythagorean disciple of Socrates. And in later decades some Stoic philosophers were also involved in political murders. We will later see Plato's own attempt at political reform, and Speusippus's involvement in the same affair.

6

The Middle Dialogues

Between the late 380s and the mid-360s, then, Plato was quietly at work in Athens, running the Academy and writing. Most, perhaps all, of our middle cluster of dialogues were written or revised into their final form in these years: *First Alcibiades*, *Charmides*, *Gorgias*, *Meno*, *Phaedo*, *Phaedrus*, *Protagoras*, *Republic*, *Symposium*, and *Theaetetus*. It was an astonishingly creative period of Plato's life. *First Alcibiades* (in which Socrates exposes inconsistencies in Alcibiades's belief-set and persuades him that he needs to work on himself) and *Charmides* (a somewhat tortuous discussion of the virtues of self-restraint and self-knowledge) are early dialogues in form. *Protagoras*, *Gorgias*, and *Meno* end with impasses that are typical of the earlier dialogues but are far richer in content. Plato's middle-period dialogues contain developments of the philosophy of the earlier dialogues, but with new influences inspired in part by his sojourn in southern Italy and Sicily in 385 and 384.

Taken as a whole, Plato's middle-period dialogues constitute probably the most famous sequence of philosophical writings that the Western world has ever produced. The first difference that strikes a reader familiar with the earlier dialogues is a difference of scale; it is not just that the middle-period dialogues are longer but also that they are far more ambitious. While Socrates still asks a lot of questions, he is more overtly steering the conversations and is now asserting positive doctrine rather than claiming to know nothing. He has views on matters such as love and its transcendent power (*Symposium*, *Phaedrus*), on the dangerous moral and social consequences of rhetoric (*Gorgias*) and what can be done to make it acceptable (*Phaedrus*), on justice and its value (*Republic*), on what an ideally just political community might look like (*Republic*), on the unsatisfactoriness of democracy (*Gorgias, Republic*), on the untrustworthiness of the senses (*Republic, Theaetetus*), on the differences between knowledge and belief (*Meno, Republic, Theaetetus*), on what it takes for something truly to be said to *be* rather than to be merely in a state of *becoming* (*Phaedo, Republic*), on the possibly dangerous moral consequences of most of what passes for poetry and theater (*Gorgias, Republic*), on the nature of virtue and whether it is something that can be taught and learned (*Protagoras, Meno*), on the immortality of the soul (*Gorgias, Phaedo, Republic*), on the nature of the soul (*Republic, Phaedrus*), and more.

When people think of or refer to Plato's thought, or "Platonism," they are invariably thinking of these doctrine-building dialogues of Plato's middle period. As we have already seen and will continue to see, there is more to Plato than this, but at the same time this approach is not unwarranted, in the sense that many of the most stimulating of Plato's ideas are developed in the middle-period dialogues. In what follows, I shall focus on Plato's distinctive and extraordinary ideas in the related fields of epistemology (the theory of knowledge) and metaphysics, insofar as they are major themes of the middle-period dialogues, and then on the ethical implications that Plato developed on the basis of his metaphysics and epistemology. But two of these dialogues famously focus on love, and I shall start with these. They do not tell us much about Plato's life, but they clearly demonstrate his brilliance.

Symposium and *Phaedrus* on Love

What Plato has to say about love in *Symposium* is displayed as a sequential argument.[1] That one step of the argument follows from the

---

1. *Symposium* 199e–207a.

previous one is occasionally more illusory than real; we are carried along by Plato's earnestness as much as by his logic. But that need not worry us now.

Love is a kind of desire, which is to say that it is always love *of* something. This something that love desires is something that it lacks—that it wants to have, or (if it already has it) to continue to have. So if love loves beauty, then love lacks beauty and wants to possess beauty. But in fact what people always love is goodness, not beauty exactly—which is to say that they long to be happy and fulfilled because only a good person is happy and fulfilled. This is the universal human condition. The love that has to do with beauty, then, is only a fraction of what love is. If love in general is for goodness, then the love that is concerned with beauty must actually be love of goodness and happiness. No one wants goodness temporarily; they want it forever. To want something forever is in a covert form to want immortality. But immortality is plainly impossible for individuals. Relative immortality, however, can be achieved through procreation of some kind—for instance, by perpetuating oneself through one's children or through producing long-lasting works of art. Procreation is impossible for anyone in a medium that they find repellent. Procreation can only take place in a beautiful medium; the connection between love and beauty is therefore that the desire for immortality—for goodness forever—requires a beautiful medium.

This is a truly extraordinary and profound argument. It is controlled largely by the following insights: the assimilation of love and desire, such that love is deficient in itself; that what we usually call "love" or "passion" is just a particular manifestation of the universal human desire for goodness and happiness; that we would like to be immortal; and that we are inherently creative. These last two insights converge in Plato's mind. He finds it relatively simple to demonstrate human creativity by appealing to a range of phenomena, from the instinctive demand (common to all species) that we should bear and raise offspring, to the particular creativity of artists and legislators.

But in creating such offspring we are simultaneously striving to per-petuate ourselves. We (in some sense of "we") are driven to outlive ourselves.

A little later in the dialogue, in a passage I shall paraphrase in the next section, Plato stops talking about love between people and takes off into the stratosphere where love becomes philosophy and the means of a person's fulfillment as a human being. But this is a change of perspective, not a change of direction. We already know that love between people is merely one manifestation of a pervasive motivating force in us; philosophy is simply the highest manifestation of the same energy that at its lowest manifests as physical lust. We all want happi-ness, and everything we do is supposed to bring us closer to that goal; falling in love with another person is one way in which we seek to achieve happiness. If love in general aims for goodness and immor-tality, the manifestation of that in the particular instance of interper-sonal relationships is the aim of procreation in a beautiful medium.

This analysis of interpersonal love has been criticized as egoistic and cold. Plato seems to be saying that I should love other people not for themselves but only for their qualities—above all, for the beauty that they happen to possess in the eyes of the beholder—and only as a means toward the end of my own happiness. But the idea that we are driven by our desire for happiness is not intended by Plato to be a description of our feelings in a relationship. It is a piece of depth psychology. It is an analysis of what *underlies* the relationship. The relationship itself, the affection I feel for the other person, may conform to whatever ideal of interpersonal love you care to hold, but that does not say anything either for or against Plato's analysis of the underlying motivation. This point bears crucially on Plato's ap-parently crude assimilation of love and desire. He is not saying that if you love something, you desire to possess it forever. He is saying that whatever you love, your underlying motivation is the permanent pos-session of goodness. In other words, the reason we love (desire perfec-tion) is precisely because it is the human condition to be imperfect. Love involves incompleteness and awareness of incompleteness. One has to be dissatisfied to be motivated at all; hence *all* desire is desire for goodness, for remedying an unsatisfactory state of affairs.

So Plato's conception of love is not altogether egoistic. To say that love is the desire for happiness begs an important question: in what does my happiness lie? There is plenty of evidence from the dialogues that Plato is what we might call a moral egoist. My pursuit of happiness can paradoxically only be fulfilled if I promote the happiness of others. (More on this later, on the philosopher rulers of *Republic*.) Love in *Symposium* is as much a desire to give as a desire to get.

A no less remarkable analysis of interpersonal love is given by Plato in the great myth of *Phaedrus*.[2] The myth begins with a description of the entire cycle of what can happen to a human soul, which has previously been shown to be immortal. We hear of the tripartite nature of souls (on which more will be said in the later section on Plato and the Pythagoreans) and how it is essential for a soul, qua winged, to rise up to the rim of heaven and attempt to see the Plain of Truth that lies beyond. There we achieve an unsteady vision of the Forms. It is such a turbulent struggle that our wings may become damaged, in which case we fall to earth (become incarnated). If or when this happens, it normally takes ten thousand years of repeated incarnations and post-life punishments and rewards to regain our wings, with only one exception: a philosophical lover can use his memory of Forms, triggered by the glimpse of Beauty in his beloved, to regrow his wings within three lifetimes, provided he can restrain to a sufficient extent the baser parts of his soul. The description of the Plain of Truth is meant to be enticing enough to explain the attraction felt by a philosopher (literally "a lover of wisdom") for abstract truth: his vision of truth was complete enough to leave him with a lingering dissatisfaction here on earth.

In the second part of the myth, we hear about the development of a human love affair; the Athenian homoerotic norm is assumed, in which the affair involves an older man and a teenage boy. The nature

2. *Phaedrus* 246a–257b.

of the affair depends entirely, we hear, on how removed the older man is from the world—on how close he is to being a philosopher. If he is fully mired in his body, all he will want is sex with the beautiful boy who arouses his love, but if he is a philosopher, the vision of worldly beauty will remind him of heavenly Beauty, as in *Symposium*, and his soul will grow wings and aspire to return to the region beyond heaven where he first caught sight of true Beauty. But Plato stresses that the philosophical lover will not want this just for himself: he also wants to bring out the philosophical potential in his beloved. The educational aspect of Athenian homoeroticism, which I mentioned in chapter 1 when discussing Plato's youth, is here properly fulfilled. So the boy comes to love his lover, which is to say that he comes to see his lover as beautiful—which, in its turn, is to say that the boy comes to see the reflection on this earth of Beauty, and so is brought to recall the world of Forms, for at some point in the past he must have glimpsed the Plain of Truth. His education as a philosopher is under way. Love can make philosophers of any of us, but Plato is not making the implausible claim that only lovers can be philosophers. Love is important only because Beauty is the most accessible Form here on earth.

There follows a description of how the beloved is captured. This account covers once again the course of a love affair, but this time from inside the skins, as it were, of the two people involved, rather than from a cosmic perspective. The kind of lover you are depends, to a large extent, on how successful you have been in seeing reality during your pre-incarnate existence. The better your grasp of reality, the more the affair can reverse the decline into incarnation. The boy may be inclined to translate love as sex, but the older partner, if he can control the baser sides of his nature, sees that this is an inappropriate response and persuades the boy of this as well. Not only does the philosophical lover educate his partner, but he also educates himself: he ascends the ladder only by pulling someone else up onto the rung he has vacated. The soul as a whole has to be redeemed, but because the soul is complex, this process of redemption involves the reasoning part gaining control of the part or parts that fill the soul with cognitive blindness. The starting point is the perception of beauty on earth, and the consequent recollection of Beauty seen before. The beloved's face is, as it were, transparent—a window onto the Form. Losing one's mind—falling in love—is a good way to find it.

The Theory of Forms

Symposium consists largely of a sequence of speeches, delivered by those present at the fictional symposium, in praise of Love (Eros). The final speech, some of which I have just paraphrased, is given by Socrates himself, although he claims he is merely acting as a mouthpiece for what he was taught by a priestess called Diotima, from the Peloponnesian town of Mantinea. The speech culminates with the following ideas. What we fall in love with is beauty, but there are grades of beauty. We start by loving beauty in another person, but it is possible to appreciate rationally that the same features you find beautiful in your beloved can be found in countless other people. So then you may begin to see that beauty of the mind is of a higher order than physical beauty. Mental beauty is manifest above all in human activities and institutions, but at this level, too, it is possible to appreciate that the particular activities and institutions that you start by finding beautiful are really no more or less so than those which other people or countries have produced. The ascent goes on until we find that what is truly attractive, the final object of love, is "true beauty":[3]

> This is, in the first place, eternal; it doesn't come to be or cease to be, and it doesn't increase or diminish. In the second place, it isn't attractive in one respect and repulsive in another, or attractive at one time but not at another, or attractive in one setting but repulsive in another, or attractive here and repulsive elsewhere, depending on how people find it. [A person who perceives this absolute beauty] will perceive it in itself and by itself, constant and eternal, and he'll see that every other beautiful thing somehow partakes of it, but in such a way that their coming

3. *Symposium* 211a–b.

to be and ceasing to be do not increase or diminish it at all, and it remains entirely unaffected.

True beauty, then, is not in the eye of the beholder but is an objective fact. I suggested earlier in the book that *Symposium* was written to be accessible to non-philosophical readers, so by the same token I think this passage was Plato's way of introducing the theory of Forms by means of a discussion of beauty, the most accessible Form here on earth.[4] We may think that the beauty of Helen of Troy or of Michelangelo's *David* is independent of individual viewpoints; Plato claims that nothing in this world has that independence. Forms are single and immutable; they are what they are absolutely, and they perfectly have the single property that they have.[5] Particular things, however, are "deficient" (as he puts it in *Phaedo*) because they no more possess one attribute than they possess the opposite attribute; they are no more beautiful than ugly: "Is there one beautiful thing, in this welter of beautiful things, that won't turn out to be ugly? Is there one moral deed that won't turn out to be immoral? Is there one just act that won't turn out to be unjust?"[6]

We talk of a "theory" of Forms, and there is no doubt that some such theory is central to Plato's thinking, but he nowhere dedicates a dialogue or a stretch of argument to developing or demonstrating any such theory. Forms are introduced as familiar entities with which we all operate anyway, as in the passage above Plato indicates that the reason we call anything beautiful is because it partakes of Beauty itself. Plato introduces Forms to point out that their existence leads to consequences of which he approved, such as the possibility of knowledge, the immortality of the soul, or to explain how we identify the qualities of things.

---

4. *Phaedrus* 250c–d.
5. The middle-period doctrine that each Form has only one property is qualified in later dialogues, especially *Sophist*. Beauty, for instance, also has the property of sameness (with itself) and difference (from other Forms).
6. *Republic* 479a.

This argumentative application of the theory is well illustrated by *Phaedo*, the topic of which is the immortality of the soul. The dialogue reports the conversation that was alleged to have taken place between Socrates and those of his friends who were with him on his last day in prison, at the end of which, as darkness drew in, he died by drinking the poison hemlock. The main topic of the conversation, poignantly suitable for the context, is whether or not the soul can be said to be immortal, or in other words, whether Socrates has any right to be confident that his soul will in some sense live on. Five arguments for the soul's immortality are proposed, not all of them very cogent. After the first two, the theory of Recollection, with which we are already familiar, is brought in: if it is right to say that we recollect Forms from a prior, disembodied existence, then the soul at least pre-exists its incarnation in a body, so perhaps it makes sense to think that it continues afterward as well. The next is an argument from affinity: the body resembles the composite things of this world, which are liable to change and dissolution, while the soul resembles the non-composite Forms, which are not so liable. A final argument takes its starting point from the Forms of Large and Small. Largeness cannot admit smallness, and vice versa; in short, opposites cannot admit opposites. Since soul is the principle of life—every Greek would have agreed that it is what animates a living creature—it cannot admit death. And so Plato's Socrates serenely lies down to die at the end of the dialogue.

The core of the theory of Forms can be presented as a short series of simple propositions, all of which are spelled out in the middle dialogues, even if not in the sequential manner in which I shall present them. Together they tell us a lot about Plato's character. I shall continue to use "beauty" and "beautiful" as placeholders for all universals and their corresponding adjectives.

First, whenever the term "beauty" occurs, it refers to the same one thing, the Form. We have already seen that this assumption is operative even in the early dialogues, but it is not quite clear there that universals are transcendent Forms that exist independently of the human mind; they may just be universals, mental constructs. Second, it is by participation in Beauty that things are beautiful. Plato is not quite sure what metaphor to choose to explain how Forms cause the properties of things: does a beautiful thing partake of Beauty, or resemble Beauty, or have Beauty present in it? It follows from these two propositions that if two or more things are beautiful, they all participate in Beauty and resemble one another just because they participate in Beauty.

What about the Forms themselves? If they are to give their properties to the things of this world, then each of them must be perfectly and paradigmatically what it is. So, third, Beauty is paradigmatically beautiful. This is a difficult proposition, and Plato himself was the first to point out the difficulty, in *Parmenides*. If Beauty is itself beautiful, and if things gain their properties by participation in Forms, then must there not be a further Form of Beauty that enables us to identify Beauty as beautiful? And then we are locked into an infinite regress of Forms of Beauty. But the final three propositions about Forms are less problematic: they are not composite; they do not exist in time; and they do not exist in space. I have already mentioned the metaphor Plato uses in *Phaedrus* that Forms exist in a "place" he calls the Plain of Truth, a "region beyond heaven."[7] But this is plainly not a place with physical dimensions; it is a place that is accessible only to the inspired rational mind.

The theory of Forms shows Plato to have been a bold and original thinker. No one nowadays believes in Forms as described by Plato; Aristotle was the first systematically to undermine the theory. But with the theory, Plato launched metaphysics on the road it has fruitfully taken ever since. I think he would have ascribed problematic aspects, such as the self-predication of Forms (that Beauty is itself beautiful), to the difficulty of what he was trying to communicate, and he would therefore not have seen them as ruining his theory but as something that future thinkers would be able to elucidate, or as something Academicians needed to puzzle out for themselves. The theory is well thought out; Plato was a methodical thinker. But also, as

7. *Phaedrus* 247c.

is revealed especially by *Phaedrus*, Plato's mind was shot through with a distinct vein of mysticism.

Plato and the Pythagoreans

This mystical or spiritual streak was nurtured by Plato's time with the Pythagoreans in Greater Greece. He returned from his visit with his head filled with new ideas. We have already looked at the place of the mathematical sciences in the *Republic's* training program for philosophers. They are to study not just arithmetic and geometry but astronomy and harmonics as well, "sibling sciences, as the Pythagoreans claim and we agree."[8] But Plato learned plenty more from the Pythagoreans. The theory of the tripartite soul—that the soul consists of rational, spirited, and appetitive parts—was based on a Pythagorean threefold analysis of people's motivations; the theory is prominent in *Republic* and *Phaedrus*. Plato was now convinced that the soul was immortal and would be reincarnated, and that it had innate knowledge of Forms (*Meno, Phaedo, Republic, Phaedrus*). Several dialogues end with fantastic myths of the soul's life after death (*Gorgias, Phaedo, Republic*), stressing the torments of an impure soul compared with the blessed existence and happy next incarnation of the soul of a righteous person. It is even possible, Plato thought, for a soul to remain conscious in the underworld, with the ability therefore to choose its next incarnation. All this stands in stark contrast with the skepticism about life after death expressed by Socrates in *Apology of Socrates*.

In this Pythagorized scheme of things philosophy becomes salvationist: it is the only way to purify one's soul, to live a better life, and to enjoy an untroubled afterlife existence. It is also salvationist at the political level. It is the job of trained philosophers to promote the well-being of all the citizens of a community. But true well-being requires knowledge, and not everyone is knowledgeable. Hence, as

8. *Republic* 530d. The phrase "sibling sciences" is borrowed from Archytas (Fragment 1 Huffman).

proposed in *Republic*, it is up to philosophers to judge what is in the best interests of the rest of the community and to put it into effect. No doubt those scholars who set out from the Academy to play a political role in some foreign city or state felt that they were playing the part of the philosophers in *Republic*, or approximating to it. In these middle dialogues, philosophy becomes a way of being a better person and of providing better service to society. Fundamentally, what Plato took from the Pythagoreans was their conception of what well-being is for a human being.[9]

Arguably, even the theory of Forms owed a lot to Pythagoreanism. The early dialogues' search for universals now became a full-blown metaphysical theory. Reflecting on Pythagorean teachings about number, Plato realized that numbers have the kind of permanence that a universal should have. When we say that $2 + 2 = 4$, we are not counting beans but saying something about immaterial and timeless entities. But if they are immaterial and timeless, then the question arises: how do we, as incarnate creatures, know them? Add the Pythagorean teaching of reincarnation and we get Plato's theory of Recollection. We would say that we acquire concepts by experience from childhood onward. We formulate an idea of "chairness" that allows us to recognize chairs and distinguish them from other things. The same kind of process happens with abstract concepts such as goodness. Plato might agree with this description, but he would say that we are not learning a concept but remembering a Form that we already unconsciously knew. It pre-existed us and will exist after us and independently of human minds; Forms would exist even if they had never been instantiated. Some of this discussion may seem naïve, but these were first steps in metaphysics. Plato was forging tools the accuracy of which would be improved by later metaphysicians.

It would be wrong to suggest that Plato was "a Pythagorean"—a member of the school, so to speak. In the first place, he always put his

---

9. At *Gorgias* 493a–b, Plato attributes a metaphor for the insatiability of desire to "a clever story-teller from Sicily, perhaps, or Italy"—that is, a Pythagorean.

own spin on whatever he borrowed or learned from others. In the second place, there is far more to these middle-period dialogues than the Pythagorean gleanings that I have sketched. But at the same time it is clear that, just as the mathematical sciences were supposed to turn the mind upward, so Plato's mind was turned in fruitful directions by his trip to Magna Graecia.

Knowledge and Belief (Again)

As we have seen earlier, and as Aristotle informs us,[10] Plato developed the theory of Forms because he was convinced by the Heracliteans that the things of this world are unstable and in flux, and so if there is to be knowledge of anything, there must exist stable and permanent things because there is no knowledge of things in flux. Forms and knowledge were essentially linked right from the start of the theory.

Implicit in the early dialogues, as we have seen, is the important distinction between knowledge and belief. But in those dialogues Plato is more concerned to find out whether anyone can be said to have knowledge than he is to say what knowledge is. The dialogue that was probably the last of the middle-period cluster to be written, the brilliant *Theaetetus*, contains his most thorough examination of knowledge, but since it is aporetic—all the attempts at defining knowledge are refuted—it is hard to know what Plato thought about it. This is particularly puzzling given that *Meno*, as mentioned earlier, seems to suggest a solution: that knowledge is true belief that has been confirmed by working out why the belief is true. But then I have already suggested that *Theaetetus* was written to provoke discussion and debate in the Academy.

A passage in *Republic* is important because there Plato tries to meet the "man on the street" on his own terms and persuade him that there is something special about knowledge.[11] There is a clear line of

10. Aristotle, *Metaphysics* 1078b12–15.
11. *Republic* 474b–480a.

thought in the passage, which the man on the street can follow because no abstruse or specialist moves appear to be made. Plato claims to establish the thesis that there are degrees of reality, falling into three bands, and that each of these three bands forms the domain of a different cognitive state. Perhaps the most startling aspect of the thesis is that, despite the fact that as human beings our hard evidence about things is provided by our senses, Plato wants to deny full reality to the world of the senses; he says that it lies between being and non-being. What are his grounds for this assertion?

In order for us to identify something, it has to have at least one quality or attribute. If we were faced, impossible though it would be, with a quality-less thing, our mental response would be one of blankness or incomprehension. This is the first band, and Plato establishes this impossibility for the sake of completeness and contrast. At the other extreme, since knowledge is a cognitive state involving certainty, it is only if something securely and absolutely possesses a quality that we can be said to know it. Only Forms securely and absolutely possess their qualities, or have full being, and are therefore the objects of knowledge. In between blankness and knowledge, there is belief and the domain of things that do not reliably have their attributes and subsist between being and non-being. It makes sense to think of belief as an intermediate state because it does not have the degree of certainty of knowledge. We say, "I believe the building is white," when we mean that we are not quite sure.

Plato says that the domain of belief is the plurality of white (etc.) things—the things of our everyday world. These are the domain of belief, not knowledge, because they cannot supply our minds with the kind of certainty required for knowledge. In the terms of the passage of *Symposium* that I discussed earlier: a white building does not seem white at night, its color will fade over time, it can be repainted, and so on. Nor is it just white: it is hard, tall, and so on. It does not present our mind with unmitigated whiteness.

Plato's ideas about knowledge are clearly not at all separable from his metaphysics; Forms are the primary and only objects of knowledge. The world of the senses is only knowable insofar as it instantiates

Forms. So throughout the middle-period dialogues, Plato claims that there are two levels of reality (excluding the aforementioned impossible quality-less state). Consider the *Republic*'s famous Cave allegory.[12] Plato asks us to imagine that we are prisoners, chained in a cave in such a way that we are able to look only straight ahead. Behind us is a fire, and between us and the fire people are constantly walking to and fro, carrying along objects, the shadows of which are projected by the fire onto the wall of the cave. Because we can only look straight ahead, these shadows are all that we see, and therefore we take them to be reality. But imagine if someone could break free and walk back and out of the cave. First, as they passed the objects that are being carried along, they would immediately see that what we take to be reality is an illusion. Second, when they emerged from the cave, they would find a whole new world of which they had previously been unaware, and they would rightly judge this new world to be the true reality.

The multifaceted allegory goes on to describe the difficulties the escapee would face if they chose to return to the cave and try to educate their fellow prisoners about the true reality outside. "There's more to the world than this!" The others would think them mad and put them on trial for impiety—as happened to Socrates. For Plato, the upper world is the world of Forms, which are real and knowable, whereas the prisoners in the cave uncritically accept the illusory world of popular culture, represented by the artifacts that are being carried along behind them and by the voices of the people doing the carrying, which are projected onto the wall of the cave and seem to emerge from the shadows. The upper world is inhabited by our souls, and the lower level of reality by our bodies and our senses. In the upper world we can gain self-knowledge, but in the cave, since we are forced to look only straight ahead, we cannot even see ourselves or our neighbors. In the upper world, we can base our actions on knowledge and therefore behave successfully and morally, while there can

12. *Republic* 514a–518b.

be no true morality based on the play of shadows, and any behavior that is describable as morally good is also describable as bad.

Ethics

There are few philosophers nowadays who would join Plato in regarding epistemology and metaphysics as closely bound together. There are perhaps no philosophers nowadays who would consider ethics, the branch of knowledge that asks what it takes to be a good person, to have just as close a relationship with metaphysics. But Plato did. However, many people nowadays and throughout the ages have thought that religious principles should guide a person's behavior, and from this perspective it immediately becomes easier to understand Plato's motivation because there is more than a tinge of religious fervor in Plato's approach to metaphysics. We have already seen that assimilation to God is one important way in which Plato expressed what he saw as the goal of human existence, and "anything divine is moral, wise, good, and has all the virtues,"[13] so that assimilation to God automatically makes a person good, and approximation to God gradually makes a person morally better. Similarly, in *Phaedrus* it is by following in the train of the god to whom one is most akin (and because there are twelve such gods, there are astrological overtones) that we may have a vision of the Forms in the Plain of Truth.[14] To do this, we have to have subdued the appetitive part of our three-part mind and harnessed the passionate part as an ally of the reasoning part.

In *Republic* Plato develops the notion that there are these three parts to the human soul and links it with morality. Following the Pythagoreans, he detected three main sources of motivation in people. There is the desire to satisfy one's instincts and appetites, and those perceived lacks that are related to one's instincts and appetites; there is the desire (that often manifests as anger or outrage) for preservation

13. *Phaedrus* 246d.
14. *Phaedrus* 246a–248b.

of one's "sense of I" or self-image; and there is the desire for understanding and truth. Everyone has all three of these psychic parts or
elements, but in different people different parts are prominent, either
overall or at different times of their lives. People may be ruled by their
appetites, in which case they are lustful, greedy, and so on; or they
may be ruled by their egos, in which case they are touchy, passionate,
proud, arrogant, brave, and so on. But a good person is one in whom
these two lower parts are ruled by the rational part. Why does this
make a person good? Because, unlike the other two parts, the rational
part has the breadth of vision to know what is good for a person,
and that includes acting morally.[15] Someone ruled by their appetitive
part would be a hedonist, and someone ruled by their passionate part
would be a status-seeker. Morality is possible only with the rule of
the rational soul.

But so far this sounds like a selfish ideal, as though moral people
were just those who do good because it is good *for them* to do good.
Somewhat later in *Republic* Plato comes up with the famous simile of
the Sun.[16] Briefly expressed, the idea is this. Just as the sun illuminates
the visible world and thereby gives us the ability to see, so the Form
of Good "gives the things we know their truth and makes it possible
for people to have knowledge." Since it is only philosophers who
know Forms, only they have the ability truly, non-accidentally, to do
good to others. Plato does not immediately bring out this moral, but
it permeates much of the rest of the dialogue. In the terms of the allegory of the Cave, philosophers are to be forced to retire from contemplation of Forms and to return to the cave to educate and improve
the lives of their fellow citizens. Since they are the only ones who
know what goodness is, only they can bring about goodness in their
communities and create an environment in which every citizen can
be good to the best of their ability. So Plato intertwines metaphysics,

15. *Republic* 444d, at the end of the first psychological section of the dialogue, that starts
    at 434d. But further insights into the psychology are provided when it is put to work
    later in the dialogue, at 580d–588a, 602c–605c, and 543a–576b.
16. *Republic* 506d–509c.

politics, and ethics. Knowledge of Forms is the essential prerequisite for rulership in a city because it gives the Guardians a kind of over-arching wisdom that enables them to see how best to govern the city in everything, great and small.

We can also approach this nest of ideas from another direction. In the field of ethics Plato, like Socrates and indeed like almost all an-cient philosophers, was a "eudaemonist," which is to say that he claims that all our actions are supposed to bring us, or at least bring us closer to, *eudaimonia*, the good state of one's *daimon*, or inner being, that may be called happiness, well-being, doing well, or flourishing. However, like Socrates, he believed that most if not all of us perform actions that actually do not bring us closer to happiness. Actions will do this only if they are performed with virtue, and since virtue is knowledge, we need to become knowledgeable. The kind of knowledge that Plato talks about in this context in the earlier dialogues is analogous to craft-knowledge or productive knowledge: conventional good things such as health, wealth, and prestige will benefit us only if they are put to good use, and putting them to good use requires a kind of know-ledge that resembles that of a carpenter or musician.[17] Without such knowledge, these things will harm us.

By the time Plato was writing the middle dialogues, the kind of knowledge in which he was interested was not craft-knowledge but knowledge of Forms. Clearly, this is not mere cleverness or knowing a lot of information. But what kind of knowledge is it? Plato is dis-tressingly vague on this point. It seems to be a kind of intuition, by which I do not mean a shortcut, an alternative to education: Plato makes it clear in *Republic* that knowledge of Forms is based on years of prior study. It is a vision that is granted one if one has put in all the prior hard work.

Plato is clearer about the results of such knowledge. A passage in *Phaedrus* is illuminating:[18]

---

17. See especially *Euthydemus* 278e–282d.
18. *Phaedrus* 268a–c.

SOCRATES: Suppose someone came up to [a couple of doctors] and said,
"I know how to treat the body in ways that allow me to raise or lower
temperatures, to get people to vomit, to make their bowels move, and
so on and so forth—whatever I choose or decide is best and since
I have this knowledge I regard myself as a professional doctor. . . ."
How do you think they would respond to him?

PHAEDRUS: I'm sure they'd ask him whether he also knew whom he should
treat in these ways, and when, and how much.

SOCRATES: And what if he said, "No, I don't. But I claim that anyone who
learned these treatments from me would be able to do what you ask"?

PHAEDRUS: I think they'd say that the man was out of his mind, and was
imagining that he'd become a doctor after having heard someone
reading from some book or other . . . but that he really had no
understanding of this area of expertise.

By the same token, then, technical knowledge enables one to know
how to do something, but knowledge of Forms enables one to know
why it is good for this thing to be done, and when it should be
done. This is the knowledge that makes a person truly good, because
he can do good to others, and therefore be truly happy. In *Republic*
philosophers have to be forced to return to the cave and do good
to their communities. They think that their happiness lies in a life
of contemplation of Forms and dialectical conversations with one
another. But they are wrong: they will be truly happy only if they
put their knowledge to work. Plato was reaffirming—in theory—his
commitment to practical politics.

Throughout the dialogues, Plato constantly asks how, given human
nature, people are to fulfill themselves and flourish. He asks his readers to accept a radically new vision of themselves, the world, and their
place in it. These middle-period dialogues are not mere academic exercises but, as were the earlier dialogues, attempts to get readers to
rethink their most basic beliefs and change their lives accordingly.
Taking just *Republic*, we are asked to consider a number of important
questions: What is morality? What, if anything, does one gain by being
a good person? Why should we not give in to the temptations of
injustice? How should one live one's life? What factors influence a

person's character for good or ill? What is it to be a human being? What is the soul (or mind) like? What is knowledge? What are the special objects of knowledge? What does one need to know in order to be a good person? Is the universe structured and ordered? What is the value of representational art and theater? Which political systems are corrupt and why? How is society to be redeemed? These are only the main issues; there are plenty of lesser ones.

In the middle dialogues, then, Plato presents us with a host of powerful and intriguing ideas, in politics, metaphysics, ethics, and many other fields. And it is all written in seductively clear prose. Plato manages the rare trick of holding our attention by the power and interest of the ideas he is presenting. I can think of no other writer who manages to pack as many ideas as Plato does into a book and still retain the reader's interest. Philosophy was scarcely more than two hundred years old, and yet *Republic* is high on most thinking people's reading list. Plato's production of the middle dialogues is the equivalent of an airplane leaving the ground only two hundred years after the invention of the kite.

7

Practicing Politics in Syracuse

Plato had kept in touch with Dion and abreast of Syracusan affairs under Dionysius I. Dion had gone from strength to strength. He was employed by Dionysius in the critical role of ambassador to the Carthaginians, who held the western parts of the island and were the perennial enemies of Syracuse, the dominant Greek city in Sicily. He was already the tyrant's brother-in-law, thanks to Dionysius's marriage to his sister Aristomache, and he became also his son-in-law when he married one of Dionysius's daughters, Arete. He seems to have been completely in the tyrant's confidence and closer to him than any other member of the court. He also amassed enormous wealth.

Dionysius I died in the spring of 367 BCE and was succeeded by his son. Dionysius II, aged in his late twenties, was not a chip off the old block: he had been softened by a luxurious and (rumor had it) dissipated upbringing, and he lacked his father's belligerence and skills as a general. This was not necessarily a bad thing, in that he made peace with the Carthaginians. But he also lacked the ability, or the ruthlessness, to maintain tight control over his subject population, and this would allow factions to emerge that opposed his rule. The Syracusans had tolerated a warlord as long as there was war to be fought against the Carthaginians, but some of them came to believe that they need not be ruled by the warlord's son.

Dion expected to be as close to Dionysius II as he had been to his father, but his hopes did not end there. After all these years, he still felt himself to be a follower of Plato, from whom he had presumably been receiving instruction by post and copies of the dialogues, and he hoped to have a benign influence on the new monarch, who was intelligent and sensitive but intellectually immature as a result of the opulent seclusion in which his father had kept him. As Dion's biographer Plutarch describes it, "Dion tried to interest the tyrant in liberal studies and to give him a taste of character-forming literature and science, in order to get him to put an end to his fear of virtue and get him used to taking pleasure in high ideals."[1] And the younger Dionysius's early measures do in fact suggest that he was inclined toward a more liberal form of tyranny and a less oppressive form of leadership than his father had displayed.

However, in the court of every monarch throughout history, courtiers jockey for position and are driven by jealousy of those who are preferred over them. Powerful forces within the court sought to undermine Dion's influence. If Dionysius was distracted by philosophy, they thought, that would leave Dion as the de facto ruler. Despite this opposition, Dion appeared to be making some headway with the young tyrant. Dion began to introduce Platonic ideas into his conversations and advice, and Dionysius found them sufficiently attractive that he was persuaded by Dion to write and ask Plato to pay a visit to his court. It would not have taken much persuasion on Dion's part: Plato was the greatest philosopher of the age, and Dionysius, who like his father had literary aspirations, wanted to maintain a splendid and cultured court. Writers hostile to the Syracusan tyrants claimed that the elder Dionysius had altogether denied his son an education, fearing that it would lead him to despise him and turn against him, but this is plainly untrue. Dion, too, wrote to Plato, saying that this was a golden opportunity, not to be passed up; and, according to Plutarch, some of the Pythagoreans of southern Italy, who lived within or close to Dionysius's realm, backed up Dion's request.

But Dion's enemies in the court arranged for the recall of the historian Philistus from exile to see whether he could satisfy Dionysius's

1. Plutarch, *Life of Dion* 9.1.

newfound longing for learning while still preserving the tyranny and keeping their clique in power in the court. Philistus was in favor of the Syracusan tyranny as long as he could advise the tyrant. Knowing this, Dion also urged Plato to come to Syracuse before others undermined Dionysius's budding idealism. For, in addition to Philistus, other Socratics, the two friends Aeschines and Aristippus, were already in Syracuse,[2] and Dion, loyal to Plato, seems to have wanted Dionysius to hear what Plato had to say, rather than any other Socratic. Aristippus, in particular, may not have been inclined to dissuade Dionysius altogether from the hedonistic ways of his earlier life.

Plato's Motives

Plato hesitated only briefly before accepting Dionysius II's invitation (see figure 7.1), though he had misgivings: young men are so fickle. The decisive factors, apart from the temptation of influencing the most powerful monarch in Europe—of bringing about "a conjunction of philosophy and power"[3]—were, first, that he owed it to Dion and to philosophy, and second, "It would have caused me acute embarrassment to find myself to be absolutely nothing more than a pure theorist, unwilling to take in hand any practical task."[4] I find it perfectly plausible that Plato would have wanted to do something practical. He was suffering from a kind of guilt. From Socrates he had absorbed the notion that political leaders should be trained experts who had enough philosophy to be good men, and that this was the way to create a state that conformed to the ideal of justice. But his revulsion for Athenian politics had made him retreat into purely

2. Diogenes Laertius, *Lives of the Eminent Philosophers* 2.61, 2.66–67; Plutarch, *Moralia* 67d–e (*How to Distinguish a Flatterer from a Friend*).
3. *Letter 7* 335d.
4. *Letter 7* 328c. The anecdotal tradition adds a fanciful motive: Plato wanted Dionysius to give him land where he could found the ideal city-state of *Republic* (Diogenes Laertius, *Lives of the Eminent Philosophers* 3.21).

Figure 7.1 Dion presents Plato to the Syracusan tyrant Dionysius II. An engraving from Hermann Gölls 1876 book, *Die Weisen und Gelehrten des Alterthums*.
366 BC, Plato visiting Dionysius the Younger or Dionysius II, c. 397 BC–343 BC, at Syracuse, Sicily

theoretical studies—not least by taking Socrates's insistence on trained political experts to extreme lengths in the utopian *Republic*. He could assume that Dionysius had some expertise—after all, he had learned monarchy at his father's knee—but he needed the preliminary philosophical training.

A passage of *Laws* is of great interest in this context. Plato is imagining what a good lawgiver needs in order to create satisfactory conditions in a state as rapidly as possible. His conclusion is surprising: "Give me a city under a tyrant. Let the tyrant be young, with a retentive memory, quick on the uptake, courageous, and with innate

nobility of character."⁵ Plato loathed tyranny, but he felt that under
such circumstances tyranny could be changed into something better.
Self-discipline and luck are added as two further necessary qualities.
If such a tyrant were to work with a true lawmaker, Plato says, that
would be the quickest and easiest way to reform a state for the best—
that is, as we shall see, to make it a blend of monarchy and democracy.⁶
Plato does not rule out other constitutions: a constitutional monarchy
is second best, then a democracy, and then an oligarchy. But in these
latter cases reformation of society would be less rapid and less straightforward. It seems that Plato saw himself as just such a lawmaker, and
Dion had convinced him that Dionysius had, or potentially had, the
required qualities. But, as it turned out, Dion was no judge of character; he allowed his hopes to sway his judgment, and Plato, blinded
by his affection for the younger man, was wrong to trust him.

Plato's support for one-man rule is not surprising in a fourth-
century context: many Greek intellectuals were reacting against what
they perceived as the weaknesses of democracy—such as the excesses
Plato witnessed during the Peloponnesian War—and were inclining optimistically toward enlightened monarchy. Xenophon portrayed King Agesilaus of Sparta as the possessor of all the virtues, and
he wrote a fictional account in praise of Cyrus the Great of Persia.
Isocrates not only wrote an encomium of Evagoras I, the king of
Salamis in Cyprus, but also advised his successor, Nicocles, to turn
himself into an enlightened monarch, ruling in the interests of his
people. Xenophon, Antisthenes, and other Socratics were using their
written works to suggest the leadership qualities a true ruler should

5. *Laws* 709e. See also *Letter* 7 328c ("Now was the time to try, because it was only necessary to win over a single man"), and *Republic* 502b ("If only one remains uncorrupted
   in a community that is prepared to obey him, that is enough: everything that is now
   open to doubt [the existence of the imaginary city] would become a fully fledged
   reality"). A historical parallel: in the 1920s, Mustafa Kemal used his position as dictator
   to re-create Turkey as a democratic republic in an astonishingly short time.
6. Compare this with the extraordinary "quickest and easiest" way of making real the
   imaginary city of *Republic*, which involves banishing everyone over the age of ten
   (*Republic* 540e–541a).

possess. Plato was simply in the forefront of this movement, both in theory (as in *Republic*) and in fact (as in his trips to Syracuse).

In *Republic*, Plato famously said, "Unless cities have philosophers as kings, or the people who are currently called kings and rulers practice philosophy with sufficient integrity, . . . there can be no end to political troubles, or even to human troubles in general."[7] Nevertheless, Plato did not go to Syracuse hoping or expecting to turn Dionysius into one of the philosopher kings of *Republic*.[8] He still maintained that the ideal political situation was one in which the rulers of a state were fully trained philosophers, who had undergone the long and arduous training outlined in *Republic*, or at least the Academic version of that training, but he was not so unrealistic as to expect that, in the time available, he could alter Dionysius's character so thoroughly.

His aim was to get Dion and Dionysius to reform Syracusan society until absolutism was reduced to constitutional rule under the law and the people were given back some degree of freedom. A tyrant is by definition an unconstitutional potentate, ruling by whim and fiat; Plato wanted to help Dion turn Dionysius into a king, working with a quasi-democratic constitution, rather than a tyrant. One of the first benefits of this, he thought, would be that Dionysius could unite the Greek cities of Sicily in an alliance, not in subservience to Syracuse, as a way of preserving Greek culture as a bulwark against the "barbarian" Carthaginians in the west of the island, who would eventually be subjugated or expelled from the island by the united Greeks.[9] Along with many others, he chauvinistically felt that Greek culture should be preserved against the pressure of the Carthaginians to the west and the Persians to the east. In *Letter 8*, he adds the Oscan-speaking peoples who were neighbors of the Greek cities of southern Italy. But the key to the whole program was getting Dionysius to see the wrongness

7. *Republic* 473c–d.
8. At *Letter 7* 328a, it is Dion, not Plato, who holds out the hope of making a philosopher king of Dionysius. This is not clear in all translations.
9. *Letter 7* 332e, 336a; see also *Letter 8* 353e and 357a.

of absolute rule. And that would take a thorough reformation of the tyrant's character.

The Second Sojourn in Sicily

So in 366,[10] aged in his late fifties, Plato made the voyage to Sicily. He was accompanied by Xenocrates, and he might (the evidence is very slight) have left Eudoxus in charge of the Academy. Despite being a relatively new arrival in Athens, Eudoxus would have been a natural choice, since he already had experience as head of his own school in Cyzicus. Plato himself tells us what happened next:[11]

> To cut a long story short, on my arrival I found Dionysius's court to be utterly filled with factionalism and with malicious reports to Dionysius about Dion. I defended him as well as I could, but there was little I could do, and after I had been there for perhaps three or four months Dionysius accused Dion of plotting against his tyranny,[12] had him put aboard a small ship, and banished him from Syracuse in disgrace. After this, those of us who were Dion's friends were all afraid that Dionysius might bring charges against one or another of us and punish him as complicit in Dion's plans. In my case, moreover, there was a rumor circulating in Syracuse that I had been put to death by Dionysius as the cause of all the troubled events of the time.
>
> But when Dionysius realized how we all felt, he was concerned that our fears might lead to something worse for himself, so he began to receive all of us in a friendly fashion, and to reassure me in particular, telling me not to worry and imploring me not to leave, whatever else I did. After all, no honor would accrue to him if I left him, but only if I stayed, and so he even made a great show of his pleading.

10. Contrary to the common view, then, Plato was still in Athens when Aristotle came as a student in 367.
11. *Letter 7* 329b–330b, 338a–b.
12. Plutarch (*Life of Dion* 14.4–7) says that Dion had written a letter to the Carthaginians, urging them not to enter into negotiations with Dionysius unless he was at the meetings as well, and that this letter fell into Dionysius's hands. At the least, the letter was an insult to Dionysius's powers of negotiation and abilities as a framer of foreign policy; but Dionysius himself took it to be a sign that Dion was actually plotting with the Carthaginians for his overthrow.

However, everyone knows that the pleas of tyrants have an element of compulsion in them, and indeed he devised a scheme for preventing my departure. He brought me into the citadel and had me lodge there,[13] in a place from which not a single shipowner would have brought me out unless Dionysius not only took no steps to prevent it, but actually sent someone with orders for my release. Nor would any merchant, any of those responsible for departures from the place, or anyone else have let me leave on my own; they would immediately have apprehended me and taken me off to Dionysius again, especially since by now the opposite of the earlier claim had made the rounds, and people were saying that Dionysius was incredibly fond of Plato.

But how did things really stand? Truth be told, with the passage of time, as he became familiar with my personality and character, his fondness for me did grow. But he wanted me to think more highly of him than Dion and to consider him more especially my friend, and it was incredible how he pushed for some such outcome. But he shied from the best way of getting that to happen (if it was going to happen at all), which was to endear himself and get close to me by becoming my student and listening to what I had to say about philosophy. He didn't want to do this because he was frightened of the danger suggested by our detractors, that he would be ensnared and Dion would have got his way in everything. I put up with all this, however, and kept to my original plan, the one that had brought me there—that is, to see if he might come to desire the philosophic life. But I was unable to break down his resistance.

...After that, I did all I could to persuade Dionysius to let me go, and the two of us came to an agreement as to what would happen when peace was restored (there was warfare in Sicily at the time).[14] Dionysius said that he would again send for Dion and me once he had made his empire more secure, and he asked Dion to think of his situation at that time not as banishment but as a temporary change of location; and I promised to come back on these conditions.

13. Lodging Plato in the citadel was ostensibly an honor, but Plato presents himself as virtually a prisoner; according to the hostile elements of the biographical tradition, however, he was just a freeloader, enjoying life in the court of the generous Syracusan tyrant.
14. We know no details of this war, not even against whom it was fought. But we do know that Dionysius prosecuted a war against the Lucanians of southern Italy, which was probably provoked by his planting of colonies on the southeastern Italian coastline (Diodorus of Sicily, *The Library* 16.5.2). Could Plato have written "in Sicily" by mistake?

A few more details emerge from other sources.[15] When Plato landed in Syracuse, Dionysius welcomed him effusively and gave him the signal honor of being driven into the city in the royal chariot. As Plato joined Dionysius in the chariot, a learned bystander was reminded of the lines in Homer's *Iliad* where the goddess Athena joins the hero Diomedes in his chariot, and quoted a version of the lines, changing one word: "And the oaken axle groaned aloud under the weight, carrying the dread *mortal* [previously "goddess"] and the best of men."[16]

Before long, seeing that Dionysius was very taken with Plato, a craze for literature and study swept the court. "The palace was filled with dust thanks to all the many people who began to study geometry,"[17] and the court as a whole became less dissipated. However fanciful Plutarch's picture may be, the tendency was there, and it was successfully undermined by Philistus and his friends when they saw to Dion's banishment. But the departure of Dion did not go down well with some of the Syracusans and, to appease those who were upset and deflect any chance of an uprising against his rule, Dionysius allowed two ships to be filled with Dion's valuables and sent after him, and Dion was allowed to receive the revenues from his estates. Hence, presumably, the tyrant's tendentious claim (at the end of the passage translated above) that Dion had not been banished but was merely living abroad. But at the same time, Dionysius must have known that there was a risk that Dion would use his wealth against him. Dion's plan as regards Dionysius seems to have been that he would either convert him to responsible rulership or overthrow him.

15. Chiefly Plutarch, *Life of Dion* 13–16, and *Moralia* 52d (*How to Distinguish a Flatterer from a Friend*).
16. Homer, *Iliad* 5.838–839.
17. In those days, geometric figures were commonly inscribed in sand because papyrus was an expensive commodity.

Dionysius II's Court

We have no direct evidence about Dionysius II's court, beyond its location, but there are commonalities to monarchical courts throughout the ages, so a certain amount can be said with confidence.

Dionysius's citadel, or palace-cum-castle, was separated from the rest of the city by a formidable fivefold entrance: an initial fortified wall, pierced by three gates, led into an open space. This space was probably used on a daily basis as a place for vendors to set up their stalls, selling to the soldiers and courtiers inside, but at a time of war, attackers who fought their way in through the first gate would be at the mercy of soldiers and artillery on the walls. Then there was a second fortified wall, pierced by two gates. Beyond this wall lay the great citadel, which was also securely fortified. That was where Plato was lodged. All this defensive building work had been carried out by Dionysius I, who evicted the last civilian residents, razed their houses, and turned the site into an impregnable extended fortress. The citadel was built on a wide man-made causeway that led to the former island of Ortygia ("Quail Island"), which was the site of the original settlement of Syracuse in the eighth century, before it expanded onto the mainland. The island embraced some of the most important Syracusan temples, and, again since Dionysius I's time, held the arsenal and the main barracks of the tyrants' mercenary forces. It also commanded the two harbors of Syracuse, both of which were protected at sea by booms. Equally important for defensive purposes was the abundant Arethusa freshwater spring.

But a royal court is more than a palace; it is also the people in orbit around the monarch, those who live or work there or who pass through on official business. Dionysius II's court encompassed, first, himself, his immediate family, and other relatives. Attached to the family were those who attended them. There might be, for instance, a royal chamberlain, responsible for managing the household; a keeper of the royal seal; a royal physician. Ushers wielding staffs guarded doorways and limited access to the monarch, who deliberately chose to remain aloof to maintain an aura of otherness. High-ranking attendants either lived in the palace or had accommodations nearby.

Then there were Dionysius's trusted advisers, such as Dion and Philistus. That is why Dionysius could present Plato's residence in the citadel as an honor; it brought him close, on a daily basis, to the royal presence. These advisers were the effective ruling class of Syracuse, so that the court was also the seat of government. Financial management of the kingdom as a whole, military planning, delegation of responsibilities to local government—all these kinds of functions were handled in court. Then there were the artists, entertainers, and intellectuals patronized by the king, and court priests to perform sacrifices and organize festivals.

If these groups constituted the inner court, those with regular access to the king's person, then the outer court was made up of the bureaucrats, secretaries, grooms, bakers, and so on, who saw to the daily running of the kingdom and the palace, and all the envoys, ambassadors, and emissaries who arrived from abroad. Envoys were expected to come not just with a request but also with a gift or an offer of services to increase the likelihood of their state's receiving the monarch's favor.

In any monarch's court, courtiers and visitors are subject to certain regulations, usually unwritten, which govern the behavior of both them and the king or tyrant. He is expected to act with splendor and dignity, they with deference. Dionysius's court was the point from which he projected his identity as monarch to the outside world, in the audiences he granted and the orders he issued. It was the setting of royal ceremonial events (state banquets, for instance, or the reception of ambassadors) and a place where a theatrical display of the king's power was presented to the wider world. From the inner chambers of the palace, the king would emerge and appear before his subjects almost like a divine epiphany. Dionysius presented himself as sacred, and as essential to his people. The statues and portraits of himself to which he gave his blessing perpetuated the same ideas of power and divinity.

Luxury and opulence were justified because they were understood to be tokens of success. Dionysius's income was enormous, largely from taxes, gifts, judicial fines and confiscations, war indemnities and booty, and the revenues from the extensive royal estates. But his expenses were also enormous: he had to make war, pay his mercenaries, build and repair fortifications and public buildings, make costly dedications in the gods' sanctuaries. And, of more relevance to the court, he had to repay gifts from other monarchs or statesmen such as Archytas of Taras with gifts of his own and reward his closest advisers (this is probably how Dion got to be so rich in the court of Dionysius I) and those whom he patronized. There is no hint in Plato's letters that he was the beneficiary of Dionysius's munificence, but it would not be surprising if he had been; the story that he was given the truly enormous sum of eighty talents may be true, or at least only exaggerated.[18] In any case, the tradition of royal patronage is why it was plausible for his detractors to present him as a parasite on the Syracusan tyrants.

Plato and Dionysius

We learn from *Letter 7* something of the content of Plato's dealings with Dionysius before Dion's banishment. Typically, for Plato, political reform started with personal reform. He insisted that moderate and self-disciplined behavior would make him a leader who deserved his position and would win him true friends and allies, so that the Sicilian cities would be governed by people he could trust. Moreover, since a monarch's courtiers imitate the monarch, Plato hoped to reform the court at the same time.

But, above all, as we learn from *Letter 3*, the three of them—Plato, Dion, and Dionysius—began to sketch out a revised constitution for Syracuse, one that would leave Dionysius as a constitutional king.

18. Diogenes Laertius, *Lives of the Eminent Philosophers* 3.9.

Plato's main contribution was to write preambles to the proposed
laws. We can see what these would have been like, because the laws
of *Laws* are prefaced by preambles. No one before Plato had con-
ceived of such a thing; there was no precedent for legal preambles.
Plato distinguished the coercive power of laws from the persuasive
power of preambles. That is, a law basically says: "Do this, or you will
be punished in such-and-such a way." A preamble, however, explains
why the law is good and is designed to get people willingly to accept
it. So, by writing preambles to the proposed new laws for Syracuse,
Plato was able to instruct Dionysius—to show him not just what a
good constitution for Syracuse might look like, but also why it was
good. His fundamental point was that all laws should have the inculcation of virtue in citizens as their purpose. Their discussions may
have ranged beyond Syracuse. According to one of the Lives of the
comic poet Aristophanes,[19] Plato recommended that Dionysius read
Aristophanes's plays in order to understand Athenian politics. The
idea is sound, even if the story is suspect.

But after Dion's banishment, Plato refused to work with Dionysius
any more on political matters, and this must be the basis of Dionysius's
claim, reflected in *Letter 3*, that Plato had actually obstructed his attempts at political reform.[20] Plato, as we have seen, says that he spent
his time instead trying to reconcile Dionysius and Dion and pro-
tecting himself against Philistus's claims that he was working with
Dion to depose Dionysius. But Dionysius continued to express enthusiasm for philosophy, even if Plato kept their discussions at a fairly
basic level. The two men remained on polite terms, then, and when
Dionysius became embroiled in warfare, he allowed the philosopher
to return to Athens.

It must have been quite a relief for Plato to be allowed to leave. He
may have failed to convert Dionysius to philosophy, but he had at least

19. J. van Leeuwen, *Prolegomena ad Aristophanem* 172.
20. Nepos, *Life of Dion* 3.3, exaggerates when he says that Plato had actually persuaded
    Dionysius to lay down the tyranny but that the tyrant was turned aside from this
    course by Philistus.

kept the door open for Dion to be able to return to Syracuse. But this was very limited success compared with the thorough reformation of Syracuse that he had set out to achieve. He claims that he had "established relations of friendship and hospitality between Archytas and the people of Taras and Dionysius,"[21] but this is something Dionysius and Archytas could have managed on their own. And the downside far outweighed any minor gains. Although it would be wrong to suggest that Plato was responsible to any considerable degree, the Syracuse he left was riven by factionalism, especially those who favored Dion against those who favored the tyranny. Everyone knew that Plato held far more affection for Dion than for Dionysius.

Idealism Tempered

Plato's disappointment in Syracuse seems to be reflected in his current views on political leadership. The dialogue *Statesman* was written after his return to Athens, and possibly not long after. At the heart of the politics of *Statesman* is the idea that rule by a wise expert who does without laws is best, and certainly better than any existing constitution. Such a *politikos*, the true statesman, is the ideal, and all those who currently occupy positions that should be occupied by statesmen are impostors. The statesman of *Statesman*, however, is not the philosopher ruler of *Republic*; he is a professional statesman, and his knowledge is knowing how to rule, not knowledge of the world of Forms. In fact, he is not a philosopher at all: as mentioned earlier, *Statesman* is the second dialogue in a projected trilogy made up of *Sophist*, *Statesman*, and *Philosopher*, so the philosopher is now distinct from the statesman.

In *Statesman*, then, Plato rethinks some of the same issues that gave rise to the philosopher rulers of *Republic*. The statesman is an expert only at political science, and all important state functions are likewise in the hands of specialists (generals, judges, educators, etc.), who

---

21. *Letter 7* 338c.

work under the direction of the statesman. The statesman lacks the all-embracing competences of the philosopher rulers of *Republic*. This may be a sign of Plato's increased realism after his Syracusan experiment. There also seems to be little or no philosophy involved in the makeup of prehistoric Athens and the original, uncorrupted Atlantis of *Timaeus-Critias*, or in the imaginary city-state of *Laws*.

Despite the continued elevation of the wise ruler, there is greater emphasis on law in *Statesman* than in *Republic*. Plenty of laws are outlined or implied in *Republic*, but they scarcely restrict the philosopher rulers; they are designed more to regulate the institutions of the imaginary city. (Hence the Roman poet Juvenal's famous tag: "But who will guard the Guardians?")[22] More is said on this issue in *Statesman*. Written law is disparaged on the ground that it lacks the flexibility to deal with the infinite variety of real-life situations; Plato assumes that a law, once made, is cast in stone or only slowly changeable. But a man of knowledge has the requisite flexibility, and he should not be handicapped by having to abide by laws if he can see a better course of action for any given situation. The same goes for other experts, such as doctors and helmsmen: it would be absurd for them to have to obey existing rules rather than respond to the situation with which they are faced. The statesman rules with laws of his own creation, designed to cover situations where his input is unavailable or unnecessary, but he has the right to change or adapt those laws as circumstances seem to him to dictate. That may not commonly happen; in most situations the laws will be perfectly adequate. But a knowledgeable statesman must be allowed to rise above the laws on those occasions when he sees the necessity of doing so: "Although from one point of view legislation and kingship do certainly go together, the ideal is for authority to be invested not in a legal code but in an individual who combines kingship with wisdom."[23]

---

22. Juvenal, *Satires* 6.347–348.
23. *Statesman* 294a.

However, in states that lack an authentic ruler—Plato was surely thinking of Syracuse—law must be sovereign. The rule of law was absolutely fundamental to Greek political thinking. Greek thinkers saw, right from the start, that the rule of law differentiated their republics from their eastern neighbors, who were ruled by kings. Law, then, in *Statesman*, takes the place of the true statesman in a second-best state; laws are the closest the general populace can get to knowledgeable leadership. Adherence to an unchanging legal code is preferable to laws being changed by people who are ignorant.

So the second-best course, and the more practicable ideal, is that the political leaders of a community, and even a single ruler such as Dionysius, should work with and within the laws. "When government by a single person is harnessed by adherence to a sound set of stipulations, that we call a legal code, it is the best of the six [non-ideal constitutions]."[24] This seems to be precisely the program Plato and Dion were working toward with Dionysius, and in *Statesman* the true statesman is also described as a king.[25] His job is to select and prepare the human material required to produce a harmonious social fabric (especially by organizing the citizens' education); to avoid factionalism by weaving the energetic and quiet elements of the citizen body together into a functioning whole, and by eliminating those of either temperament who are incapable of adjusting to this dispensation; and to create a strong political body by ensuring that all citizens are indoctrinated into holding the same beliefs about what is good, fine, and just.[26] Thus the citizens form a community of the virtuous. Statesmanship is a theoretical rather than productive science, but one which is also practical in that it prescribes to those officials whose job it is to run the state. The statesman-king is in a position to prescribe

24. *Statesman* 302e. The six non-ideal constitutions are kingship and its bad counterpart, tyranny; aristocracy (the rule of the few men who are best suited to rule) and oligarchy; and democracy and mob rule. In each pairing, the distinction depends on the presence or absence of law.

25. The identification of the true statesman and the king had already been floated as an idea in an intriguing, aporetic stretch of an early dialogue: *Euthydemus* 291c–292e.

26. *Statesman* 308b–311c.

because he is the only one with the ability to recognize the right time for any particular action to be done by any of the other arts, those that are ruled by his ruling art. So a general is an expert at waging war, but the statesman knows when war is and is not to be fought.

As I have already said, I do not think that Plato went to Syracuse expecting to turn Dionysius into a philosopher king. Nevertheless, his Syracusan experience relegated the idea of the philosopher ruler to fantasyland, if it was not there already. Even the expert statesman seems to be an unattainable exemplar. The idealism expressed in *Republic* has been tempered by a new awareness of how difficult it would be, in the real world, to bring about such an ideal. In Syracuse, as he himself says,[27] Plato attempted to set in motion something approximating to his second-best constitution, the rule of a king who is constrained by a sound legal code. He failed, but worthy goals are worth striving for even in the face of likely failure.

The Third Visit to Syracuse

Plato was back in Athens sometime in 365. Aristotle had been in the Academy for about two years, and Dion was now studying there, too, for at least some of the year—a prince in the Academy. Dion was also made an honorary citizen of Sparta; this may have been a reward for services rendered while Dionysius I was tyrant, or it may have been a "golden passport," a reward for financial investment in the country. At any rate, he seems to have had property in the Peloponnese and spent time there as well. In Athens, he was lodging with a friend of his, the astronomer Callippus,[28] and had bought property in the countryside outside Athens. He also formed a close friendship with Speusippus.

27. *Letter 8* 356b–357a.
28. One often reads that Callippus was an Academician, but this is expressly denied by Plato at *Letter 7* 333e–334c (where he is writing, without naming them, of Callippus and his brother Hippothales), and Plato is followed by Plutarch, *Life of Dion* 54.1. The mistake (if it is a mistake) stems from Diogenes Laertius, *Lives of the Eminent Philosophers* 3.46.

Plato returned to the quiet life of writing, teaching, and fostering the Academy.

Meanwhile, in Syracuse, in his spare time from warfare, Dionysius II had remained enthusiastic about philosophy. After all, Plato's project for him had foundered not because Dionysius was not interested in philosophy but because of the deterioration of the relationship between the tyrant and Dion. Dionysius surrounded himself with intellectuals, took an interest in the subject himself, and expressed regret that he had not taken it more seriously while Plato was by his side. Two of these intellectuals, as we know from *Letter 7*, were the Pythagoreans Archytas and Archedemus; Aristippus was still there, and possibly Aeschines, but we do not know the names of the others.[29] In *Letter 7*, written some years later, Plato had this to say:[30]

> It seems that after this Archytas arrived in Dionysius's court . . . and that there were other people in Syracuse who had learned this and that from Dion, and yet others who had learned from them. Their minds were stuffed with misconceptions as regards philosophy. They were apparently trying to engage Dionysius in discussions about philosophical topics, on the assumption that he had been thoroughly instructed in my views.

Dionysius, however, was aware that he had hardly been instructed at all by Plato, but the glimpses that he was receiving from Archytas and others made him want more. Or at least they made him want to crown his court with the philosopher whom all the others considered the greatest. So at the end of 363 he invited Plato to return to Syracuse. He had said that he would send for him again when the war was over, and it was now over. Dion, too, as well as Plato, had been receiving reports about Dionysius's renewed interest in philosophy, and he urged Plato to go—not least because he knew that if anyone could

secure his return to Syracuse, Plato could. But Plato refused, implaus-
ibly pleading old age.

In 361, Dionysius tried again:[31]

> On this occasion, Dionysius sent me a trireme to ease the journey, and
> he also sent a few of my Sicilian acquaintances, including Archedemus,
> one of Archytas's associates, because he reckoned that I valued him
> more highly than anyone else in Sicily. All these people told me the
> same thing, that Dionysius was making wonderful progress with regard
> to philosophy. Knowing how I felt about Dion, and knowing of Dion's
> desire that I should make the voyage to Syracuse, Dionysius wrote me
> a very long letter [promising to settle things with Dion according to
> my wishes, with the threat that if I refused to come, the rift with Dion
> would remain]. Other letters kept coming to me from Archytas and
> from people in Taras,[32] commending Dionysius's knowledge of phil-
> osophy and saying that if I didn't come now, I would wreck the friend-
> ship I had brought about between them and Dionysius, which was of
> no slight political importance.
>
> So my summons to Sicily at that time was like this: people in Sicily
> and Italy were pulling me, and people in Athens were more or less lit-
> erally pushing me out with their entreaties. Under these circumstances,
> the same consideration occurred to me as before, that I ought not to
> let Dion down or my friends and companions in Taras. And another
> thought that came to mind was that it wouldn't be at all surprising if
> an intelligent young man, on hearing some discussion of worthwhile
> matters, were to be seized by the desire to perfect his life. I felt that I was
> therefore obliged to test the situation, to find out for certain on which
> side the truth lay, and I thought that I should on no account leave
> him unaided in this regard or expose myself to the blame that I would
> rightly incur if what people were telling me about Dionysius were
> true. I set out, therefore, cloaked with this reasoning, even though I had
> many fears and, naturally, anticipated no particularly favorable outcome.

Plato left Heraclides of Pontus in charge of the Academy and took
two Academicians with him. Helicon of Cyzicus was one of them, and
while he was there, he foretold a coming solar eclipse, allowing us to

31. *Letter 7* 339a–340a. There is also a summary of the third visit to Syracuse in *Letter 3*
    317a–319c.
32. According to Plutarch, *Life of Dion* 18.5, they had been manipulated by Dionysius
    into writing these letters.

know that Plato and his companions were in Syracuse on May 12, 361. The other Academician who accompanied Plato was Speusippus.[33] Dionysius greeted them effusively, though the story that Plato alone was admitted into the tyrant's presence without being searched seems unlikely, especially given Plato's closeness to Dion and the habitual paranoia of tyrants.[34]

The first thing he did on arrival, Plato continues in *Letter 7*, was test Dionysius to see whether he was truly on fire with philosophy. Plato explained to Dionysius what was involved in becoming a philosopher by outlining the fundamental tenets and principles of his philosophy and by showing how arduous the work was that was required to realize them. In other words, he outlined the curriculum of the Academy. He stressed in particular what Dionysius would have to give up in order to reform his character, which was the necessary starting point. The premise of this test was that the prospect of hard work will arouse enthusiasm in someone who genuinely yearns to become a philosopher but will put off others. He also pointed out that Dionysius would need to subject himself to a teacher—Plato himself, in the first instance—"until he had reached the end of the journey or had become capable of doing without a guide and finding the way on his own." That would be hard for someone used to wielding power over others—and would fuel other courtiers' fears that Dionysius's interest in philosophy would leave them out in the cold.

Dionysius spectacularly failed the test: there was no way that he was going to change. He arrogantly thought that, in the interval between his first invitation to Plato and Plato's arrival a couple of years later, he had gained enough from Archytas and the others who had been instructing him. In fact, Plato tells us, Dionysius later even wrote a handbook of Platonism. Throughout the dialogues, Plato has Socrates make his interlocutors feel ashamed of their ignorance, wielding

---

33. An anecdote told by Aelian, *Historical Miscellany* 7.17, has Eudoxus in Syracuse as well, but only for a short time, to visit Plato.
34. Plutarch, *Life of Dion* 19.3; Aelian, *Historical Miscellany* 4.18.

shame like a lever to prize open a crack in their psychological de-
fenses; but Dionysius had no sense of shame. At any rate, he recognized no need of further instruction, and Plato gave up trying to
instruct him, realizing that all the tyrant wanted was a reputation as
a philosopher, not actually to be one. His philosophy was no more
than skin deep, like a suntan.[35] No further preambles to prospective
laws, designed to reform Syracuse, were written; no further attempts
were made to see whether he might come to desire the philosophic
life; no further talks about responsible leadership took place. Instead,
on those occasions when Plato had an audience with the tyrant, he
focused on trying to reconcile Dion and Dionysius, even though it
was already clear that Dionysius had no intention of allowing Dion
back to Syracuse as he had promised. By now Plato surely knew that
Dion was at least tempted by the idea of overthrowing the tyrant, and
his attempt to reconcile the two men was an attempt to prevent civil
war in Syracuse.

The relationship further soured when Plato found out that Dionysius
had stopped sending Dion the money that was due to him from his
estates. Dionysius claimed to be keeping the money for Dion's son
Hipparinus, who was his nephew and, with Dion banished, his ward.
Plato was angry—with himself for having been sucked in once again,
with Dionysius, and with Archytas and the rest for giving Dionysius
the idea that Platonism was a matter of doctrine alone, rather than
being based on the reformation of character. As on his previous visit
to Dionysius, Plato felt himself to be a prisoner in the castle. He asked
to be allowed to leave immediately. Dionysius delayed him by suggesting a compromise: he would continue to let Dion have his money
provided Plato personally, or someone he trusted, was responsible for
doling it out to Dion and for making sure that it was never enough
for Dion to use against him, by raising an army, for instance. He asked
Plato to stay until the following year on these conditions.

---

35. *Letter 7* 340d.

Throughout this visit, Dionysius seems to have been toying with Plato, and this in particular was a clever move, because it put Plato, who was very loyal to his friends, in a quandary. If he accepted the bargain, it would make him Dion's minder and Dionysius's lackey; if he refused, Dion's funds would be cut off, Dionysius and others could plausibly make out that Plato was to blame, his relationship with Dion would be severely jeopardized, and there would be a risk of civil war in Syracuse. Dionysius's outmaneuvering of Plato perhaps reveals a certain naiveté or unworldliness in the philosopher's character.

The next day Plato went to Dionysius and told him he would accept the bargain and stay on, but only if Dion himself agreed to the financial arrangements Dionysius was proposing. But the letter to Dion was never sent because behind Plato's back, Dionysius next sold all of Dion's estates and property. Before long the rift was complete. Dionysius banished Plato from the citadel, and he went to stay with his friend Archedemus. That was doubtless congenial to him, but since there were elements in Syracuse who were hostile to him, he was more vulnerable outside the citadel. He certainly felt his life to be in danger. Philodemus of Gadara says that Plato was suspected of conspiring with Dion with the aim of assassinating Dionysius, and that was why his life was threatened; this is supported by Plutarch's assertion that Speusippus had been sounding out people in Syracuse to see how much sympathy a coup by Dion might encounter. Plato was fearful that a hit squad of Dionysius's mercenaries would be sent for him;[36] this is what it is like to live under a tyrant. The fear was compounded by the fact that Plato was on good terms with a man called Heraclides, an associate of Dion's whom the mercenaries blamed for an attempt to slash their pay. Nor did it help that Dionysius thought—rightly, as events would prove—that Heraclides was a prominent member of Dion's conspiracy against him.

---

36. Philodemus, *Index Academicorum* col. X, 35–43; Plutarch, *Life of Dion* 22.1–2; Plato, *Letter 7* 350a.

Plato badly needed to get out of Syracuse. He wrote to Archytas
to get him to intercede with Dionysius on Plato's behalf. Archytas
sent a man called Lamiscus to Syracuse, making out that this was just
a regular diplomatic visit; Lamiscus successfully interceded on Plato's
behalf, no doubt subtly twisting Dionysius's arm by pointing out how
important it was that the friendship between Syracuse and Taras remained intact, and Plato left on the Tarentine ship. Dealing with monarchs is a tricky business; at least Plato avoided execution, but not all
philosophical advisers are so lucky: Seneca was forced to commit sui-
cide by the Roman emperor Nero, and Thomas More was executed
by King Henry VIII of England.

There is a nice story, too good to be true, that as Plato was getting
ready to leave, Dionysius said to him, "I suppose you'll have plenty
of bad things to say about me to your fellow philosophers." Plato
replied with a smile, "God forbid that we should have such a scar-
city of things to talk about in the Academy that we would mention
your name at all."[37] Presumably Speusippus and Helicon traveled with
Plato, if they had not already left. Plato probably stayed in Taras for
a while to relax and recover. It was perhaps while he was there that
he heard that Dionysius had remarried Dion's wife, Arete, to another
man, one of his supporters whom he wanted to bind more closely to
the royal family. The third visit to Syracuse had been a complete and
utter failure, and Plato's hands-on engagement with practical politics
came to a bitter end.[38]

We have no way of knowing what people back in Athens thought
of his interventions in Syracuse. Did his failure cause a dip in his
reputation? Did his fellow Athenians, who lived under a democratic

---

37. The story was commonly retold, among others that are supposed to illustrate Plato's
blunt candor: Riginos, *Platonica* 79–83. Diogenes Laertius assigns the story to the
elder Dionysius.
38. There is an apocryphal story that the philosopher Martin Heidegger, who was a
member of the Nazi Party, wanted to turn Adolf Hitler into a philosopher king.
When he gave up, he was greeted by a friend with the words, "Hello, Martin. So
you're back from Syracuse."

constitution, think badly of him for working with a monarch? But the Athenians always seem to have let Plato get on with his work and to have tolerated it, even though he was explicitly perpetuating the work of Socrates, who was killed by the democracy, and even though anyone reading Plato's books knew how hostile he was toward democracy. They did not see a theoretician as a practical threat, and Plato returned to his quiet, scholarly life in the Academy.

Dion's Coup and Death

It was now the summer of 360. Plato landed on the west coast of the Peloponnese and, since it was an Olympic year, he made straight for Olympia, a few kilometers inland in the district of Elis. Every four years many thousands of Greeks went to Olympia for the festival in honor of Zeus; they ranged from the great and the good, lodging in their costly pavilions, down to ordinary folk sleeping in the open, and people selling food and drink to the crowds—or snatching their purses. They were there to watch the best athletes in the Greek world compete, but far more went on than that. There were sacrifices and feasting, political and diplomatic announcements, lectures by philosophers and scientists, display speeches by orators, various entertainments, a commercial fair. It was rightly considered the most glorious panhellenic meeting. Visitors and competitors came from all over the Greek world—from Sicily and southern Italy, from mainland Greece, and from Asia Minor—so it was also an occasion to form international relationships and shape foreign policy.

There is a nice anecdote about Plato at Olympia, though it is not clear that it stems from this visit to the festival; it would not be surprising if he had gone on other occasions as well. He was chatting with a group of strangers and introduced himself only as "Plato" (which, as we have seen, was a common enough name). Later, these new friends of his paid him a visit in Athens and asked to be shown the way to the Academy because they wanted to meet Plato the famous philosopher.

At this point Plato revealed his full identity.[39] Be that as it may, on the occasion in question, Plato met Dion there, probably by arrangement, and updated him on the news from Syracuse. It may be that Dion had not yet heard about the forced remarriage of his wife. Calling on Zeus as his witness, Plato tells us,[40]

> he immediately ordered me, my family, and my friends to prepare ourselves for vengeance on Dionysius. He assumed that we would want vengeance for Dionysius's breach of hospitality . . . just as he did for his unjust banishment and exile. When I heard this, I told him that he could ask my friends if they wanted to help him, "but as for me," I said, "you and the others forced me, in a sense, to share Dionysius's table, hearth, and religious rites. And although he might have believed all the malicious tales that were circulating about me, that I was plotting against him and his tyranny, he still didn't put me to death, but held back from doing so. Besides, I'm rather too old now to help anyone make war, though I'm with you both if you should ever need to be reconciled with one another and want to do something positive. But as long as you desire to do evil, you should look elsewhere for help."

So Plato returned to Athens and Dion began to prepare for war. The meeting at Olympia may have been the last time the two men met. Dion was encouraged by Speusippus, who told him that he had met with a favorable response when he had tested the waters in Syracuse. Dion was not planning to return to Greece, so he gave his estate outside Athens to Speusippus; we have no idea what happened to his estate in the Peloponnese, if it was not just rented. Heraclides arrived from Syracuse. Mercenaries were enrolled and encamped on the island of Zacynthos; extra arms and armor were forged; a professional seer called Miltas, who had studied in the Academy, was recruited (no military expedition was complete without someone to study and interpret the sacrifices for good and bad omens); Eudemus, a friend of Aristotle's and an exile from Cyprus, volunteered, as did others, including some Syracusans who had been sent into exile by

39. Aelian, *Historical Miscellany* 4.9–13.
40. *Letter* 7 350b–d.

Dionysius; Callippus, the man with whom Dion had been staying in Athens, also went along. But in the end Dion had a fighting force of only eight hundred men, and he was going up against one of the most powerful cities in the Mediterranean. Nevertheless, he was successful.[41]

> Dion, the son of Hipparinus, returned to Sicily to overthrow Dionysius' tyranny, and to everyone's surprise, given that no one had ever had more meager resources, he succeeded in overthrowing the greatest power in Europe. Who could have believed it? He landed with only two transport ships, and overcame a tyrant who had four hundred warships and an army of about a hundred thousand foot and ten thousand horse, and who had stockpiled all the weaponry, grain, and money that he was likely to need in order to supply these forces handsomely—a tyrant, moreover, who ruled the greatest of the Greek cities, who controlled harbors, dockyards, and unassailable citadels, and who had a great many powerful allies. The factors contributing to Dion's success were above all his noble spirit, his courage, and the support of his fellow freedom-fighters, but more important than all of these were the cowardice of the tyrant and the loathing his subjects felt for him. It was the conjunction of all these factors at a single critical moment that made it possible for Dion to succeed, contrary to expectations, where success had been considered impossible.

Dion sailed for Sicily in 357—on August 10, to be precise, the day after a recorded lunar eclipse. Rather than hug the coast, as was normal in those days for reasons of safety, he chose to sail from Zacynthos across the open sea because he knew that Philistus was lying in wait for him in southeast Italy. He disembarked at Heraclea Minoa, in the southwest of the island. As he marched toward Syracuse, several thousand more from various Syracusan cities joined him; Dionysius's empire was beginning to crumble. When Dion reached Syracuse itself, the citizens made him welcome, just as Speusippus had predicted. Dion had brought plenty of equipment from Greece, and he armed

---

41. The breathtaking, violent events, worthy of a major motion picture, are told at considerable length by Plutarch in his *Life of Dion*. Much of his account is based on that of Timonides, who sailed with Dion and was therefore an eyewitness, even if a biased one. For more details, see the accounts of the historian Diodorus of Sicily, from whom the following paragraph is extracted (*The Library* 16.9).

Figure 7.2 A half-drachma coin issued during the brief rule of Syracuse by Plato's friend Dion. The head is that of Zeus the Giver of Freedom, because Dion felt he had liberated Syracuse from tyranny.
Credit: Photo by Classical Numismatic Group, LLC. http://www.cngcoins.com/

the Syracusans; the paranoid tyrant had made the possession of weaponry by ordinary citizens illegal. Dionysius's troops were, however, safe on Ortygia, behind their formidable defensive walls. Before long, they were joined by Dionysius himself, who had been in the toe of Italy when he was recalled by the news of Dion's arrival. Dion's numbers were swelled when Heraclides arrived from Greece with further recruits, but so were Dionysius's when Philistus returned from southeast Italy. After victories and defeats on both sides, Heraclides won a major sea battle, in which Philistus lost his life, and Dionysius stealthily fled, leaving his troops on Ortygia under the command of his son, Apollocrates.

Eventually, however, Dion managed to force the surrender of the citadel, and Apollocrates sailed away to join his father in Locri, in southern Italy. Great power was at stake—effectively the control of Sicily, rich in agricultural products and timber—and bitter rivalry broke out among the leading rebels. Heraclides, for instance, was now heading up a populist movement, and Dion acquiesced in his murder. Eventually Dion became supreme in Syracuse. He could have made himself tyrant, and it was widely believed that this was his aim, but that was perhaps only because the Syracusans were accustomed to tyrants. For, according to Plutarch, he was planning to reform the constitution and make it the blend of democracy and monarchy that Plato and he had earlier wanted to create. Dion was still trying to see Plato's agenda through to completion.[42] But Callippus, who had assumed leadership of the democrats since Heraclides's death, had Dion murdered in 354.

Callippus himself soon lost Syracuse and his life, and the city descended into chaos for the next decade. The chaos included the return of Dionysius as tyrant for a couple of years before he was finally banished to Corinth in Greece, where he died in 343 in considerably reduced circumstances. Since Plato died in 347, he did not live to see the restoration of Syracuse and Greek Sicily by Timoleon of Corinth in the late 340s and early 330s and never knew that Timoleon turned Syracuse into a democracy. It did not last long, but Timoleon showed that the reformation of Syracuse was a possibility—at any rate, provided it was pushed through by military means.

Plato's Reaction

What did Plato make of all this? *Letter 7* was written to Dion's friends not long after their leader had been assassinated and is in effect Plato's response to questions that must have been on their minds. Why had Plato not left Syracuse after Dion's banishment? Why had he returned in 361? Why had he not done more to reconcile Dionysius and Dion, and secure Dion's restoration? Why did he stay in Syracuse after Dionysius had stolen Dion's property? It almost looked as though Plato had betrayed Dion. These were publicly known events, and Plato's letter supplies readers with the inside story that explains them.

42. *Laws* 756e–757a.

In the letter[43] he says that he considers himself to be indirectly responsible for the whole mess because it was he who, on his first visit to
Syracuse, when Dionysius I was on the throne, had converted Dion to
the cause of virtue. This is a rather odd thing to say, and I suspect that it
is deliberately disingenuous. For in fact Plato did have a greater share
in responsibility for Dion's coup, or at least for its success, than he admits in *Letter 7*. *Letter 3* was written sometime between 358 and 356.[44]
It is an open letter in which he rebukes Dionysius II and justifies
himself in the face of certain charges the tyrant, probably influenced
by Philistus, had published against him. But by doing this, given the
date at which the letter was written, he was almost overtly encouraging
the friends of Dion in Syracuse by stirring up indignation against
Dionysius. All the wrongs of Dionysius's rule are laid by Plato at the
door of Dionysius himself—and, it is implied, they need to be put
right by someone. Dion's supporters would have taken heart from the
fact that the greatest thinker of the age was on their side.

Plato says that he loathed bloodshed and therefore approved of
Dion's original intention to try to reform Dionysius and Syracuse
while avoiding violent revolution. Even after it became clear that
trying to reform Dionysius was flogging a dead horse, he was still
sympathetic to Dion's aim of replacing Dionysius with himself, on
the grounds that Dion would use his position to do good to the
city by creating a just constitution and an equitable legal code. So
he approved of the end but not the means that it became necessary
to use: as we have just seen, he considered Dion's making war on
Dionysius an "evil." Plato was, of course, saddened by Dion's murder
and pays him a poignant tribute, but he concludes that Dion was
a poor judge of character and in particular put too much trust in
Callippus and Hippothales, who murdered him. Nevertheless, Plato
wrote this stirring epitaph: "It is altogether right and honorable for

43. *Letter 7* 326e–327a and passim.
44. It must have been written around then, because 315d–e makes it plain that Dionysius
    was already aware of Dion's intention to depose him.

anyone who aims at what is best for himself and his community to suffer whatever he turns out to suffer."[45]

Plato probably approved and disapproved of Dion's coup to the same degree as he did the coups of other Academicians such as Python of Aenus and Chion of Heraclea. Dion's coup was merely on a larger and more world-changing scale, given the importance of Syracuse. It would not be right to say that the affair was a blot on Plato's reputation because he tried his best under difficult circumstances. But the idea of imbuing Dionysius with enough philosophy to get him to agree to reform Syracuse does suggest a certain naiveté and lack of judgment. Plato allowed his affection for Dion and his adherence to Socratic political thought to tempt him with the idea of making a significant and lasting difference in the real world.

45. *Letter 7* 334e.

8

Last Years

There is a unique suggestion of a fourth overseas journey by Plato, to southern Italy in 349 BCE. Writing in the first century BCE, Cicero, in his work *On Old Age*, has his character Cato say:[1]

> Nearchus of Tarentum . . . told me of the tradition that Archytas put forward these views [against hedonism] in the presence of Gaius Pontius, the Samnite . . . Indeed, he said that Plato of Athens was present at the conversation, and I have verified that Plato did come to Tarentum in the year of the consulship of Lucius Camillus and Appius Claudius.

The story is suspect because of the anecdotal tradition's predilection for linking Plato with thinkers from unusual places. Here he meets "Gaius Pontius, the Samnite," a famous Italian wisdom teacher whose first language was Oscan, not Latin (and whose son would humiliate the Romans at the Caudine Forks in 321). But the story is not impossible. Plato would have been seventy-five at the time of this journey. That, it is true, makes him elderly, especially by the standards of the day. But seventy-five is not too old to travel if one is fit enough,[2] and the fact that Plato died in 347 says nothing about the state of his health in 349. On balance, however, I think the story is

---

1. Cicero, *On Old Age* 12.41. Cicero employs the usual Roman method for pinpointing years, by the names of the two consuls for that year. There is also a version of the story, though without any mention of Plato, at Plutarch, *Life of Cato the Elder* 2.3; here Nearchus himself, not Archytas, is the antihedonist speaker.
2. Seneca, writing in the first century CE, reports that sea voyages used to exhaust Plato (*Letters* 58.30). But this is probably his invention because he wants to make the point that frugal living can help one recover from exhaustion.

probably fiction, though that leaves us to puzzle over why Cicero, a highly reputable writer, chose to perpetuate it.

Plato and the Followers of Dion

Letter 7 was written late in 353 or early in 352 and Letter 8 later in 352; both are addressed to "the friends and companions of Dion," following Dion's death. So after his return from Syracuse in 360, Plato had kept in touch with Sicilian affairs. Much of the advice he offers in Letter 7 is rather vague. He tells them to avoid tyrannical power and work for the common good of the whole city, to imitate Dion's love for Syracuse and his moderate lifestyle, to try to carry out his plans for Syracuse—that is, to reform the constitution until it was a Platonic blend of monarchy and democracy—and to invite settlers from all over the Greek world to repopulate the devastated Greek cities of Sicily. This program of repopulation was carried through some years later by Timoleon of Corinth.

Letter 8 is far more specific—as it had to be, because conditions were critical. The Carthaginians were encroaching from the west and Dionysius II was based nearby in Locri. Political leaders—tyrants, in effect—came and went in Syracuse and in other Sicilian Greek cities. After Dion's assassination, his friends and followers had fled from Syracuse and had taken over Leontini, less than thirty kilometers northwest of Syracuse. They were inclining to make a figurehead of Dion's son Aretaeus, an infant born after his death to his wife, Arete, whom he had reclaimed on his defeat of Dionysius. They entered into an agreement with Hipparinus, a half-brother of Dionysius II. He was also a nephew of Dion, but he had not embraced Dion's ideals. Nevertheless, they united with Hipparinus against the common enemy and helped him take over Syracuse while Callippus was away with the majority of his troops on a military expedition. Syracuse was seething with factions: not just Dion's friends and those who supported Hipparinus, but the democratic faction that had formerly been led by Heraclides, and those who wanted to restore Dionysius to power. This was the situation when they wrote to Athens for advice; *Letter 8* is Plato's response.

The starting point, Plato insists, must be a set of impartial laws that favors no faction over any other. He recommends inviting fifty senior and responsible men from all over the Greek world to draw up these laws, and he outlines the kind of constitution that he thinks would satisfy all parties. He puts the words into dead Dion's mouth, indicating to Dion's friends that this constitution would have met his approval. Somewhat on the model of the Spartan dyarchy (joint rule by two kings), he suggests a triarchy, three kings: Aretaeus, Hipparinus, and Dionysius. Under the circumstances, this seems a sensible suggestion. The infant Aretaeus would need a guardian or guardians, much as the infant Alexander IV of Macedon did after the death of his father Alexander the Great in 323 (and Macedon had a dyarchy at that time: Alexander IV was joined by his uncle, Philip III).

Plato particularly stresses the point in the case of Dionysius, but all three kings are to be constitutional monarchs, subservient to the laws that the fifty lawmakers will have drawn up. He leaves it for the Syracusans themselves to decide whether the kings will have the authority of the Spartan kings (such as nominal command of armies in the field and certain judicial functions) or more restricted powers.[3] The three kings are to be supreme in ceremonial and religious matters, but "matters of war and peace" are to be decided by thirty-five "guardians of the laws," along with the popular assembly and the council.[4] The kings are not to act as judges in cases involving death or exile because as religious leaders they have to remain unpolluted by blood. Such cases are to be in the hands of the thirty-five, and, as in historical Athens, various other courts are to assess other kinds of case.

---

3. Spartan history demonstrates, however, that even kings with limited powers can use their prestige and their popularity to get their political way.

4. *Letter 8* 356b–357a. The number of the law-guardians is significant because in *Laws* Plato has thirty-seven of them. If *Letter 8* were a forgery, the forger would have made sure not to alter Plato's number.

The kings, the law-guardians (chosen, presumably, by the popular assembly), the council, and the assembled people would check and balance one another, so that no single faction would be able to become
dominant and promote its own interests.

There have been successful triarchies in history, if relatively short-
lived. In the first century BCE, three men acted as guardians of the
Chinese child emperor Zhao until he came of age; the "Three Pashas"
guided the affairs of the Ottoman empire during the First World War.
But given the fraught and rivalrous history of Syracuse, one may
doubt whether Plato's proposal was workable. We cannot know, because it was overtaken by events and never put into effect, nor do
we even know what kind of reception Plato's suggestions received
from Dion's friends and followers. At any rate, it seems that Plato did
not entirely give up on practical politics after his disappointment in
Syracuse; he just resorted to writing rather than face-to-face inter-
vention. But *Letter 8* was, as far as we know, the end of his involvement
in Syracusan affairs.

Laws

Plato's political views continued to evolve and to be influenced by his
experiences in Syracuse. In *Letter 8* Plato merely sketches the constitutional changes he wants to see put in place in Syracuse, but even
so, we can see similarities with some of the proposals of *Laws*. In this
dialogue, the longest and arguably the most ambitious that Plato ever
wrote, he imagines three elderly men—Megillus of Sparta, Cleinias
of Cnossus in Crete, and an "Athenian Visitor" (a patent stand-in for
Plato himself)—constructing in words a city-state, called Magnesia.
The Athenian is called a "visitor" because the dialogue is set in Crete.

What these three come up with is a very detailed, if not quite
comprehensive, imagining of a political community: all the magistrates are enumerated, the sizes of their boards, and their spheres of
operation; the functions of the assembly and council are itemized;

checks and balances are put in place to prevent individuals or groups becoming dominant; the courts and court procedure, penology, the educational system, the city's religion and religious officials—all are described, sometimes in minute detail. It is a theoretical model, but the whole book is written with practical intent, as is shown above all by its frequent borrowings from existing constitutions, especially those of Athens and Sparta. It may not be a blueprint for founding an actual city in the real world, but specific regulations are meant to be implementable, and I have suggested that they acted as models for Academicians in their practical political interventions. The city-state imagined in *Laws* may be a utopia, but it is not a *mere* utopia, one that even the author could not realistically expect to be realized in an approximate form or in part.[5] So it is arguably another manifestation of the realism that Plato's experiences in Syracuse forced upon him.

As we saw, there are as many similarities between the political thought of *Statesman* and *Republic* as there are differences, but the differences are telling and seem to suggest ways in which Plato's dealings with Dionysius II changed his mind about political leadership. And the changes that are outlined in *Statesman* achieve further prominence in *Laws*. Compared not only to *Republic* but also to *Statesman*, there is a far greater emphasis on law in *Laws*. The Age of Cronus, when humans were ruled by gods, is over. Now mortals rule mortals, but since no mortal can be entrusted with unfettered power,[6] obedience to the laws by all the political officers of Magnesia—and even women are eligible for the lower grades of office—is inculcated by a carefully thought out system of education that includes studying the explanatory preambles to the laws. In effect, the entire state of Magnesia is an educational institution. The preambles are meant to be rationally persuasive, but they sometimes descend to sermonizing and even appeals to superstition. We are probably meant to think of the ideal rhetoric

5. Plato expresses doubt that it could be realized in all its details at 745e–746c.
6. Lord Acton was well read in Plato, and it is likely that *Laws* is the source of his most famous saying: "Power tends to corrupt, and absolute power corrupts absolutely." See especially *Laws* 691c–d, 713c, and 875a–d.

of *Phaedrus*, where the kind of speech employed is tailored to the kind of audience. The purpose of the preambles is persuasive, partly to get the general population of Magnesia to accept the laws, and partly to supply them with models of behavior that make up for gaps or deficiencies in the laws.

Magnesia is a highly regulated society, but Plato believed that he was curing some of the great civic ills of his own time: the massive gulf in wealth between the richest and poorest members of society that led to strife and even civil war (in Magnesia, the difference is only 4:1); the lack of a clearly defined law code; the low valuation of education, especially of women; and legislation's lack of focus on the well-being of the citizens. The citizens are to be "voluntary slaves to the laws"[7] because they have been educated to be good people and good citizens, and because they recognize that the laws are designed to promote their interests. The laws here take the place of human leaders in Plato's earlier thoughts on the subject. As in *Statesman*, Plato still believed that the leadership of a wise political expert is best, but in *Laws*, unlike in *Statesman*, he makes it perfectly clear that "such a person is absolutely nowhere to be found, except for a few faint traces."[8] The laws embody reason, the divine element in us, and Plato makes them almost unchangeable. Since law is the embodiment of reason, the rule of law is the closest one can realistically get to the rule of philosophers or ideal statesmen.

The constitution of the imaginary city-state fills out Plato's sketchy remarks in *Letter 8*. It is to be a blend of monarchy and democracy. This might make one think of the constitutional monarchy that Plato and Dion were urging on Dionysius. In *Laws*, however, there is no monarchy as such; the "monarchic" elements of the constitution are to be found in the powers awarded to the senior officers of the state, which would all be in the hands of a king in a true monarchy. Democracy inclines toward excess freedom, while monarchy inclines

7. *Laws* 700a.
8. *Laws* 875d.

toward excess authoritarianism; *Laws* is Plato's attempt to find the mean between the two. The democratic elements ensure the participation and representation of citizens, while the monarchic elements provide the competence to guide the city and all its citizens toward virtue and its concomitant, well-being. Executive power is not in the hands of philosopher rulers, as in *Republic*, but in those of the property-owning citizens of the state. It is distributed among many boards of magistrates, and they check one another, since each board is responsible to some other organ of state, and all officers are liable to interrogation by auditors. These checks and balances ensure the supremacy of law. No officeholder in Magnesia is above the law; none is the expert statesman of *Statesman*.

However, there is one maverick board—the Nocturnal Council, so called because it meets, every day, in the hours between dawn and sunrise. The members of the council (who are co-opted, not chosen by democratic means) are some of the senior officers of the state, but each of the senior members also invites a promising younger citizen, aged between thirty and forty, to attend meetings, to enable him to improve his understanding of the way the state is organized and run. These younger members are to retire from the council when they reach the age of forty and be replaced by others. In this way, there will be a pool of people in the city who are capable of applying, as political leaders, what they learned from their time in the council. We hear again echoes of the Socratic cry that political leaders should be experts.

One of the councilors' jobs is to visit atheists in the prison cells to which they have been condemned for their views and attempt to re-educate them, but their primary function is to discuss Magnesia's laws, with a view to attaining a theoretical understanding of law. In this they are aided by the fact that a number of fifty-year-old citizens of good repute are sent abroad for up to ten years to observe others' laws and institutions, and when they return, they report to the Nocturnal Council. Without some people in the city having this understanding, Plato says, the laws cannot safely endure, but the council's job is also to decide whether any of Magnesia's laws could be improved. As the head of the civic body, the council exists to make sure that changes to the laws are guided by reason, not impulsiveness.[9]

The Nocturnal Council is also to inquire into the nature of virtue because the inculcation of virtue is the overall aim of the laws, as it should be the aim of responsible political leaders. To do their jobs, councilors need to have gone through a program of higher education, including dialectic, metaphysics, theology, psychology (the nature of the soul), arithmetic, geometry, harmonics, and astronomy.[10] This program resembles the one which the philosopher rulers of *Republic* go through (or that of the Academy), but the councilors are, technically, not the rulers of Magnesia. In the event that a law needed changing, they would not make the change themselves; that would be the job of the board of law-guardians, though it would presumably follow the recommendations of the council.[11] Otherwise, it makes little sense for Plato to have described the council as the "anchor" of the city. The councilors wield influence in the city, but they do not rule. They influence events by nurturing and educating the younger councilors who will later hold various offices in the city and because some of their colleagues are already officeholders in the city. Rather than philosopher rulers, the councilors are closer to the political experts of *Statesman*, except that they are not regarded as superior to the laws. Or, from another point of view, they are the Academy of Magnesia—a moral and intellectual advisory aristocracy.

Given the similarities between *Laws* and the political provisions of the three letters—especially the mixed constitution of *Letter 8* and the preambles to the laws of *Letter 3*—it seems safe to say that the city-state of *Laws*, or something like it, is what Plato would have liked to have achieved in Syracuse. It is not the unrealizable ideal of rule by philosophers or flawless statesmen, and Plato therefore calls it a second

---

9. *Laws* 960b–969c.
10. *Laws* 817e–818a, 964d–968e.
11. See *Laws* 770a–b and 772c–d for the tweaking of laws by the law-guardians.

best.[12] Plato always believed that it was possible for people to live well
and flourish under wise leadership; *Republic, Statesman*, and *Laws* represent three attempts to describe how this might be possible, and they
form a sliding scale from utopianism to relative realism. By the time
he wrote *Laws*, he had come to believe that people were not capable
of flourishing on their own, without the rule of law.

The Late Dialogues

In its mundane realism, *Laws* is in many ways different from the rest
of Plato's written works, even from the rest of the dialogues that we
have identified as the "late cluster." These are *Sophist, Statesman, Timaeus,
Critias*, and *Philebus*. They form a mixed bag, and it is not easy to sum-
marize them as a group, as was possible for the early and middle dialogues, but they are united by features of Plato's late style, even if not
so much by their content. Compared with their predecessors, the late
dialogues read almost as if they had come from a different pen. They
are less conversational and more didactic and systematic. The interlocutors scarcely come to life, and they are never responsible for changes of
direction in the conversation, as they are in earlier dialogues. There is
very little scene-setting or characterization. In fact, the main speakers
of *Sophist, Statesman*, and *Laws* are deliberately anonymized: the Eleatic
Visitor in the first two, and the Athenian Visitor in *Laws*. Socratic themes
are still prominent in the late dialogues, but the disappearance of Socrates
as spokesman allows Plato to reappraise ideas proposed by Socrates in
earlier dialogues. It also makes these dialogues virtually timeless, rather
than being set in the fifth century of Socrates's lifetime. Socrates re-
appears as the protagonist in *Philebus*, and although this is the lightest
and most accessible of these later dialogues, Socrates himself has lost the
sparkle that is typical of earlier dialogues.

Almost all of *Timaeus* is a monologue, as is the fifth chapter (or
"book") of *Laws*. Because of Plato's desire to avoid hiatus in these

---

12. *Laws* 739a–e, 807b, 875d. In the first of these two passages, the fictional city of *Laws* is
    expressly compared to the higher ideal of *Republic*; see also *Laws* 807b–c.

late dialogues,[13] the writing is often far more crabbed and difficult. In general, one might call his late style "weighty"—accepting the implication that it is sometimes heavy going. The best explanation for these choices by Plato is that the books were primarily intended to generate discussion within the Academy, rather than to be read by a wider audience. They assume an audience of people who are already steeped in philosophy and who are prepared to work at understanding a text. These dialogues are no longer inquiries into human nature and ways of life; there is scarcely a whisper of the axiom that reformation of character is the foundation of philosophy because this is something the target audience already knows.

We have already looked at the main political aspects of *Statesman*. It shares with its sister dialogue, *Sophist*, an emphasis on methodology, specifically by displaying and making use of what is known as the "method of division." This is a way of arriving at a definition by narrowing the field of search, or, to put it another way, a way of uncovering the structure of reality. The thing to be defined is assigned to its genus, and then the genus is successively divided into species and sub-species. Each division is usually dichotomous, and after each division you ask yourself to which of the two species your quarry belongs and reject the other one. So in *Sophist*, the sophist is assigned to the genus "image-making," which is divided into "likeness-making" and "apparition-making" (that is, the making of what are only apparent likenesses). It is decided that he belongs to "apparition-making," which is itself divided into the making of apparitions with tools or by imitation—and we finally end up with the definition of a sophist as one who makes apparitions by imitation, out of ignorance, and with a lack of sincerity.

As in *Statesman*, there is much more in *Sophist* than the search for a definition of "sophist." Above all, the idea that a sophist makes things seem to be when they are not leads to an important digression on what "what is not" might mean, because the sophist produces something that *is not* but which at the same time really *is* an apparition.

13. See pp. 86–7.

For the first time, Plato sorts out the various meanings that the Greek verb "to be" could have. Another important development is a focus on Forms that are shared by all the various special branches of knowledge, and are not isolated, as middle-period Forms were, but communicate with all other Forms. Typical such Forms are being and non-being (once properly understood), sameness and difference, similarity and dissimilarity, unity and plurality, motion and rest, generation and destruction.[14] These concepts are indeed fundamental for our thinking about almost anything.

Timaeus and *Critias* are best known to the general public for the Atlantis story. The story is sketched in *Timaeus*, and *Critias* would have told it in full, if Plato had not stopped writing the dialogue. Despite its incompleteness, hardly anything else Plato wrote has sparked as much interest, and many books have been written as if the story of an advanced civilization on a now-sunken island in the Atlantic Ocean were true. It is, however, clearly a Platonic invention. There is no trace of the story earlier; Plato was its originator. Although *Timaeus* and *Critias* were written many years later than *Republic*, the conversations are supposed to take place on the day after the conversation of *Republic*, and they show, at Socrates's request, an idealized society (not that of *Republic*, but a fictional, antediluvian Athens) at war against the rapacious Atlantian invaders. Atlantian society, far from being enlightened, has been corrupted by wealth, whereas in Athens the rulers (like the Guardians of *Republic*) have no private property.

Given the unfinished status of *Critias*, some guesswork is involved, but in all likelihood ancient Athens is supposed to remind readers of historical Athens around the start of the fifth century—aristocrats such as Plato found much to admire in Athenian society at that time—and Atlantis is supposed to remind us of Athens at the end of the fifth century, which Plato saw as having been corrupted by personal wealth and radical democracy. The Atlantis story was invented by Plato as a political allegory, but generations of unwary readers have been taken

14. The two main passages on these "common notions" are *Theaetetus* 185a–186b and *Sophist* 254c–259b.

in by a standard device of ancient fiction-writing, stressing the historical accuracy of the fiction that is being created. Thus, for instance, the conversations of Socrates written by Xenophon often start with an affirmation of their historicity such as "I was there when Socrates spoke to so-and-so"—even when there is no way that Xenophon could have been present.

Timaeus is one of Plato's richest and most impressive works (see figure 8.1). It consists largely of an attempt to develop an account,

Figure 8.1 Plato's mathematized conception of the work of the creator god in *Timaeus* is the source of the Christian image of God as a geometer. This picture was the frontispiece of a thirteenth-century French Bible. Codex Vindobonensis 2554, f.1 verso.

both scientific and suggestive, of pretty much everything about our universe—the macrocosm and the microcosm, the visible and the invisible, the divine and the human. Everything about this account is startling and innovative, from its powerful teleological thrust (that is, why it is best that the world and all its parts are as they are) to its specific conceptions of God, the gods, the structure and origin of the universe, and the principles that make it what it is. A rational and benevolent deity imposed mathematical structure on the pre-existent chaos, thus creating a model of orderliness for beings with rational souls (human beings) to emulate. *Timaeus* is noteworthy for the fact that the physical world, treated largely with contempt in earlier dialogues, is now considered to deserve serious study. Plato's conception of Being had been expanded by discussion in the Academy.

God made the universe mathematical: the world soul is structured by musical ratios, and the world body is made up of elementary triangles. It is clear that Plato's interest in Pythagoreanism, boosted during his first visit to southern Italy and Sicily in 384, was still informing his written work.[15] *Timaeus* constitutes an ingenious adaptation of the basic Pythagorean axioms that the universe is mathematical in structure and that mathematical principles are responsible for the beauty and goodness of the world: "The god wanted everything to be good, marred by as little imperfection as possible. He found everything visible in a state of turmoil, moving in a discordant and chaotic manner, so he led it from chaos to order, which he regarded as in all ways better."[16]

The main topic of *Philebus* is familiar from earlier dialogues (hence the reinstatement of Socrates): what constitutes the good life for people, one in which their potential as human beings is fulfilled. One might speculate that it was written as a kind of response to the puzzlement his lecture "On the Good" had met with—that Plato wanted to present a more accessible version of his views on the human good,

---

15. Aristotle wrote a book, now lost, comparing Archytas's work with Plato's *Timaeus*.
16. *Timaeus* 30a.

without bringing mathematics into it. The basic choice presented in the dialogue is between hedonism, taking pleasure to be the good and the cause of human happiness, and intellectualism, ascribing these properties to rationality and knowledge. Not surprisingly, by the end of the dialogue, knowledge has defeated pleasure. Along the way, Plato has the opportunity not just to develop his own theory of what pleasure is and does but also to take note of others' views so that, as I have remarked before, the dialogue serves as a kind of repository of Academic views on pleasure and is to that extent evidently a discussion document.

Plato again employs Pythagorean principles to bring about the victory of knowledge. A "Prometheus" figure is said to have claimed that "while the things that are ever said to exist consist of a one and many, yet they also innately have within themselves limit and unlimitedness."[17] The Prometheus figure is therefore Philolaus of Croton, the most important Pythagorean theoretician after Pythagoras himself. Philolaus asserted, in the dogmatic way that was typical of fifth-century philosophy, that the world as a whole and everything in it were made out of "limiters" and "unlimiteds." In *Philebus*, Plato argues that nothing good can come from things that are unlimited; they need to have determinacy imposed on them by a limiter. Knowledge is assigned to the class of things that are limited, and pleasure to the class of things that are unlimited. Plato's final words on the good life and what constitutes human well-being are a sophisticated development of his earlier thoughts.

Death and Heroization

Plato died in 347, aged about seventy-six. We do not know the time of year: in chapter 1, I rejected the fanciful idea that he died on his

17. *Philebus* 16a. Prometheus was a Titan (a member of an earlier race of deities than the Olympian gods) who defied Zeus and gave fire to humankind, thus launching human civilization.

birthday—as if we could be sure of the date of his birthday. Nor
do we know what he died of, though the earliest of the surviving
biographies reports that he had had a fever for a few days before his
death.[18] If anything more dramatic had occurred, we would probably have heard of it. Nevertheless, the biographical tradition invented
some odd circumstances for his death, such as that he died at a wed-
ding feast, or of an infestation of lice. A less suspect tradition has him
working, his mind still active, right up to his death; hence perhaps the
tradition that he died because he would not be confined to his bed
by his fever. He died "pen in hand," and after his death, a tablet was
discovered on which he had been writing several different versions
of the opening sentence of *Republic*.[19] He spent some of his last days
in the company of a visiting "Chaldaean"—that is, a Mesopotamian
astrologer—who seems to have tried to heal him by means of music.[20]

Plato had seen Athens and Greece go through many changes. While
he was growing up, his native city was arguably the greatest in the
Greek world—but then it was defeated by Sparta in the Peloponnesian
War. Despite the attempts of the Athenians and their allies to topple
Sparta from its dominance in the Corinthian War (in which Plato
probably fought), Spartan ascendancy lasted more than thirty years,
until the Spartans were finally humbled by Thebes at the battle of
Leuctra in 371. Theban ascendancy lasted only ten years, and then the
major states of the Greek mainland returned to an uneasy standoff.
But the handwriting was on the wall for the freedom of the Greeks. A
new power was growing in the north: Macedon under Philip II. Philip
came to the throne in 359, and once he had consolidated Macedon, he
began to take over the Greek cities of the northern Aegean and claim
them for the nation-state he was constructing. Several of these Greek
cities were Athenian possessions or former allies, and in 357 Athens
declared war on Macedon. This was largely a cold war; nothing much
happened, and nothing had been resolved at the time of Plato's death.

18. Philodemus, *Index Academicorum* col. III.42.
19. Cicero, *On Old Age* 5.13, 7.23; Dionysius of Halicarnassus, *On Literary Composition* 25.
20. Philodemus, *Index Academicorum* col. III.40—V.18.

For Plato's successors, Philip was the new great power with which they had to reckon.

In the field of literature, Plato had seen the freedom of Old Comedy give way to the gentler humor of Middle Comedy, and lived through the end of the great age of Athenian tragedy. He must have read Thucydides's monumental, unfinished history of the Peloponnesian War, and its continuations by Xenophon, Theopompus, and Cratippus. He had familiarized himself with the technical treatises that were being composed in many fields, especially medicine. He had viewed with alarm the rise of professional oratory, and he had seen and overseen the rise of professional philosophy by himself, his fellow Socratics, and the scholars of the Academy.

The travel writer Pausanias, who had seen Plato's tomb (or what remained of it in his day, the second century CE), says that it was "not far from the Academy [park]," but Diogenes Laertius says that it was "in the Academy," meaning the grounds of the Academy school. Diogenes's account is confirmed by fragmentary Philodemus, who says that the tomb was near the shrine of the Muses in the garden of Plato's school.[21] The tomb was adorned with an eagle and a statue of Plato, which in one account was dedicated by a visiting sage from Central Asia.[22] The funeral procession was apparently well attended by ordinary Athenians.[23] They recognized that a good measure of the fame of their city in the fourth century was owed to its tolerance of philosophers and other intellectuals, and Plato, a native son, was the most famous philosopher in the Greek world. Athens had finally shed the illusion of itself as a military power and was beginning its long drift toward becoming a "university town."

---

21. Pausanias, *Guide to Greece* 1.30.3; Diogenes Laertius, *Lives of the Eminent Philosophers* 3.40; Philodemus, *Index Academicorum* col. II.31–33.

22. Diogenes Laertius, *Lives of the Eminent Philosophers* 3.25. The eagle is an inference from the fact that one of the alleged epitaphs (see below) starts as follows: "Eagle, why have you landed on this tomb?"

23. Diogenes Laertius, *Lives of the Eminent Philosophers* 3.41; Olympiodorus, *Commentary on Plato's Alcibiades* 2.164.

The tomb was also adorned with a poetic epitaph. Half a dozen epitaphs claiming to be the original have been preserved in anthologies and biographies. They share two common motifs. The first is that the god Apollo had two significant children: Asclepius, the healer of human bodies, and Plato, the healer of human souls. The second is the dualistic contrast between the earthly location of Plato's body and the heavenly location of his soul.

The majority of the epigrams are certainly inauthentic; they were not inscribed on Plato's tomb but are later, literary compositions. As we found earlier for the epigrams ascribed to the youthful Plato,[24] they bear all the hallmarks of composition in the third century or later. The inauthenticity of one of them, the first quoted by Diogenes Laertius, is further demonstrated by the fact that it calls Plato "Aristocles," which, as we found, was never his name. The epitaph with the best claim to authenticity is the two-liner ascribed, almost certainly falsely, to Speusippus:[25]

> Although Earth here holds in her bosom the body of Plato,
> His soul is in the rank of the blessed, equal to that of the gods.

After Plato's death, he became the object of a hero cult—as, possibly, Socrates was within the Academy. Certainly, a statue of Socrates was consecrated in the Academy. A hero, in the technical Greek religious sense, was a mortal who, after his death, was regarded as having been so especially favored by the gods that he was effectively more than human. Typical heroes were founders of cities or particularly successful athletes—or people, like Plato, whose achievements were extraordinary. On the anniversary of his birth or death (which in Plato's case were taken to be the same day), Plato was honored as the founder of the Academy and its way of life, and as the offspring of Apollo. Libations would have regularly been poured at his tomb, and on the anniversary more elaborate rituals took place. An animal sacrifice was

24. See pp. 21–3.
25. With some variations, it also forms the first two lines of the second epitaph quoted by Diogenes Laertius.

performed at the tomb, and prayers of thanks were offered to the gods for his life and achievements. Probably a modest feast took place, with the meat of the sacrifice shared among those present; perhaps some of his work was read out. The purpose was to gain his goodwill and to foster a sense of community among the worshippers. And so Plato lived on, not just through the dialogues and the school that he left to posterity but also in the hearts and minds of those who called themselves Platonists, as one who was utterly dedicated to the quest for truth and knowledge.

The Academy after Plato's Death

Speusippus was chosen to be the next head of the Academy. We think of Aristotle as the best of the younger generation in the Academy, but there is no reason to think that Plato and the other scholars thought the same. The loss of Speusippus's work and the survival of much of Aristotle's inevitably skews our perception. Besides, Speusippus was about sixty years old, while Aristotle was only thirty-seven, and Speusippus, with his deep interest in mathematics, was more embedded in the heart of the Academy than was Aristotle, who had little interest or ability in the subject. And, of course, Speusippus was Plato's nephew. Plato had probably chosen Speusippus as his successor before his death because Philodemus tells us that he "took over from Plato himself the directorship of the school."[26]

After Plato's death, both Aristotle and Xenocrates left Athens together and went to Atarneus in northwestern Asia Minor. Did they leave in a huff because of Speusippus's appointment? This seems unlikely in the case of Xenocrates, who became head of the school upon Speusippus's death in 339, but there is a tradition that Aristotle

26. Philodemus, *Index Academicorum* col. VI.28–30. After Speusippus's death, Xenocrates was chosen by the junior scholars. In the subsequent history of the Academy, scholarchs might be appointed either by election or by the personal choice of the outgoing head.

had "broken off with Plato" shortly before Plato's death. Anecdotes about Aristotle's relationship with Plato go both ways, some implying mutual esteem, others hinting at friction. A combination of the two—both esteem *and* friction—seems quite possible. Aristotle himself, when he is about to launch into a critical discussion of the idea that there is a universal Good, says that an obstacle is that "those who introduced the Forms are friends of mine."[27] And if the poetic "Elegy to Eudemus" was written by Aristotle, as it may well have been, it contains praise of Plato as "a man who proved clearly, the only or the first to do so, by his own life and by his philosophy, that a person's happiness and goodness are inseparable."[28]

Plato had presumably made his will known in this matter sometime before his death, so perhaps Aristotle was miffed at being passed over for the headship and that was the occasion of the rift. The same thing happened when Xenocrates was chosen as head of the school in 339/8. Heraclides of Pontus and Menedemus of Pyrrha were the runners-up, and this was when Heraclides returned to his native city of Heraclea Pontica, and Menedemus started his own school in the Academy gymnasium. Although Aristotle eventually returned to Athens in 335, he never returned to the Academy but instead founded his own school. Yet grief rather than resentment might have been the reason for his and Xenocrates's departure. For thirty-five years, Plato had been the lodestar of the Academy, and upon his death there was a real danger of the school fragmenting. Aristotle may have felt that without Plato the Academy was no longer an attractive place for him to work. Besides, his philosophical principles had already departed fundamentally from those of Plato and other Academicians. It was time for him to set up on his own.

---

27. Aristotle, *Nicomachean Ethics* 1096a13. Aristotle immediately goes on to say, in paraphrase, "I am a friend of Plato, but a greater friend of truth." For the anecdotes, see Riginos, *Platonica* 129–134. The tradition of a rift between the two is recorded by Diogenes Laertius, *Lives of the Eminent Philosophers* 5.2.
28. Aristotle, Fragment 673 Rose.

But, thanks in the first instance to the authority and fundraising abilities of Speusippus, the Academy did not fall apart. Scholarch succeeded scholarch in an orderly progression, and the school continued for more than 250 years in the same premises, the Academy gymnasium; Polemo, who died in 269, was the last to use Plato's house as a school. In the year 307/6 the Athenians passed a law that no philosopher should be allowed to run a school in Athens without permission from the government. Some philosophers left Athens, but it is unlikely that there was a hiatus in the activities of the Academy. It seems to have continued despite the fact that the proposer of the law, a certain Sophocles, had singled out some of the Academicians' undemocratic political activities as proving the undesirability of the institution. In any case, the law was repealed after only a few months.

In 200 BCE the troops of Philip V of Macedon badly damaged the park. In 86, troops under the Roman general Lucius Cornelius Sulla inflicted more serious damage during the siege of Athens, which had foolishly chosen to side with Mithridates VI of Pontus in his attempt to drive the Romans altogether out of Asia Minor and the eastern Mediterranean. The sources speak only of Sulla's men chopping down trees in the Academy park with which to make siege engines, but since (as far as we can tell) no further teaching went on in the Academy afterward, the destruction may have been more thorough, or at least enough to make the park a depressing place to teach and study. The Lyceum gymnasium was also destroyed at the same time. Academic teaching moved into the city of Athens, and Platonism was being studied elsewhere in the Mediterranean as well, especially in Alexandria in Egypt, now the center of Greek culture. Even after the loss of the physical school, philosophers in Athens continued to identify and teach as Platonists and "Academics," and in 176 CE the philosophically inclined Roman emperor Marcus Aurelius, author of the work known to us as *Meditations*, established Imperial Chairs in Athens for the teaching of the four main philosophical traditions: Platonism, Aristotelianism, Stoicism, and Epicureanism.

So versions of Plato's ideas persisted, perpetuated often through the writing of learned commentaries on the dialogues. Two main trends emerged. For almost two hundred years from the middle of the third century BCE, Academicians stressed the questioning aspect of the dialogues, which is especially prominent in the early dialogues, and the difficulty of pinning down what might count as Platonic doctrine. They held that the dialogues were skeptical works, and that philosophers should doubt whether the truth can ever be found on any topic and should question others' opinions rather than commit themselves to views of their own. Then, after the destruction of the Academy, the thinkers scholars today called "Middle Platonists" and "Neoplatonists" reverted to the position that the dialogues contained positive doctrine.

In the late fourth century CE, a Platonist called Plutarch of Athens refounded the physical school, though not in the Academy park. Then in 529 the Christian emperor Justinian made it illegal for non-Christians to teach; they were either to convert to the "true faith" or be sent into exile from their native cities. In Athens, Justinian's target was chiefly the Academy because the Platonism of that era was deeply spiritual, with an inclination toward occultism and magic; it was a direct rival to Christianity. Despite the strength of the Church in Athens, however, the law was not rigidly enforced, and the teaching of Platonism continued in Athens for some decades, presumably in a more muted fashion. But after 529 the Academy was in decline, and by the final quarter of the century, probably as a result of the Slavic sack of Athens in 582, it had ceased to exist.

A Life in Philosophy and a Philosophical Afterlife

What Plato accomplished in his lifetime is astounding, but his achievements extend beyond his lifetime. He started a tradition that has sent ripples down to our own time. The vibrancy of the tradition is not marred but proved by the courses that it took. It was capable of being skeptical in one era and dogmatic in another; it was capable of stimulating thinkers as diverse as Aristotle and Speusippus. Just as Socrates generated about half a dozen lines of work, all of which were authentically Socratic, so his greatest student created a philosophy that was capacious enough to include contradictions and yet remain intact. There surely can be no higher praise for an innovative philosopher. Plato did this by his aloof presence in the Academy, and above all by the multifaceted nature of the dialogues. They are and are not dogmatic; they invite readers in and then compel them to fall back on their own resources; they make everything seem straightforward and then pull the rug out from under their feet. To aid him in this work he invented a character called Socrates, and the homage to his teacher lies precisely in the fact that he is a Platonic invention, a vehicle for perpetuating the work that, on Plato's understanding, Socrates initiated. Other Socratics also made the attempt according to their own understanding of Socrates, but the survival of Plato's work and the loss of theirs tells a tale.

Plato opened up infinite possibilities for the future of philosophy—not just for academic philosophers but for any of us who think and who care about what we are and what we may become, as individuals and as the human species. For anyone who strives to value knowledge over belief and to practice critical thinking rather than blind acceptance, who knows that there is more to the world than meets the eye, who thinks that virtue is not just a stuffy Victorian value and is prepared not just to sweep that insight under the rug but let it alter their world forever, however difficult and unpopular that may be—for all these people, Plato's life is a paradigm and his instruction deeply rewarding.

Philosophy addresses the big questions: What is the meaning of life? What is consciousness? What is the best form of government? What is goodness? What is truth? Should we trust our reasoning capacity? Do we have free will? And a host of other questions. Human beings are naturally endowed with curiosity, and philosophy is the ultimate way of attempting to satisfy curiosity. Philosophy begins in wonder,

as Plato said.[29] If we lose that sense of wonder—if we become im-
mersed in the trivia of everyday life and what passes for popular "culture"—we risk living in a stale universe. Plato's thought has lasted well
because there will always be those who refuse to quell their curiosity.

The particular spin that Plato put on doing philosophy also remains
important. By writing philosophy as conversation, he expressed the
notion that searching for truth is an ongoing quest. Knowledge is possible, but it is just as important to keep looking for it and to doubt that
one has ever found it. Philosophy, as Plato practiced it, trains the mind
and endows one with problem-solving skills; it teaches one to think
clearly, and without clear thinking, we are less likely to be successful
in any of our endeavors. There can hardly be a better introduction to
philosophical thinking than reading Plato's dialogues and reflecting
on both the ideas and the methodology. It does not really matter
whether or not he was "right." Reading the dialogues stimulates one
to think for oneself about philosophical issues.

Plato started practicing philosophy with Socrates and others at an
early age. He found that there was no field of human endeavor where
philosophy could not help. He perpetuated the practice of philosophy
and philosophical principles in everything he did. It is not just that
he wrote stimulating and profound books, but he himself returned
to the murky cave of the real world. After his first failure in Syracuse,
one might think that he would not have returned, but he did, and by
doing so, he left us with a model of dedication to a cause and of how a
philosopher might try to make himself useful in a political context—a
model taken up by recent thinkers such as Bernard Williams. And
he founded the Academy, a school that perpetuated philosophy for
almost a thousand years. Plato's life was truly a life in the service of
philosophy, and that is why his life should still matter to us. The big
questions do not go away.

29. *Theaetetus* 155d.

Further Reading

Since this book is intended to be an introduction to Plato as well as a biography, a reasonably lengthy bibliography is in order to guide readers to further studies. The secondary literature on Plato is vast. What follows is only a small selection of works written in English, but enough to express a range of differing interpretations, including those with which I disagree. Apart from particular works relevant to issues raised in the book, I have chiefly focused on general works, rather than works devoted to single dialogues or issues, and on works suitable for beginners or relative beginners in philosophy and literature. Where I list an edited volume of essays, it may be assumed that at least several of the essays it contains are worth reading, so that I have not separately listed the essays.

TRANSLATIONS OF PLATO

There are many good, recent translations of Plato's works, most of them also annotated and containing useful introductions to the individual dialogues. Many publishers offer such translations, but four stand out: Oxford University Press, for its Oxford World's Classics series and the Clarendon Plato series; Penguin Books, for the Penguin Classics; Cambridge University Press, for Cambridge Texts in the History of Philosophy and Cambridge Texts in the History of Political Thought; and Hackett. I myself have translated sixteen of Plato's dialogues in eleven volumes, for Oxford University Press, Penguin, and Cambridge University Press. Hackett has also issued a single-volume complete works: J. M. Cooper and D. S. Hutchinson (eds.), *Plato: Complete Works* (Hackett, 1997). Readers who want only key passages will find a good selection in T. Chappell, *The Plato Reader* (Edinburgh University Press, 1996).

TRANSLATIONS OF OTHER THINKERS

Presocratics: R. Waterfield, *The First Philosophers: The Presocratics and Sophists* (Oxford University Press, 2000), or J. Barnes, *Early Greek Philosophy* (Penguin, 1987).

Sophists: in addition to Waterfield, *The First Philosophers* (just above), J. Dillon and T. Gergel, *The Greek Sophists* (Penguin, 2003). Ranging wider than just the sophists, but with a narrower focus: M. Gagarin and P. Woodruff, *Early Greek Political Thought from Homer to the Sophists* (Cambridge University Press, 1995).

Socratics: G. Boys-Stones and C. Rowe, *The Circle of Socrates: Readings in the First-Generation Socratics* (Hackett, 2013).

Isocrates: J.D. Mikalson, *The Essential Isocrates* (University of Texas Press, 2022).

TRANSLATIONS OF ANCIENT BIOGRAPHIES OF PLATO

Anonymous: L.G. Westerink, *Anonymous Prolegomena to Platonic Philosophy* (North Holland Publishing, 1962).

Apuleius: R.C. Fowler, *Imperial Plato: Albinus, Maximus, Apuleius* (Parmenides, 2016).

Diogenes Laertius: P. Mensch (trans.) and J. Miller (ed.), *Diogenes Laertius: Lives of the Eminent Philosophers* (Oxford University Press, 2018; compact ed. 2020), or S. White, *Diogenes Laertius: Lives of Eminent Philosophers: An Edited Translation* (Cambridge University Press, 2021).

Hesychius: online audio text: https://archive.org/details/hesychius (posted 2016).

Olympiodorus: M. Griffin, *Olympiodorus:* Life of Plato *and* On Plato, First Alcibiades 1–9 (Bloomsbury, 2015).

Philodemus: P. Kalligas and V. Tsouna, "Philodemus' *History of the Philosophers*: Plato and the Academy (PHerc. 1021 and 164)," in P. Kalligas, C. Balla, E. Baziotopoulou-Valavani, and V. Karasmanis (eds.), *Plato's Academy: Its Workings and Its History* (Cambridge University Press, 2020), 276–383. But the text will be superseded by K. Fleischer, *Philodems Geschichte der Akademie: Edition, Übersetzung, Kommentar* (Brill, 2023).

OTHER MAIN SOURCES FOR PLATO'S LIFE

Plutarch, *Life of Dion*, in I. Scott-Kilvert and T. Duff, *Plutarch: The Age of Alexander* (Penguin, 2011).

Cornelius Nepos, *Life of Dion*, in J.C. Rolfe (ed.), *Cornelius Nepos* (Harvard University Press, 1929). Also available online at www.attalus.org/translate/nepos10.html.

HISTORY AND CULTURE

J. Billings, *The Philosophical Stage: Drama and Dialectic in Classical Athens* (Princeton University Press, 2021).

B. Caven, *Dionysius I: War-Lord of Sicily* (Yale University Press, 1990).

K.J. Dover, *Greek Homosexuality*, new ed., with forewords by S. Halliwell, M. Masterson, and J. Robson (Bloomsbury, 2016).

M. Golden, *Children and Childhood in Classical Athens*, 2nd ed. (Johns Hopkins University Press, 2015).

S. Goldhill, *The Invention of Prose* (Oxford University Press, 2002).

W.V. Harris, *Ancient Literacy* (Harvard University Press, 1989).

M. Joyal, I. McDougall, and J.C. Yardley, *Greek and Roman Education: A Sourcebook* (Routledge, 2009).

C.H. Kahn, "Writing Philosophy: Prose and Poetry from Thales to Plato," in H.Yunis (ed.), *Written Texts and the Rise of Literate Culture in Ancient Greece* (Cambridge University Press, 2003), 139–61.

C. Moore, *Calling Philosophers Names: On the Origin of a Discipline* (Princeton University Press, 2019).

J. Ober, *Political Dissent in Democratic Athens: Intellectual Critics of Popular Rule* (Princeton University Press, 1998).

T.E. Rihll, "Teaching and Learning in Classical Athens," *Greece & Rome* 50 (2003): 168–90.

A. Rubel, *Fear and Loathing in Ancient Athens: Religion and Politics during the Peloponnesian War*, trans. M.Vickers and A. Piftor (Acumen, 2014).

L. Sanders, *The Legend of Dion* (Edgar Kent, 2008).

E. Turner, *Athenian Books in the Fifth and Fourth Centuries* (Lewis, 1952).

R. Waterfield, *Creators, Conquerors, and Citizens: A History of Ancient Greece* (Oxford University Press, 2018).

H. Yunis, *Taming Democracy: Models of Political Rhetoric in Classical Athens* (Cornell University Press, 1996).

THE PRESOCRATICS

P. Curd, "Presocratic Philosophy," in Edward N. Zalta (ed.), Stanford Encyclopedia of Philosophy (Fall 2020 Edition), https://plato.stanford.edu/archives/fall2020/entries/presocratics/.

234 FURTHER READING

G.S. Kirk, J.E. Raven, and M. Schofield, *The Presocratic Philosophers*, 2nd ed. (Cambridge University Press, 1983).

R.D. McKirahan, *Philosophy before Socrates*, 2nd ed. (Hackett, 2010).

J. Warren, *Presocratics* (Acumen; University of California Press, 2007).

PYTHAGOREANISM

G. Cornelli, R. McKirahan, and C. Macris (eds.), *On Pythagoreanism* (De Gruyter, 2013).

C.A. Huffman, *Archytas of Tarentum: Pythagorean, Philosopher and Mathematician King* (Cambridge University Press, 2005).

C.A. Huffman (ed.), *A History of Pythagoreanism* (Cambridge University Press, 2014).

C.H. Kahn, *Pythagoras and the Pythagoreans: A Brief History* (Hackett, 2001).

THE SOPHISTS

M. Bonazzi, *The Sophists* (Cambridge University Press, 2020).

W.K.C. Guthrie, *The Sophists* (Cambridge University Press, 1971) = Part I of *A History of Greek Philosophy*, vol. 3, *The Sophists and Socrates* (Cambridge University Press, 1969).

G.B. Kerferd, *The Sophistic Movement* (Cambridge University Press, 1981).

C. Moore and J. Billings (eds.), *The Cambridge Companion to the Sophists* (Cambridge University Press, 2022).

C.C.W. Taylor, and Mi-Kyoung Lee, "The Sophists," in Edward N. Zalta (ed.), Stanford Encyclopedia of Philosophy (Fall 2020 Edition), https://plato.stanford.edu/archives/fall2020/entries/sophists/.

H. Tell, *Plato's Counterfeit Sophists* (Center for Hellenic Studies, 2011).

SOCRATES

J. Bussanich and N.D. Smith (eds.), *The Bloomsbury Companion to Socrates* (Bloomsbury, 2013).

W.K.C. Guthrie, *Socrates* (Cambridge University Press, 1971) = Part II of *A History of Greek Philosophy*, vol. 3, *The Sophists and Socrates* (Cambridge University Press, 1969).

D.R. Morrison (ed.), *The Cambridge Companion to Socrates* (Cambridge University Press, 2011).

D. Nails, and S. Monoson, "Socrates," in Edward N. Zalta (ed.), Stanford Encyclopedia of Philosophy (Summer 2022 Edition), https://plato.stanford.edu/archives/sum2022/entries/socrates/.

S. Peterson, "Plato's Reception of Socrates: One Aspect," in C. Moore (ed.), *Brill's Companion to the Reception of Socrates* (Brill, 2019), 98–123.

W.J. Prior, *Socrates* (Polity, 2019).

G. Rudebusch, *Socrates* (Wiley-Blackwell, 2009).

C.C.W. Taylor, *Socrates: A Very Short Introduction* (Oxford University Press, 1998).

R. Waterfield, *Why Socrates Died: Dispelling the Myths* (Faber, 2009).

THE SOCRATICS

F. Decleva Caizzi, "Minor Socratics," in M.L. Gill and P. Pellegrin (eds.), *A Companion to Ancient Philosophy* (Blackwell, 2006), 119–35.

A. Ford, "The Beginnings of Dialogue: Socratic Discourses and Fourth-Century Prose," in S. Goldhill (ed.), *The End of Dialogue in Antiquity* (Cambridge University Press, 2008), 29–44.

A. Ford, "*Sōkratikoi logoi* in Aristotle and Fourth-Century Theories of Genre," *Classical Philology* 105 (2010): 221–35.

D.M. Johnson, *Xenophon's Socratic Works* (Routledge, 2021).

S. Prince, *Antisthenes of Athens: Texts, Translations, and Commentary* (University of Michigan Press, 2015).

H.D. Rankin, *Sophists, Socratics and Cynics* (Croom Helm, 1983).

L. Rossetti, "The Context of Plato's Dialogues," in A. Bosch-Veciana and J. Monserrat-Molas (eds.), *Philosophy and Dialogue: Studies in Plato's Dialogues*, vol. 1 (Barcelonesa d'Edicions, 2007), 15–31.

L. Stavru and C. Moore (eds.), *Socrates and the Socratic Dialogue* (Brill, 2018).

R. Waterfield, "Xenophon's Socratic Mission," in C. Tuplin (ed.), *Xenophon and His World* (Steiner, 2004), 79–113.

U. Zilioli, *The Cyrenaics* (Acumen, 2012).

U. Zilioli (ed.), *From the Socratics to the Socratic Schools: Classical Ethics, Metaphysics and Epistemology* (Routledge, 2015).

ISOCRATES

R. Johnson, "Isocrates' Methods of Teaching," *American Journal of Philology* 80 (1959): 25–36.

M. McCoy, "Alcidamas, Isocrates, and Plato on Speech, Writing, and Philosophical Rhetoric," *Ancient Philosophy* 29 (2009): 45–66.

K. Morgan, "The Education of Athens: Politics and Rhetoric in Isocrates and Plato," in T. Poulakos and D. Depew (eds.), *Isocrates and Civic Education* (University of Texas Press, 2004), 125–54.

D.J. Murphy, "Isocrates and the Dialogue," *Classical World* 106 (2013): 311–53.

E.J. Power, "Class Size and Pedagogy in Isocrates' School," *History of Education Quarterly* 6 (1966): 22–32.

T. Wareh, *The Theory and Practice of Life: Isocrates and the Philosophers* (Center for Hellenic Studies, 2012).

THE EARLY ACADEMY

W.H.F. Altman, *Plato and Demosthenes: Recovering the Old Academy* (Lexington Books, 2022).

M. Baltes, "Plato's School, the Academy," *Hermathena* 155 (1993): 5–26.

F.A.G. Beck, *Greek Education, 450–350 BC* (Methuen, 1964).

P.A. Brunt, "Plato's Academy and Politics," in *Studies in Greek History and Thought* (Oxford University Press, 1993), 282–342.

H. Cherniss, *The Riddle of the Early Academy* (University of California Press, 1945).

A.-H. Chroust, "Plato's Academy: The First Organized School of Political Science in Antiquity," *Review of Politics* 29 (1967): 25–40.

R.M. Dancy, *Two Studies in the Early Academy* (State University of New York Press, 1991).

R.M. Dancy, "Speusippus," in Edward N. Zalta (ed.), *Stanford Encyclopedia of Philosophy* (Fall 2021 Edition), https://plato.stanford.edu/archives/fall2021/entries/speusippus/.

R.M. Dancy, "Xenocrates," in Edward N. Zalta (ed.), *Stanford Encyclopedia of Philosophy* (Summer 2021 Edition), https://plato.stanford.edu/archives/sum2021/entries/xenocrates/.

D.R. Dicks, *Early Greek Astronomy to Aristotle* (Thames and Hudson, 1970).

J. Dillon, *The Heirs of Plato: A Study of the Old Academy (347–274 BC)* (Oxford University Press, 2003).

D. El Murr, "The Academy from Plato to Polemo," in L. Perilli and D. Taormina (eds.), *Ancient Philosophy: Textual Paths and Historical Explanations* (Routledge, 2018), 337–53.

D. Frede, "A Superannuated Student: Aristotle and Authority in the Academy," in J. Bryan, R. Wardy, and J. Warren (eds.), *Authors and Authority in Ancient Philosophy* (Cambridge University Press, 2018), 78–101.

F. Fronterotta, "Eudoxus and Speusippus on Pleasure (according to Aristotle): A Debate in the Ancient Academy," *Revue de Philosophie Ancienne* 4 (2018): 39–72.

H.B. Gottschalk, *Heraclides of Pontus* (Oxford University Press, 1980).

P. Kalligas, C. Balla, E. Baziotopoulou-Valavani, and V. Karasmanis (eds.), *Plato's Academy: Its Workings and Its History* (Cambridge University Press, 2020).

H.I. Marrou, *A History of Education in Antiquity*, trans. G. Lamb (Sheed and Ward, 1956).

C. Natali, *Aristotle: His Life and School*, ed. D.S. Hutchinson (Princeton University Press, 2013).

A.F. Natoli, *The Letter of Speusippus to Philip II* (Steiner, 2004).

A. Nehamas, "The Academy at Work: The Target of Dialectic in Plato's *Parmenides*," *Oxford Studies in Ancient Philosophy* 57 (2019): 121–52.

T.J. Saunders, "The RAND Corporation in Antiquity? Plato's Academy and Greek Politics," in J. Betts, J. Hooker, and J. Green (eds), *Studies in Honour of T.B.L. Webster*, vol. 1 (Bristol Classical Press, 1986), 200–210.

E. Schütrumpf (ed.), *Heraclides of Pontus: Text and Translation* (Transaction, 2008).

D. Sedley, "Xenocrates' Invention of Platonism," in M. Erler, J.E. Hessler, and F.M. Petrucci (eds.), *Authority and Authoritative Texts in the Platonist Tradition* (Cambridge University Press, 2021), 12–37.

L. Trelawny-Cassity, "Plato: The Academy," *Internet Encyclopedia of Philosophy* https://iep.utm.edu/academy.

E. Watts, "Creating the Academy: Historical Discourse and the Shape of Community in the Old Academy," *Journal of Hellenic Studies* 127 (2007): 106–22.

S.A. White, "Socrates at Colonus: A Hero for the Academy," in N.D. Smith and P.B. Woodruff (eds.), *Reason and Religion in Socratic Philosophy* (Oxford University Press, 2000), 151–75.

R.E. Wycherley, "Peripatos: The Athenian Philosophical Scene II," *Greece & Rome* 9 (1962): 2–21.

L. Zhmud, "Plato as 'Architect of Science,'" *Phronesis* 43 (1998): 211–44.

PLATO: LETTERS AND BIOGRAPHICAL DETAILS

G.J.D. Aalders, "The Authenticity of the Eighth Platonic Epistle Reconsidered," *Mnemosyne* 22 (1969): 233–57.

R.S. Bluck, *Plato's Seventh and Eighth Letters* (Cambridge University Press, 1947).

G. Boas, "Fact and Legend in the Biography of Plato," *Philosophical Review* 57 (1948): 439–57.

C.M. Bowra, "Plato's Epigram on Dion's Death," *American Journal of Philology* 59 (1938): 394–404.

M.F. Burnyeat and M. Frede, *The Pseudo-Platonic Seventh Letter*, ed. D. Scott (Oxford University Press, 2015).

J. Dillon, "Aristoxenus' *Life of Plato*," in C.A. Huffman (ed.), *Aristoxenus of Tarentum: Discussion* (Transaction, 2012), 283–96.

L. Edelstein, *Plato's Seventh Letter* (Brill, 1966).

M.C. Farmer, "Playing the Philosopher: Plato in Fourth-Century Comedy," *American Journal of Philology* 138 (2017): 1–41.

M.I. Finley, "Plato and Practical Politics," in *Aspects of Antiquity*, 2nd ed. (Penguin, 1977).

M.I. Finley, "Plato, Dion and Dionysius II," in *Ancient Sicily*, 2nd ed. (Chatto & Windus, 1979), 88–93.

P. Gooch, "The Celebration of Plato's Birthday," *Classical World* 75 (1982): 239–40.

N. Gulley, "The Authenticity of Plato's Epistles," in K. von Fritz (ed.), *Pseudepigrapha I* (Fondation Hardt, 1972), 103–30.

R. Hackforth, *The Authorship of the Platonic Epistles* (Manchester University Press, 1913; repr., Olms, 1985). Citations refer to the Olms edition.

T.H. Irwin, "The Inside Story of the Seventh Platonic Letter: A Sceptical Introduction," *Rhizai* 2 (2009): 127–60.

N.F. Jones, "Plato: Deme, Place of Residence, and Urban Outlook," in *Rural Athens under the Democracy* (University of Pennsylvania Press, 2004), 235–45.

C.H. Kahn, review of *The Pseudo-Platonic Seventh Letter*, by M.F. Burnyeat and M. Frede, ed. D. Scott, Notre Dame Philosophical Reviews, November 9, 2015, https://ndpr.nd.edu/news/the-pseudo-platonic-seventh-letter/.

G.E.R. Lloyd, "Plato and Archytas in the Seventh Letter," *Phronesis* 35 (1990): 159–74.

W. Ludwig, "Plato's Love Epigrams," *Greek, Roman, and Byzantine Studies* 4 (1963): 59–82.

D. Massimo, "Defining a 'Ps.-Plato' Epigrammatist," in R. Berardi, M. Filosa, and D. Massimo (eds.), *Defining Authorship, Debating Authenticity: Problems of Authority from Classical Antiquity to the Renaissance* (De Gruyter, 2020), 47–66.

G.R. Morrow, *Plato: Epistles* (Bobbs-Merrill, 1962).

D. Nails, *The People of Plato: A Prosopography of Plato and Other Socratics* (Hackett, 2002).

N. Notomi, "Plato, Isocrates, and Epistolary Literature: Reconsidering the *Seventh Letter* in Its Context," *Plato Journal* 23 (2022): 67–79.

J.A. Notopoulos, "The Name of Plato," *Classical Philology* 34 (1939): 135–45.

J.A. Notopoulos, "Porphyry's Life of Plato," *Classical Philology* 35 (1940): 284–93.

J.A. Notopoulos, "Plato's Epitaph," *American Journal of Philology* 63 (1942): 272–93.

W.H. Porter, "The Sequel of Plato's First Visit to Sicily," *Hermathena* 61 (1943): 46–55.

F. Poulsen, "A New Portrait of Plato," *Journal of Hellenic Studies* 40 (1920): 190–96.

H. Reid and M. Ralkowski (eds.), *Plato at Syracuse: Essays on Plato in Western Greece* (Parnassos, 2019).

A.S. Riginos, *Platonica: The Anecdotes Concerning the Life and Writings of Plato* (Brill, 1976).

L. Sanders, "Nationalistic Recommendations and Policies in the Seventh and Eighth Platonic Epistles," *Ancient History Bulletin* 8 (1994): 76–85.

L. Tarán, "Plato's Alleged Epitaph," *Greek, Roman, and Byzantine Studies* 24 (1984): 63–82.

M. Trapp, review of *The Pseudo-Platonic Seventh Letter*, by M.F. Burnyeat and M. Frede, ed. D. Scott, *Histos* 10 (2016): 76–87, https://research.ncl.ac.uk/histos/documents/2016RD08TrapponFredeBurnyeat.pdf).

G. Verhasselt, "Philodemus' Excerpt from Dicaearchus on Plato in the *Historia Academicorum* (PHerc. 1021, coll. 1*-1–2): Edition, Translation, and Commentary," *Cronache Ercolanesi* 47 (2017): 55–72.

M. Ypsilanti, "Lais and Her Mirror," *Bulletin of the Institute of Classical Studies* 49 (2006): 193–212.

PLATO AND POLITICS

G.J.D. Aalders, "Political Thought and Political Programs in the Platonic Epistles," in K. von Fritz (ed.), *Pseudepigrapha I* (Fondation Hardt, 1972), 145–75.

D. Allen, "Culture War: Plato and Athenian Politics, 350–330 BC," in C. Tiersch (ed.), *Die Athenische Demokratie im. 4. Jahrhundert: Zwischen Modernisierung und Tradition* (Steiner, 2016), 279–92.

C. Bobonich, *Plato's Utopia Recast: His Later Ethics and Politics* (Oxford University Press, 2002).

J.R. Cohen, "Rex aut Lex," *Apeiron* 29 (1996): 145–61.

G.C. Field, "Plato's Political Thought and Its Value Today," *Philosophy* 16 (1941): 227–41.

G. Klosko, *The Development of Plato's Political Theory*, 2nd ed. (Oxford University Press, 2006).

M. Lane, "Plato's Political Philosophy," in M.L. Gill and P. Pellegrin (eds.), *A Companion to Ancient Philosophy* (Blackwell, 2006), 170–91.

V.B. Lewis, "*Politeia kai Nomoi*: On the Coherence of Plato's Political Philosophy," *Polity* 31 (1998): 331–49.

V.B. Lewis, "The *Seventh Letter* and the Unity of Plato's Political Philosophy,"
   Southern Journal of Philosophy 38 (2000): 231–50.

S. Monoson, *Plato's Democratic Entanglements: Athenian Politics and the Practice
   of Philosophy* (Princeton University Press, 2000).

C.J. Rowe and M. Schofield (eds.), *The Cambridge History of Greek and Roman
   Political Thought* (Cambridge University Press, 2000).

M. Schofield, "The Disappearing Philosopher King," in *Saving the City:
   Philosopher-Kings and Other Classical Paradigms* (Routledge, 1999), 31–50.

M. Schofield, *Plato: Political Philosophy* (Oxford University Press, 2006).

T. Shiell, "The Unity of Plato's Political Thought," *History of Political Thought*
   12 (1991): 377–90.

ORDERING THE DIALOGUES

*In addition to the sources in this section, several of the books listed in the subsequent
section "Plato in General" have relevant chapters, especially Annas and Rowe 2002
and Nails 1995.*

W.H.F. Altman, "The Reading Order of Plato's Dialogues," *Phoenix* 64
   (2010): 18–51.

L. Brandwood, *The Chronology of Plato's Dialogues* (Cambridge University
   Press, 1990).

J. Howland, "Re-Reading Plato: The Problem of Platonic Chronology,"
   Phoenix 45 (1991): 189–214.

G. Ledger, *Re-Counting Plato: A Computer Analysis of Plato's Style* (Oxford
   University Press, 1989).

C. Poster, "The Idea(s) of Order of Platonic Dialogues and Their Hermeneutic
   Consequences," *Phoenix* 52 (1998): 282–98.

PLATO IN GENERAL

*I have asterisked a few books that would make suitable starting points for the study
of Plato. I particularly recommend the books by Evans and Mason.*

J. Annas, *Platonic Ethics Old and New* (Cornell University Press, 1999).

*J. Annas, *Plato: A Very Short Introduction* (Oxford University Press, 2003).

J. Annas, *Virtue and Law in Plato and Beyond* (Oxford University Press, 2017).

J. Annas and C.J. Rowe (eds.), *New Perspectives on Plato, Modern and Ancient*
   (Center for Hellenic Studies, 2002).

J.A. Arieti, *Interpreting Plato: The Dialogues as Drama* (Rowman &
   Littlefield, 1991).

H.H. Benson (ed.), *A Companion to Plato* (Blackwell, 2006).

J. Beversluis, "A Defence of Dogmatism in the Interpretation of Plato," *Oxford Studies in Ancient Philosophy* 31 (2006): 85–111.

D.L. Blank, "The Arousal of Emotion in Plato's Dialogues," *Classical Quarterly* 43 (1993): 428–39.

R. Blondell, *The Play of Character in Plato's Dialogues* (Cambridge University Press, 2002).

T.C. Brickhouse and N.D. Smith, *Plato's Socrates* (Oxford University Press, 1994).

L. Brisson, *Plato the Myth Maker*, trans. G. Naddaf (University of Chicago Press, 1998).

R. Brock, "Plato and Comedy," in E. Craik (ed.), *"Owls to Athens": Essays on Classical Subjects Presented to Sir Kenneth Dover* (Oxford University Press, 1990), 39–49.

M.F. Burnyeat, "Plato on Why Mathematics Is Good for the Soul," in T. Smiley (ed.), *Mathematics and Necessity: Essays in the History of Philosophy* (Oxford University Press, 2000), 1–81.

N.G. Charalabopoulos, *Platonic Drama and Its Ancient Reception* (Cambridge University Press, 2012).

D. Clay, *Platonic Questions: Dialogues with the Silent Philosopher* (Pennsylvania State University Press, 2000).

C. Collobert, P. Destrée, and F.J. Gonzalez (eds.), *Plato and Myth: Studies on the Use and Status of Platonic Myths* (Brill, 2012).

J.A. Corlett, *Interpreting Plato's Dialogues* (Parmenides, 2006).

A.K. Cotton, *Platonic Dialogue and the Education of the Reader* (Oxford University Press, 2014).

I.M. Crombie, *An Examination of Plato's Doctrines*, 2 vols. (Routledge & Kegan Paul, 1962, 1963).

★I.M. Crombie, *Plato: The Midwife's Apprentice* (Routledge & Kegan Paul, 1964).

★D. Ebrey and R. Kraut (eds.), *The Cambridge Companion to Plato*, 2nd ed. (Cambridge University Press, 2022).

★J.D.G. Evans, *A Plato Primer* (Acumen, 2010).

G.C. Field, *Plato and His Contemporaries: A Study in Fourth-Century Life and Thought*, 3rd ed. (Methuen, 1967).

J. Findlay, *Plato: The Written and Unwritten Doctrines* (Routledge & Kegan Paul, 1974).

G. Fine (ed.), *Plato*, 2 vols. (Oxford University Press, 1999).

★G. Fine (ed.), *The Oxford Handbook of Plato*, 2nd ed. (Oxford University Press, 2019).

M. Finkelberg, *The Gatekeeper: Narrative Voice in Plato's Dialogues* (Brill, 2019).

K. Gaiser, "Plato's Enigmatic Lecture 'On the Good,'" *Phronesis* 25 (1980): 5–37.

L.P. Gerson, *From Plato to Platonism* (Cornell University Press, 2013).

L.P. Gerson, "The Myth of Plato's Socratic Period," *Archiv für Geschichte der Philosophie* 96 (2014): 403–30.

C. Gill, "The Platonic Dialogue," in M.L. Gill and P. Pellegrin (eds.), *A Companion to Ancient Philosophy* (Blackwell, 2006), 136–50.

C. Gill and M.M. McCabe (eds.), *Form and Argument in Late Plato* (Oxford University Press, 1996).

★R.N. Goldstein, *Plato at the Googleplex: Why Philosophy Won't Go Away* (Random House, 2014).

F.J. Gonzalez, *Dialectic and Dialogue: Plato's Practice of Philosophical Inquiry* (Northwestern University Press, 1998).

F.J. Gonzalez (ed.), *The Third Way: New Directions in Platonic Studies* (Rowman & Littlefield, 1995).

J. Gordon, *Turning toward Philosophy: Literary Device and Dramatic Structure in Plato's Dialogues* (Pennsylvania State University Press, 1999).

J.C.B. Gosling, *Plato* (Routledge & Kegan Paul, 1973).

A. Gregory, *Plato's Philosophy of Science* (Duckworth, 2000).

C.L. Griswold (ed.), *Platonic Writings, Platonic Readings* (Routledge, 1988).

★G.M.A. Grube, *Plato's Thought* (Methuen, 1935).

★W.K.C. Guthrie, *A History of Greek Philosophy*, vol. 4, *Plato: The Man and His Dialogues: Earlier Period* (Cambridge University Press, 1975).

★W.K.C. Guthrie, *A History of Greek Philosophy*, vol. 5, *The Later Plato and the Academy* (Cambridge University Press, 1978).

P. Hadot, *What Is Ancient Philosophy?*, trans. M. Chase (Harvard University Press, 2002).

★R.M. Hare, *Plato* (Oxford University Press, 1982).

R. Hathaway, "Skeptical Maxims about the 'Publication' of Plato's Dialogues," in R. Freis (ed.), *The Progress of Plato's Progress* (ΑΓΩΝ Supplement 2, 1969), 28–42.

R. Hunter, *Plato and the Traditions of Ancient Literature: The Silent Stream* (Cambridge University Press, 2012).

D.A. Hyland, "Why Plato Wrote Dialogues," *Philosophy and Rhetoric* 1 (1968): 38–50.

T.H. Irwin, *Plato's Ethics* (Oxford University Press, 1995).

T.H. Irwin, "Art and Philosophy in Plato's Dialogues," *Phronesis* 41 (1996): 335–50.

C. Janaway, *Images of Excellence: Plato's Critique of the Arts* (Oxford University Press, 1995).

W.A. Johnson, "Dramatic Frame and Philosophical Idea in Plato," *American Journal of Philology* 119 (1998): 577–98.

C.H. Kahn, *Plato and the Socratic Dialogue: The Philosophical Use of a Literary Form* (Cambridge University Press, 1996).

C.H. Kahn, *Plato and the Post-Socratic Dialogue: The Return to the Philosophy of Nature* (Cambridge University Press, 2013).

E. Kaklamanou, M. Pavlou, and A. Tsakmakis (eds.), *Framing the Dialogues: How to Read Openings and Closures in Plato* (Brill, 2021).

R. Kamtekar, *Plato's Moral Psychology: Intellectualism, the Divided Soul, and the Desire for the Good* (Oxford University Press, 2017).

J. Klagge and N.D. Smith (eds.), *Methods of Interpreting Plato and His Dialogues* (Oxford University Press, 1992).

★R. Kraut, *How to Read Plato* (Granta, 2008).

★R. Kraut, "Plato," in Edward N. Zalta (ed.), *Stanford Encyclopedia of Philosophy* (Spring 2022 Edition), https://plato.stanford.edu/archives/spr2022/entries/plato/.

★R. Kraut (ed.), *The Cambridge Companion to Plato* (Cambridge University Press, 1992).

A.A. Krentz, "Dramatic Form and Philosophical Content in Plato's Dialogues," *Philosophy and Rhetoric* 7 (1983): 32–47.

★M. Lane, *Plato's Progeny: How Plato and Socrates Still Captivate the Modern Mind* (Duckworth, 2001).

A.G. Long, "Plato's Dialogues and a Common Rationale for Dialogue Form," in S. Goldhill (ed.), *The End of Dialogue in Antiquity* (Cambridge University Press, 2008), 45–59.

A.G. Long, *Conversation and Self-Sufficiency in Plato* (Oxford University Press, 2013).

★S. Lovibond, "Plato's Theory of Mind," in S. Everson (ed.), *Psychology*, Companions to Ancient Thought 2 (Cambridge University Press, 1991), 35–55.

★A.S. Mason, *Plato* (University of California Press; Acumen, 2010).

M.M. McCabe, *Plato and His Predecessors: The Dramatisation of Reason* (Cambridge University Press, 2000).

M. McCoy, *Plato on the Rhetoric of Philosophers and Sophists* (Cambridge University Press, 2008).

★C. Meinwald, *Plato* (Routledge, 2016).

★A.I. Mintz, *Plato: Images, Aims, and Practices of Education* (Springer, 2018).

M.L. Morgan, *Platonic Piety: Philosophy and Ritual in Fourth-Century Athens* (Yale University Press, 1990).

G.R. Morrow, "Plato and Greek Slavery," *Mind* 48 (1939): 186–201.

D. Nails, *Agora, Academy, and the Conduct of Philosophy* (Springer, 1995).

D. Nails and H. Thesleff, "Early Academic Editing: Plato's *Laws*," in S. Scolnicov and L. Brisson (eds.), *Plato's* Laws: *From Theory into Practice* (Academia Verlag, 2003), 14–29.

A. Nehamas, "Eristic, Antilogic, Sophistic, Dialectic: Plato's Demarcation of Philosophy from Sophistry," in *Virtues of Authenticity: Essays on Plato and Socrates* (Princeton University Press, 1999), 108–22.

*A.W. Nightingale, *Genres in Dialogue: Plato and the Construct of Philosophy* (Cambridge University Press, 1995).

A.W. Nightingale, *Philosophy and Religion in Plato's Dialogues* (Cambridge University Press, 2021).

C. Partenie (ed.), *Plato's Myths* (Cambridge University Press, 2009).

G. Press (ed.), *Plato's Dialogues: New Studies and Interpretations* (Rowman & Littlefield, 1993).

G. Press (ed.), *Who Speaks for Plato? Studies in Platonic Anonymity* (Rowman & Littlefield, 2000).

*G. Press (ed.), *The Continuum Companion to Plato* (Continuum, 2012).

W.J. Prior, *Unity and Development in Plato's Metaphysics* (Croom Helm, 1985).

W.J. Prior, "Why Did Plato Write Socratic Dialogues?" in M.L. McPherran (ed.), *Wisdom, Ignorance, and Virtue: New Essays in Socratic Studies* (Academic Printing & Publishing, 1997), 109–23.

M. Ralkowski, "The Place of Doctrines in Plato's Philosophy," *Journal of Practical Philosophy* 8 (2007): 21–26.

G. van Riel, *Plato's Gods* (Ashgate, 2013).

C.J. Rowe, *Plato*, 2nd ed. (Bloomsbury, 2004).

C.J. Rowe, *Plato and the Art of Philosophical Writing* (Cambridge University Press, 2007).

D. Russell, *Plato on Pleasure and the Good Life* (Oxford University Press, 2005).

R.B. Rutherford, *The Art of Plato* (Duckworth, 1995).

K. Sayre, *Plato's Literary Garden: How to Read a Platonic Dialogue* (University of Notre Dame Press, 1995).

M. Schofield, "When and Why Did Plato Write Narrated Dialogues?" in E. Moutsopoulos and M. Protopapas-Marneli (eds.), *Plato: Poet and Philosopher: In Memory of Ioannis N. Theodorakopoulos* (Academy of Athens Research Centre on Greek Philosophy, 2013), 87–96.

*D. Sedley, "An Introduction to Plato's Theory of Forms," *Royal Institute of Philosophy*, Supplement 78 (2016): 3–22.

D. Sedley, "Plato's Self-References," in B. Bossi and T.M. Robinson (eds.), *Plato's* Theaetetus *Revisited* (De Gruyter, 2020), 3–9.

P. Shorey, *The Unity of Plato's Thought* (University of Chicago Press, 1903).

D. Sider, "Did Plato Write Dialogues before Socrates' Death?" *Apeiron* 14 (1980): 15–18.

N.D. Smith (ed.), *Plato: Critical Assessments*, 4 vols. (Routledge, 1998).

T. Szlezák, *Reading Plato*, trans. G. Zanker (Routledge, 1999).

H. Tarrant, *Plato's First Interpreters* (Duckworth, 2000).

H. Tarrant, D.A. Layne, D. Baltzly, and F. Renaud (eds.), *Brill's Companion to the Reception of Plato in Antiquity* (Brill, 2018).

V. Tejera, *Plato's Dialogues One by One: A Dialogical Interpretation* (University Press of America, 1999).

H. Thesleff, *Platonic Patterns: A Collection of Studies* (Parmenides, 2009).

*E.N. Tigerstedt, *Interpreting Plato* (Almqvist & Wiksell International, 1977).

N. Tuana (ed.), *Feminist Interpretations of Plato* (Pennsylvania State University Press, 1994).

I. Vasiliou, *Aiming at Virtue in Plato* (Cambridge University Press, 2008).

G. Vlastos, *Plato's Universe* (University of Washington Press, 1975).

K.M. Vogt, *Belief and Truth: A Skeptic Reading of Plato* (Oxford University Press, 2012).

C. Warne, *Arguing with Socrates: An Introduction to Plato's Shorter Dialogues* (Bloomsbury, 2013).

A. Wedberg, *Plato's Philosophy of Mathematics* (Almqvist & Wiksell, 1955).

N.P. White, *Plato on Knowledge and Reality* (Hackett, 1976).

D. Wolfsdorf, *Trials of Reason: Plato and the Crafting of Philosophy* (Oxford University Press, 2008).

C.H. Zuckert, *Plato's Philosophers: The Coherence of the Dialogues* (University of Chicago Press, 2009).

Index